The Story of Western Philosophy

The Story of Western Philosophy

Francis H. Parker

New Introduction by Peter Kreeft

ST. AUGUSTINE'S PRESS
South Bend, Indiana

Manufactured in the United States of America

1 2 3 4 5 6   20 19 18 17 16 15 14

Library of Congress Cataloging in Publication Data
Parker, Francis H.
The story of western philosophy / Francis H. Parker;
new introduction by Peter Kreeft. – 2nd edition.
pages cm
Includes bibliographical references and index.
ISBN 978-1-58731-820-7 (paperbound: alk. paper)
1. Philosophy – History. I. Title.
B72.P3 2014
190 – dc23   201400945

∞ The paper used in this publication meets the minimum requirements of
the American National Standard for Information Sciences – Permanence of
Paper for Printed Materials, ANSI Z39.481984.

ST. AUGUSTINE'S PRESS
www.staugustine.net

Contents

Introduction

It is a privilege to write an introduction to the reissuing of a classic.

Why is this book a classic among histories of philosophy?

(1) Not just because it takes philosophy seriously and literally, as the love of wisdom, not the cultivation of cleverness.

(2) Not just because it takes history seriously, as the history of consciousness itself, not just of its objects.

(3) Not just because it manifests, without chauvinism, the distinctive greatness of the Western mind.

(4) Not just because it masterfully selects and condenses all this into a single, quite short volume.

(5) Not just because the author's point of view is generic common sense, associated more with the philosophy of Aristotle than any other, yet very fair to alternatives (Plato, Descartes, Hobbes, Hume, Kant, Hegel).

(6) Not just because the author treats philosophy as a human instrument, reminiscent of the title of his classic Aristotelian logic text, *Logic as a Human Instrument*.

(7) Not just because the writing is sharp.

(8) Not just because the arguments are summarized so clearly that a good high school student can follow them.

(9) Not just because it has an exciting story line. (Thus the second word in the title.)

(10) Not just because it offers an original point of view or "big picture"—essentially "the one and the many"—that makes unified sense of this incredibly commodious and diverse enterprise.

(11) Note just because it has the sense to end with Hegel, since the unified plot line of Western philosophy, clear for 2230 years, from the death of Socrates to the death of Hegel, branches out into cancerous confusion after that.

(12) And not just because most other histories of philosophy lack many of these eleven virtues.

(13) But because it has power. It sticks in your mind; it changes your thinking.

This book helped me immensely as an undergraduate philosophy major. It helped me when I was writing my own history of philosophy (*Socrates' Children*), which is four times as long and covers four times as many philosophers.

Introductions—*all* introductions–should be shorter than they are. ("Heeeere's Johnny!" was a classic.) Most philosophy books should be shorter than they are. All the more, then, it follows that an introduction to a mercifully short philosophy book should be mercifully short.

Peter Kreeft

Preface

This book was born of the paperback boom, and it is meant as an aid in the interpretation of the history of Western philosophy. It is designed especially for use in a course in the history of philosophy, but I hope that it may also prove useful for other purposes, such as an historical introduction to philosophy or a comprehensive review of the history of philosophy or just as a help to the general reader trying to make some sense out of the history of Western philosophy.

When I began teaching the standard course in the general history of philosophy I used a textbook, like most other teachers, because I thought the works of the historical philosophers were too expensive for students to buy, and for a whole class to read them in the library was too difficult and inconvenient. The arrival of the boom in paperback and other inexpensive editions changed this situation, for it then became feasible—indeed, almost mandatory—to require a class to buy the basic writings of the great philosophers, so my assignments in my history of philosophy course changed from a textbook to the philosophers themselves. This resulted in a gratifying improvement in the substance, vitality, and freshness of the course both for the students and for myself, but it soon made me realize that I must now do more lecturing in order to help the students to analyze, interpret, organize, and unify this mass of primary material. This in turn meant—I was not long in discovering—that I had little time left for class discussion. Thus I found myself in the dilemma of having to slight either class discussion or else the analysis, organization, and interpretation necessary in order to prevent the readings from appearing chaotic and meaningless to the students. To return to the use of a textbook did not seem an adequate solution, for the existing interpretive textbooks were too long to be assigned as a whole in addition to a sufficient amount of source material, and assignment of only parts of them left the students with a fragmented and ununified impression of the history of philosophy.

What was needed, I thought, was a companion to the paperbacks—a book which presented a unified interpretation of the history of philosophy without competing with source books. By leaving most of the historical facts to the many excellent editions of the philosophical texts now available, and by focusing on the interpretation of those facts and of the philosophical history they compose, such a book could remain short enough, I hoped, to be used along with the source materials and yet also thorough enough to help illuminate those materials. The present book is the result of my attempt to meet that need.

This emphasis upon interpretation rather than presentation of the historical facts has resulted in the condensation of all the factual material and even in the complete omission of some philosophers and topics often treated in history of philosophy books. The chief examples of such omission are much of medieval philosophy and everything after Hegel. These two omissions result partly from such practical considerations as my desire to keep the book as short as possible, but they also result from the interpretation of the history of philosophy which the book presents. The fundamental theme of this interpretation is that the history of philosophy is the most abstract expression of the growth of human existence—at least of Western man—and that the main stages in this development are three: an original state of the self's undifferentiated objective union with the whole of reality, a withdrawal of the self from this whole to win subjective freedom but at the price of isolation and estrangement, and a return to the whole in a reunion of a no longer isolated and merely subjective self with a no longer merely undifferentiated objective world. Ancient and medieval philosophy are viewed as the philosophical expression of the first stage, modern philosophy of the second, and the third stage is considered to lie in the future. Thus the interpretive reason for a condensed treatment of medieval philosophy is my belief that the objectivism basic to philosophy prior to modern times approaches its full development in Plato and Aristotle and that the philosophical as distinct from the theological concepts of the medieval philosophers are drawn mostly from ancient philosophy. The interpretive reason for ending this book with Hegel is my belief (whose truth I try to demonstrate in the course of the book) that Hegel expresses the essence of modern philosophy in absolute form, that in his philosophy the developing subjectivism definitive of modern philosophy receives its ultimate logical expression. For a fuller and clearer statement of this organizing interpretation the reader may wish to consider the Prologue and Epilogue before turning to the body of the book.* The reader may well, probably will, and in one sense even should, disagree with this interpretation, for such disagreement has the great merit that its formulation and defense forces him to work out his own interpretation of the history of Western philosophy.

Finally, I must not fail to record my deep gratitude to those who have helped me in writing this book. In addition to the many students in my history of philosophy courses who have supplied both the occasion for the book and the stimulus for many of its ideas, I must mention at least the following: Professor Henry Veatch of Northwestern University and Professor John Wild of Yale University, especially for my appreciation of the tradition of realistic philosophy in ancient and medieval times but more generally for all the philosophy to which they have exposed me both by precept and by example; Professor William Harry Jellema of Calvin College and Grand Valley College, to whom I am indebted generally for his embodiment

---

* Also this interpretive theme has been published as "The Temporal Being of Western Man," *Review of Metaphysics,* XVIII, 4 (June 1965), 629–46.

of the love of wisdom and especially for an appreciation of the nature and role of reason in traditional and modern philosophy; Professor Donald Williams of Harvard University, especially for ideas about the philosophers of the seventeenth century; Professor Edgard McKown of Evansville College, under whom I first studied the history of philosophy; Professor Robert Brumbaugh of Yale University, as a philosophical companion and historical resource during a too-brief sojourn in Greece; Professor Victor Gourevitch of Wellesley College, for helpful criticisms and suggestions; my former colleagues at Haverford, Professors Martin Foss, Douglas Steere, Paul Desjardins, Gerhard Spiegler, and Louis Aryeh Kosman, especially for all our discussions of the history of philosophy; and, above all, my wife, whose unflagging cheerfulness and courage are primarily responsible for the completion of this book.

F. H. P.

The Story of Western Philosophy

Prologue:
The
Philosophical Story
Previewed

This book is a guide to the interpretation of the history of Western philosophy. Is there, as the word "history" suggests, a story or plot in the history of Western philosophy, or in any of its parts? We shall see that there is a story in the whole of the history of Western philosophy (although its end still lies in the future), a story in each of the major parts of that story, and a story in each of the main subdivisions of those parts. Thus, the story of Western philosophy has stories within stories, wheels within wheels. Moreover, the stories we shall follow in this book are doubtless not the only stories in the history of Western philosophy, and they may also not be the most important ones. Our task as students both of the history of philosophy and of philosophy itself, therefore, should be to try to discover these most important stories or plots, to reflect upon them, and thereby to advance our own philosophizing.

The stories in the history of Western philosophy are stories in a double sense: they develop over time and they have a plot. Like all stories, they have a beginning, a middle, and an end, and the beginnings and ends are logical as well as chronological ones. Each beginning is a premise and each end a conclusion of

3

a logical sequence of thought, whether or not it is a valid one. Of course the conclusion of one logical sequence may also be the premise for a second, whose conclusion may in turn be a premise for a third, and so on. Yet the major conclusions are sufficiently final to mark the ends of divisions or subdivisions in the history of philosophy. These logical stories are quite distinct from, and even independent of, the chronological stories in which they are imbedded, just as the logical sequence of propositions in Euclid's system of plane geometry is quite independent of Euclid's dated discovery and the transient rediscovery of it. From this point of view, the stories we shall be studying can rightly be regarded as alternative philosophical systems, alternative logical developments of thoughts about life and the world, so the study of these stories can and should be regarded as material for the development of our own philosophies, our own logical developments of our own thoughts about life and the world. What is spread out in time is also logically timeless. As historians our task will be to discover these plots as they are imbedded in time. As philosophers our task will be to understand the logical sequences involved and to use that understanding to advance our own philosophizing.

In addition to being historians and philosophers, however, we who investigate the history of philosophy should also try to be both at once; we should try to be philosophical historians or historiological philosophers of the history of philosophy. After discovering the plots composing the history of philosophy, and in addition to reflecting upon their logical sequences to advance our own philosophizing, we should also try to understand these stories and the overall story which they compose as human history, as the expression of the developing nature of temporal man in his natural and social world. As has already been foreshadowed in the Preface and as will become fully explicit in the Epilogue, this study will indicate that the history of Western philosophy is the abstract and general expression of the temporal being of Western man and that the stages in this history reflect the stages in the development of Western man as a natural individual and social being.

To see this connection between Western man's philosophy

and his historically developing nature, however, it is neither necessary nor advisable to explain each philosopher's views immediately in terms of his cultural setting. It is not necessary to do so because the point will emerge from the structure of the history of Western man's philosophy itself without immediate reference to the cultural settings in which it is developed. In addition, any immediate explanation of a man's philosophy in terms of the special features of his life and culture runs the risk of committing the genetic fallacy, the fallacy of reductionism—of psychologism or sociologism—the fallacy of explaining, or explaining away, a philosophy in terms of its psychological or sociological origins. What is needed is a mean between the extremes of reducing philosophy to and isolating it from its origins in the developing historical existence of natural and social man. The author has aimed at this golden mean by confining himself in the chapters composing the body of this book to a purely philosophical investigation of historical philosophies, at least for the most part trying to understand them in their own terms, and by using this Prologue and especially the Epilogue to see how this purely philosophical understanding of the history of Western philosophy expresses and reflects the developing nature, the temporal being, of the Western man whose philosophy it is.

To understand something of the nature of such a story or history which is both philosophical and also expressive of the evolution of natural and social man, and also to introduce ourselves to the first period as well as to the plot of the whole story of Western philosophy, let us now consider a preliminary account of the story of ancient Greek philosophy. (A concluding account accompanies the discussion of Aristotle, p. 82 and Ch. 4-6).

The motto of this preliminary account of the story of ancient Greek philosophy might well be "Phylogeny Recapitulates Ontogeny." The reader may already have encountered the reverse maxim, "Ontogeny Recapitulates Phylogeny," perhaps in studying biology; it means that the development of the individual embryo repeats the various stages in the development of the whole species. The central theme of this preliminary interpretation of ancient Greek philosophy is this idea in reverse: the development of the species repeats the development of the individual. The species meant is the philosophical species, here ancient Greek philosophy, and the individual meant is any human, especially a child, since a child's development is more rapid and hence more noticeable than an adult's. The developmental theme which occurs in the child and which is repeated in ancient Greek philosophy, according to this interpretation, is the increasing awareness of parts and the whole and their interrelation.

At the ontogenetic level, the level of the child, linguistic-conceptual growth seems to be from *whole* to *parts* to *whole-of-parts*. When a child first begins to think and talk he does not see the myriad distinctions which adults find among things. Differences are overlooked, and all things tend to be fused together into one whole approximating what William James called "a blooming, buzzing confusion," and F. S. C. Northrop has more recently called "the undifferentiated esthetic continuum." The first and broadest of these wholes in which the young child fuses all the parts is simply being or reality itself. Everything is something-or-other, whatever else it may later be learned to be. When a little child who is just learning to talk begins his wearisome questioning as to "What's this?" and "What's that?" he already knows that this and that are at least something; he is aware of everything fused together into one whole and is busy trying to disentangle its parts. Thus the first stage in his linguistic-conceptual development is a confused grasp of everything as one, an awareness of the whole of everything.

The second stage is the untangling of this whole into various of its parts. As some of these parts appear in many of the other parts, the child tends to identify the whole with some one or more of these relatively ubiquitous parts. As Aristotle says, the little child calls all men father; he reduces the whole class of men to that one with whom he is most familiar. All men are "daddies," all women are "mammas," "We always have to go to school," "Why do I always have to practice the piano?" A glutton is all belly, the athlete all muscle, and the intellectual all head. In this second stage, then, he withdraws from the primordial, all-obliterating whole of the first stage and identifies it with some one or more of its parts. Thus the formula for this second stage is *pars pro toto,* the substitution of a part for a whole.

The third and final stage is a return to the whole of being or reality with all its parts seen in it—seen distinctly from the whole and from each other as merely parts, yet also viewed as parts of the whole. The milkman, the postman, and Daddy are all different from each other, and no one of them is the only man there is, yet all of them are recognized as men. They are different and yet the same. Life is neither all work nor all play nor all rest, but it is partly each of these. The world is not all matter nor all mind; it is partly each of these. This third stage is obviously an ideal limit which can only be approximated, but it seems to be the ultimate stage toward which the individual moves.

Each of these three stages is itself distinguishable into stages, of course, and those stages into further stages, etc., yet the whole, part, whole-of-parts division seems to be the most general and fundamental one. Compare, for example, the structure of the curriculum of a liberal arts program. It probably starts with a year of general studies to provide a survey of the whole of human knowledge. It proceeds to a period of specialization in which some one part of this whole of knowledge is studied in detail. Finally, it probably aims at the ideal (though doubtless not very closely approximating it) of seeing the relation of the specialized part to the whole body of human knowledge. Whole, part, whole-of-parts—this three-stage sequence appears at the ontogenetic or individual level, and this sequence is repeated at the phylogenetic level of ancient Greek philosophy.

Ancient Greek philosophy may be divided into three main periods: the Cosmological Period, extending from about 600 to 425 B.C., the Anthropological Period, extending from about 450 to about 399 B.C. (the death of Socrates), and the Systematic Period, extending from about 399 to about 322 B.C. (the death of Aristotle). As its name indicates, the Cosmological Period is chiefly concerned with the cosmos or world as a whole; and this period therefore is, at the phylogenetic level, the first in the three-stage sequence. In this period the philosophers make no clear distinction between man and nature, the living and the nonliving, sentience and nonsentience, mind and its objects. The Cosmological philosophers are hylozoists (*hylē* = matter, *zoē* = life); they view all matter as infused with life and consciousness. They are also philosophical extroverts; their attention is turned outward away from themselves toward the outside world, and they are hardly conscious of themselves as distinct from it. These philosophers represent the first stage, the concentration on the whole; but they also represent the beginning of the second stage, the withdrawal from the whole and the identification of it with some one of its parts. What is everything? Water for Thales and air for Anaximenes. Furthermore, a withdrawal from and return to the whole exists even within this Cosmological Period: Thales begins the sequence with water and Democritus ends it with being and nonbeing, with atoms and the void. Yet however small or large the part with which reality is identified, for the Cosmological philosophers it is almost always some form of matter; hence Aristotle calls them physicists. For this reason we may say (modifying the famous dictum of Protagoras which will be considered shortly) that the motto of the Cosmological Period is that "Matter is the measure of all things."

In the Anthropological Period, as its name indicates, the philosophers turn their attention away from the whole of reality and from its material part to that sub-part of reality which is man, so the withdrawal from the whole in this period is more complete. Philosophy is now introverted and anthropocentric; man is divorced from nature. While the whole of being is never quite identified with man, attention is focused primarily upon man and all other things are seen in relation to him. Furthermore, as in the Cosmological Period, a withdrawal and return takes place even within this period: the Sophists' withdrawal into momentary sensations and Socrates' return to the Cosmological philosophers' concern with eternal truths. Yet however man is regarded, all things are still seen in relation to him. Hence the motto of the Anthropological Period may be taken as the famous saying of the Sophist, Protagoras, "Man is the measure of all things."

In the Systematic Period, finally, there is a return to the

whole. Matter and man, the two parts which previously had been separated from the whole, are now rejoined to the reality of which they are parts. The parts are viewed as parts of the whole—hence the name, the "Systematic Period." As in the other two periods, this period also contains a certain withdrawal and return: Plato tends to emphasize the stable, abstract, timeless part of reality in separation from the changing, concrete, and temporal part, and Aristotle returns to the whole by attempting to bind these two parts together. Because reality as a whole concerns the two great philosophers of the Systematic Period, we may say that the motto of this period is "Being is the measure of all things."

Thus original union with the whole, withdrawal to that part which is man, and return to the whole viewed as a whole of its human and other parts emerge as the general plot of the story of ancient Greek philosophy. Furthermore, this movement also emerges in a more general form as the fundamental plot of the story of Western philosophy as a whole. For this reason the reader might wish to look at the Epilogue before turning to Chapter One of the book. From that final perspective, after having studied the development of the whole history of Western philosophy, we shall see that ancient philosophy together with its medieval development is analogous to the Cosmological Period within ancient philosophy as the expression of an original whole world within which the knowing subject and his natural objects have not yet been fundamentally distinguished; man is at home in the world and hardly knows himself as distinct from it.

Modern philosophy will be viewed as analogous to the Anthropological Period within ancient philosophy, for in modern times man as the knowing subject or mind is born out of the primordial undifferentiated whole and knows himself to be radically other than and free from the world; the subject and his freedom are certain, but the world as his object is problematic. This stage of the complete freedom of the knowing and acting subject or self receives its absolute logical formulation in the philosophy of Hegel, and for this reason this study ends with Hegel even though the chronology of Western philosophy and its modern period has of course now left Hegel more than a hundred years behind.

The final chapter in the story of Western philosophy will be seen to be abstractly analogous to the Systematic Period of ancient Greek philosophy, to Plato and Aristotle—a reunion of the subject or self with the objective world, with which it was one in ancient and medieval philosophy, but from which it will have won its freedom in modern philosophy, yet a reunion which preserves the freedom and maturity of the subject. Since this final stage of philosophical reunion of the subject and the object remains as a future accomplishment, however, its concrete details cannot yet be ascertained.

This Prologue is only a synoptic preview of the story of ancient Greek philosophy and of Western philosophy as a whole, however. An examination of the philosophers' works will reveal to what extent this interpretation makes sense.

Part I

ANCIENT AND MEDIEVAL OBJECTIVISM

Chapter 1

The Cosmological Philosophers

Like most beginnings, the beginning of Western philosophy is obscure. It is far removed from us in time and, more importantly, very little of what the early philosophers taught and wrote is extant; much of the available information comes from secondary reports and those even further removed. Hence it should be stressed from the outset how very tenuous our understanding of these early thinkers is. The first notable group of these thinkers is the Milesians.

1-1. *The Milesians*

The Milesian philosophers take their name from the city of Miletus on the west coast of Asia Minor. Their writings, and also those of the later Cosmological philosophers, seem to be a mixture of what would be regarded today as philosophy, science, religion, and poetry. Fundamentally they tend to see all things as more or less fused together in one whole. Philosophy, science, religion, and poetry as separate subjects are just being born;

13

and indeed, the word "philosophy" was not even coined until the middle of the Cosmological Period. This holism is also connected with the mythological background and origin of ancient Greek philosophy;[1] the Milesians are the first Western philosophers precisely because they begin to handle rationally the questions which had previously been handled mythically. From this primordial fusion of philosophy, science, religion, mythology, poetry, etc. this study extracts only the gradually emerging philosophical considerations, rational considerations of ultimates.

The question the Milesians seek to answer is, in briefest terms, What is reality? What does everything come down to, in the last analysis? The historical, phylogenetic beginning of philosophy is thus much the same as the ontogenetic beginning of conscious philosophizing in an individual person when he begins to wonder what the ultimate nature of reality is. Is it matter? Is it mind? Is it spirit? Is it some other, unknown, something? Since the attention of the philosophers of this earliest period is turned away from themselves toward the changing, physical world of nature, the question which they try to answer is, somewhat more specifically, "What is the stuff or substance out of which everything is made?" And since they mean the *one* stuff of *every*thing, their question is also, "What is the single constant that abides through all change?"

The criteria for evaluating their answers are tautologically contained in their question. Since they are looking for the stuff of *all* things, any answer they give to this question is faulty if there is at least one thing which cannot be reduced to the proposed stuff. This may be called the criterion of *universality*. And since they seek the one stuff of all things, a *single* substance, a proposed ultimate substance is faulty if it is not *one*, not single. This may be called the criterion of *simplicity*. At this stage the desire is for a single ultimate—though we shall later see a tendency to abandon a single ultimate in favor of two or more. This desire for universality and simplicity, which is recognizable in the human mind even today, thus seems to have been present from these early times.

To this Milesian question—What is the stuff of all things?— the most notable answers are those of Thales, Anaximander, and Anaximenes. *Thales,* who flourished about 585 B.C., held that the ultimate stuff of all things is water. Whatever may have been Thales' reason for holding this view, it seems clear (as Anaximander will later suggest) that water cannot be the stuff of *all* things, that it violates the criterion of universality, for there are some things which ordinary observation shows to be irreducible to and even incompatible with water. Fire, for example, is put out by water. Hence historically the first answer to the question of the stuff of all things seems, like so many first answers, not to stand up under scrutiny.

Anaximander, who probably flourished about 570 B.C., declared that the ultimate stuff of all things is an indeterminate, indefinite, infinite something: the *apeiron* (a = no, *peiras* = boundary). Exactly what Anaximander himself meant by his *apeiron,* and exactly what his reasons were for maintaining it, are problematic. But the concept of the indeterminate, which had already been foreshadowed by the "chaos" of the eighth-century poet Hesiod and which will become a most important and enduring concept, is the first great insight in the history of Western philosophy. The ultimate stuff must be an *apeiron,* an indeterminate, in two senses. In the first place, the ultimate stuff must be indeterminate in the sense of being *externally unbounded,* because anything which is externally bounded (like Thales' water) would have to be bounded by something else outside it (like earth) and hence it would not be truly universal, not the stuff of *all* things. In the second place, the world stuff must be indeterminate in the sense of being *internally indefinite,* because that which assumes all forms whatsoever, even incompatible forms like water and fire, cannot possess any definite form of its own. If it did possess any definite form, it would by that fact be excluded from, and hence not be the stuff of, anything with a different form. What can be changed into any definite thing cannot itself be a definite thing. The ultimate stuff of all concrete things cannot itself be one of those concrete things; it must rather be something indeterminate. Hence the world stuff is the *apeiron*.

If Anaximander's indeterminate is the first great insight in the history of Western philosophy, it is also only an incomplete one, however, for his views (so far as we have knowledge of them) do not explain how the determinate things of the world could be generated out of the *apeiron*. If the world stuff is indeterminate, how does it form the many determinate things which make up the world we experience? Anaximander has no other ultimate than the *apeiron*. Hence he has to say that all determinate things are already present in the indeterminate at the beginning. If these determinate things are present in the indeterminate *actually* (which seems to be his position), then the indeterminate is *not* indeterminate but actually determinate. Furthermore, when Anaximander says that there are pairs of opposites (like hot and cold, wet and dry) which separate themselves out of the indeterminate, he is presupposing another kind of determinate, a determinate *activity* as well as determinate *things,* for this separating out is itself something determinate. If, on the other hand, these determinate things are originally in the indeterminate *only potentially,* then there must be something actually determinate to actualize those potential determinate things, as well as the actually determinate activity of actualizing them.

Hence Anaximander's theory is faced with a dilemma. If, on the one hand, the world stuff is truly indeterminate, originally containing determinate things only potentially, then a second principle is needed—one of *definiteness* and *determination*—to actualize out of that indeterminate world stuff the many determinate things we experience. This alternative will be taken by the Pythagoreans and after them by Plato and Aristotle. If, on the other hand, the primordial stuff contains the actually determinate things which make up the world, then it is not truly indeterminate at all but really quite determinate. This alternative will be taken by Parmenides and the Pluralists. Parmenides and his Eleatic followers will hold that this determinate world stuff is one, and the Pluralists that it is many. Thus

Anaximander's theory is a fork in the road of philosophical history:

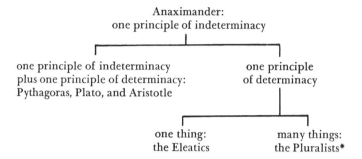

Anaximander:
one principle of indeterminacy

one principle of indeterminacy
plus one principle of determinacy:
Pythagoras, Plato, and Aristotle

one principle
of determinacy

one thing:
the Eleatics

many things:
the Pluralists*

Anaximenes, who flourished around 550 B.C., held that the stuff of all things is air, vapor, or breath. The apparent universality of air comes out better in Greek than it does in English, for air is what things breathe *(psycho)* and is thus the very breath of life and soul *(psychē)*. Note here the hylozoism of Anaximenes' position, its fusion of matter and life. Air seems to be more indeterminate than Thales' water, thus profiting from the insight of Anaximander, yet more determinate than Anaximander's *apeiron;* thus Anaximenes attempts to fill the gap in Anaximander's theory. Anaximenes also presents a clear and quantifiable view of the process of the generation of the many things of our experience from the one primordial world stuff. This process consists in the condensation and rarefaction of air to produce the other three of the traditionally accepted four "elements" (fire, air, water, and earth) and through them all other things. Hence the difference between the one stuff and the many things in the world is a difference only in degree and not in kind, and this tends to preserve the unity of all things.

In spite of these advantages of Anaximenes' account of the origin of things from the one world stuff, his air as a world stuff is clearly subject to essentially the same difficulty as Thales' water. From an observational point of view rocks, for example,

---

* However, Democritus also has in his "void" something approximating a principle of indeterminacy.

seem to shove air aside and thus to be other than and incompatible with merely compressed air, just as fire is incompatible with Thales' water. And from a logical point of view, as we saw in connection with Anaximander's *apeiron* as internally indefinite, in so far as air has a specific nature of its own it must be different from all things with different specific natures and hence not their basic stuff. Once more Anaximander's fundamental insight reasserts itself: no determinate, restricted substance can be absolutely universal. Air is too concrete.

1-2. *The Pythagoreans*

To Pythagoras, who flourished about 530 B.C., is attributed the coining of the word "philosophy," "the love of wisdom" (*philia* = love, *sophia* = wisdom). Previously the men we are studying were known just as wise men or teachers (*sophistēs,* sophist), but Pythagoras was supposed to have objected that only a god can be wise and that the most that men can hope to achieve is a love of wisdom. Pythagoras and his followers are probably best known for their work in mathematics (note the Pythagorean theorem in geometry) and for their numerology. They held that all things are numbers, Aristotle tells us, and from this point of view they may be regarded, like the Milesians, as putting forth a doctrine of one ultimate world stuff. More important to the story of Western philosophy, however, is the less well known Pythagorean theory of the Limited and the Unlimited. This theory seems to have been closely tied up with the Pythagoreans' numerology and perhaps even derived from it. All things are numbers, and numbers are either odd or even. Hence all things are either odd or even, and the odd are Limited and the even Unlimited. They identified the Unlimited with breath and darkness, the passive, female, principle in the world, the *apeiron* or indeterminate of Anaximander. The Limit *(peras)* they identified with light and perhaps fire; it is the active, male, principle in the world. Everything in the universe is viewed as the product of these two opposing yet complementary principles or forces: mother and father, earth and sky.

The Pythagoreans thus preserve the principle of the indeterminate, Anaximander's contribution, while also, in their principle of the Limit, removing the flaw in Anaximander's theory. There is now, in addition to Anaximander's primordial indefiniteness, an equally primordial principle of determinacy which makes possible the emergence of determinate things from the matrix of the indeterminate. Just as the production of a determinate ingot of steel requires both the molten steel and the die that stamps it, so does the origin of every definite thing require both an indeterminate, maternal matter and a determining, paternal form. Hence there are now two ultimates instead of only one; in this sense the desire of the Milesians for complete unity is rejected as unachievable. And yet in another sense the Pythagoreans do achieve this unity through their concept of harmony, a union of the two conjointly universal principles of determinacy and indeterminacy, which is to be found everywhere—even in the renowned "music of the spheres."

The Pythagoreans thus solve the problem of the Milesians by recognizing that the explanation of things requires two complementary principles. Yet this differentiation of the ultimate into two is still not a sufficiently complete differentiation, as we shall see, for is the Pythagorean principle of the Limit the principle of determinate*ness* or the principle of determin*ation*, the determin*ate* or the determin*ing*? Is it, for example, the shape of the steel ingot, or is it the shaping die? The Pythagoreans' position on this issue is not clear, and the reason it is not clear is probably that they did not even raise the question of this distinction between the limited and the limiting. This distinction becomes explicit as the story unfolds further.

1-3. *The Problem of Change*

The problem which confronted the Milesian philosophers may be expressed in two different ways: What is the stuff of which everything is made, and what is the constant that abides through all change? The Milesians and Pythagoreans emphasized the first aspect of the problem, that of the world stuff, although they also dealt with the problem of change. The reverse is true

of Heraclitus and the Eleatic philosophers: while they deal
with the question of the world stuff, they emphasize the question of a constant that abides through all change.

The problem of change is a riddle: How can a thing change
and yet remain the same thing? A green leaf which becomes
yellow remains the same leaf throughout its change—yet how
can it, since it has become different? This is the riddle facing
Heraclitus and the Eleatics. How can a thing change and yet
remain the same thing? Their joint answer to this paradoxical
question is that it really cannot. Change is real, Heraclitus
maintains, and experience agrees, so there cannot be any unchanging stuff. Reason tells us that there must be one unchanging stuff; so change must be unreal, Parmenides and the other
Eleatic philosophers maintain. While we must not steal the
thunder of later philosophers or reveal the outcome of the
story, it may already be noted that the tacit assumption behind
both of these positions is an all-or-none principle, that a thing
must either change entirely or else not at all.

1-3.1 *Heraclitus*

Heraclitus, who flourished about 500 B.C., expressed his basic
position in the famous dictum that "everything flows" *(panta
rhei)*. Everything is constantly changing; one cannot step into
the same river twice, because with the second step the river has
changed and hence is no longer the same. Does nothing at all
then remain constant? Yes, one thing: change itself—and also,
as we shall shortly see, the fundamental nature or law of change.

What is change? "The identity of opposites," Heraclitus says.
In change opposites are identical with each other, and everything in the universe is the same as everything else. Why does
Heraclitus maintain this view, which seems so contrary both to
experience and to logic? Although we cannot know for sure
what Heraclitus, "the obscure," had in mind, there is a good
reason for maintaining that change is the identity of opposites.
Take again the autumn leaf changing from green to yellow. If
there is in this change no identity of opposites, no overlap, no
point at which the leaf is both green and yellow, then it follows
that no change takes place at all: a leaf is simply unchangingly

green for a certain period of time; it is then annihilated at an instant and is followed by the *ex nihilo* creation of another leaf which remains unchangingly yellow. Not only must the two opposites overlap and be identical at one time, moreover; they also must overlap and be identical even at *all* times during the change from green to yellow. At every instant throughout the process of actually changing from green to yellow, the changing leaf can be defined only by both of these opposite states. Also this identity of opposites must be true of the whole world because the whole world, our senses tell us, is in a constant and continual process of change. Hence all things are identical—a conclusion which Heraclitus may also have experienced quasi-mystically. Heraclitus' identity of opposites includes in a new form Anaximander's pairs of opposites imbedded in the primordial *apeiron;* it also encompasses the Pythagoreans' harmonious union of the two fundamental, opposed, principles of the Limit and the Unlimited.

This identity of opposites seems to be the meaning of Heraclitus' *logos,* a word meaning "word," "thought," "reason," "mind," "law," etc.[2] The *logos* is the law of change, the rational order imbedded in all things, the wisdom and the divinity immanent in the world, "Zeus and yet not *Zeus.*" This law is not only descriptive, like what we today call scientific, natural law; it is also prescriptive, like the statutory "law of the land." It not only describes what does happen but also prescribes what ought to and must happen on pain of retribution. Thus the *logos* determines what must happen in both senses of the word "must."

Heraclitus also at times seems to identify this *logos* with fire and to regard it as the world stuff. In this sense he is true to the spirit of the Milesians, and in this sense also he denies that everything changes, that nothing is constant. In so far as he regards fire as the world stuff he also presents a theory of the generation of all things from it, a theory rather like that of Anaximenes. The "downward" way of the coming into being of things from fire goes through the other three traditionally accepted elements of air, water, and earth; and the "upward" way of the passing away of things back into their eternal source goes from earth back up through water and air to fire. What we regard as a stable, unchanging state is actually an equilibrium in the strife or war between the downward way of life and the upward way of death—although these two ways, like all opposites, are really identical.

> Life and death upon one tether
> And running beautiful together.[3]

When we recall that the world stuff, fire, is itself not a substance but a process, however, and also that it symbolizes process better than anything else that we sense, we see that Heraclitus is still primarily concerned with the problem of change and also that he has not abandoned his principle that everything flows.

How, then, can a thing change and yet remain the same? Heraclitus' answer is that it cannot. If a thing changes, it changes and does not remain the same, and everything does change. In fact, everything *is* change and nothing but change, the fundamental nature and law of this universal change being the identity of the opposites which are involved in it.

1-3.2. *The Eleatics*

The Eleatic philosophers (from the lower Italian city of Elea) take the other alternative. How can a thing change and yet remain the same? It cannot, they agree with Heraclitus, but for a different reason and with a different conclusion. If a certain thing is said to change, why then *it* changes; and this *it* must, therefore, remain unchangingly itself throughout the supposed change. Hence nothing changes substantially at all; change is merely a superficial appearance. Even though our experience tells us that everything changes, when our reason reflects upon the experience of change, it tells us that really nothing at all changes. And reason, not experience, must be accepted as the source and standard of truth. Thus the Eleatics are the first rationalists.

Xenophanes of Colophon in Asia Minor (who was somewhat older than Heraclitus) is said by Plato and Aristotle to be the originator of the theory developed by Parmenides and the other Eleatics; but his monism seems to be primarily of a theological form, consisting in the repudiation of polytheism and anthropomorphism and in the insistence that God is one and all-controlling.

Parmenides (born about 516 B.C.) is most important of the philosophers who deny the reality of change. Change must be unreal and illusory, Parmenides argues, because for a real thing or being to change is, by definition, for it to become something different; and to be different from the real or being is to be unreal or nonbeing, which is nothing at all. Hence *being* or what is *real* cannot change, and of course *nonbeing* or what is *unreal* cannot really change either. Hence logic requires that there cannot really be any such thing as change, that the appearance of change is mere illusion.

Parmenides also argues that plurality is unreal and illusory, that only one thing can really be. If a second thing existed, as second it would have to be different from the first thing. But to be different from the first thing, which is real, is to be different from the real; and to be different from the real is to be unreal, that is, nothing at all. Hence there cannot really be any second or third thing. The real must be one. Plurality, like change, is illusory.

The important presuppositions in these arguments are two. The first is that the laws of logic, and especially the law of non-contradiction, are true of objective reality as well as of thought. For Parmenides thought and being are one. Where there is a conflict between sensation and reason, as there seems to be in the case of change and plurality, sensation must be forfeited and reason must be followed. The second of the presuppositions essential to Parmenides' arguments for the unreality of change and plurality is that the term "real" (or "being") is, like a proper name, applicable to a single thing only. While this presupposition might seem to be a conclusion proven by the above argument that plurality is illusory, it is actually presupposed by that argument. When Parmenides uses the word "being" it is as if he were talking about George Washington, the first president of the United States. A second being, a second real thing, cannot exist any more than there can be a second George Washington, a second first president of the United States. Of course Parmenides may be right; "being" and "reality" may truly be proper names, applying to only one thing. Here we must be careful not to anticipate distinctions not made until later.

For Parmenides change and multiplicity are therefore unreal because they both involve something's being other than the real and because being other than the real is self-contradictory and impossible. Being, for Parmenides, is therefore unchanging, eternal or timeless (since time involves change), homogeneous, and indivisible. This is "the way of truth." Hence the world of nature which we sense is unreal, and to accept it as real is "the way of opinion." Here arises the problem of the status of illusion. Let us grant Parmenides that the physical world is illusory. So it really and truly *is* illusory, and hence has the reality, at any rate, of being an illusion. But where in Parmenides' unchanging, monolithic being is there any place for *apparent* multiplicity and change? This difficulty is faced by every philosopher whose concept of the world is too small to include false concepts of the world.

Zeno (born about 490–485 B.C.) formulated his famous paradoxes to defend, probably against Pythagoreans, the view of Parmenides that reality is one and unchanging. This use of paradox amounts to indirect or *reductio ad absurdum* argument, the proof of a proposition by showing that its contradictory is self-contradictory or absurd. Probably the most famous of these paradoxes is that of Achilles and the tortoise. Achilles can never overtake the tortoise because when he has covered half the distance to the tortoise he must still cover the other half, and when he has covered half of that he must still cover the other half of that half, and so on ad infinitum. Achilles continually approaches but never reaches the tortoise—even if the tortoise is not moving at all. Furthermore, not only can Achilles not catch the tortoise, but, as shown in another one of the paradoxes, he cannot even get started. Before he reaches any given point on the race course he must reach the point halfway to it, but before he can do that he must reach the point halfway to that halfway point, and the point halfway to that point, and so on ad infinitum. So Achilles cannot even move.

The essential presupposition behind these paradoxes is that the infinite divisibility of spatial and temporal continua by reason must also be an infinite divisibility in reality. Since the infinite divisibility of time and space in our thought leads to the concept of infinitesimals, for one who believes in time and space there really must be infinitesimals which are spatially and temporally unextended. Since all space and time are infinitely divisible in thought, all space and time must consist of non-spatial, nontemporal infinitesimals—which is to say that there is really nothing spatial or temporal at all, and hence really no change or motion at all. Finally, since all these infinitesimals must collapse into one, since they have no extension by which they are distinguished from each other, they cannot really have any multiplicity either. This assumption that what is divisible by reason is divisible in reality will be rejected by Democritus, but it logically follows from Parmenides' belief that being and reason are identical.

Melissus (who flourished about 440 B.C.) defended Parmenides' theory against the Pluralists by arguments similar to those of Parmenides and Zeno. Motion cannot exist, he argues, for it requires a void (which Democritus also will concede) and a void is self-contradictory and impossible, a nothing which is something (which Democritus will not concede). However, Melissus introduces two important modifications into Parmenides' theory. Being must be infinite, not finite as Parmenides apparently held, for if it were finite it would have to be bounded by something outside it, in which case there would be a being other than the universal Being. Hence also Being cannot be material as Parmenides seems to imply that it is, for all material beings are finite or bounded. Being must be infinite and immaterial. Here we can see the logic behind Anaximander's *apeiron* applied to Eleatic monism to reassert Anaximander's fundamental insight that reality must in some sense be infinite and indeterminate.

How then can a thing change and yet remain the same? Heraclitus' and the Eleatics' answer is that it cannot. For Heraclitus everything changes except the fact and law of change itself, and this law of change is the identity of opposites. For the Eleatics, however, nothing can change, for the real could change only to what is unreal, or vice versa, which would be no change at all; and only one real thing can exist, for any second thing would be other than the real and hence unreal. This dilemma between all change and no change is the crucial problem faced by the Pluralist philosophers.

1-4. *The Pluralists*

The Pluralists—Empedocles, Anaxagoras, and the Atomists (Leucippus and Democritus)—are equally concerned with both aspects of the Milesians' problem, the problem of the world stuff and the problem of change. Their treatment of these problems represents, in different ways, an attempted reconciliation of the position of Heraclitus with that of the Eleatics. In contrast to Heraclitus and the Eleatics, who represented the two extremes of all change and all stability, the Pluralists try to hit a golden mean which will preserve both change and stability, multiplicity and unity, experience and logic. Our sense experience tells us that there is a real world of many changing things, and our reason—at least as interpreted by the Eleatics—tells us that reality at its basic level must be immutable. The essential characteristic of the Pluralists' reconciliation of these two extremes is the recognition of reality as a plurality of immutable elements with changing interrelations. The Eleatics' immutable Being becomes a number of immutable beings, and the fact that there are more than one of these permits the retention of Heraclitus' change considered as rearrangements of these immutable beings.

Empedocles (about 494–434 B.C.) takes as the immutable beings or "elements," fire, air, water, and earth. Each of these "roots," as he called them, is like the Being of Parmenides, except that it moves. However, this movement does not occur in a void because, as Empedocles agrees with Melissus, the idea of a void is self-contradictory. Empedocles, however, rejects the conclusion which Melissus drew from the impossibility of a void, the conclusion that change and motion are therefore impossible, and maintains that motion exists in a plenum, a completely full world. It is not necessary that any space be empty in order for something to move; each moving thing replaces some other moving thing, which replaces some other moving thing, etc., so that, apparently, the movement of any one thing requires the movement of everything else in the world.

The agencies ultimately causing this motion are love and hate. These agencies seem to be grasped hylozoistically as both the emotional forces which we call love and hate and the physical forces of attraction and repulsion. Furthermore, love and hate seem to be conceived by Empedocles both as the forces themselves and as agents exercising those forces. Here again we have manifestation of the holism and hylozoism, the absence of distinction, characteristic of the early stages of thought. With his principles of love and hate Empedocles does, however, introduce one distinction which had not yet been made, at least not clearly. In seeing the Pythagoreans add a principle of determinacy to Anaximander's principle of indeterminacy, we noted that they apparently did not make any distinction between the determinate and the determining, between the Limited and the Limiting (p. 18). This distinction Empedocles clearly makes. Love and hate are for him determining agencies or forces which are quite distinct from the principle of determinateness supplied by the four "roots": fire, air, water, and earth. Empedocles thus distinguishes out of the original whole of reality a third kind of principle, a principle of agency, to add to the principles of indeterminacy and determinateness extracted earlier by Anaximander and the Pythagoreans.

The resulting process of change is the mingling and separation of the four roots—fire, air, water, and earth—by the two agencies, love and hate. Such mingling and separation—which is similar to Anaximander's concept of the separating out of pairs of opposites from the indeterminate—has four main logical and temporal stages. The original condition is one of homogeneity, a fusion of all the roots by the agency of love or attraction. Love reigns over hate. The second stage is one of gradual separation of the roots from each other under the power of repulsion or hate. Hate is in the ascendancy, and in this period distinct individual things come into existence. The third stage is one of complete heterogeneity, the completest possible separation of the roots from each other so that individual things pass out of existence. Hate reigns over love. The fourth and final stage is one of a mingling of the roots with each other to bring individual things into existence once more. Love is in the ascendancy. These four stages continually follow each other in an endless cycle of production and destruction of worlds. Worlds are born in the second and fourth stages, and they die in the first and third stages.

Anaxagoras (born around 500 B.C.) criticizes the four Empedoclean roots as insufficiently elemental and general. More different kinds of elements are needed to account for the things we experience; in fact, Anaxagoras argues, every distinct kind of thing must have a corresponding element. Hence these elements, which Anaxagoras regarded as the "seeds" or "germs" of all things, are infinite in number and variety. Every compound thing contains, in different amounts, all the different kinds of seeds. No matter how pure a piece of "pure" gold may be, it also contains the seeds of other metals and of all other things whatsoever. In this way he accounts for the possibility of anything changing into anything else.

For Anaxagoras these seeds are essentially qualitative rather than quantitative. Whether they have any quantitative size at all seems unclear. In some of the extant fragments of Anaxagoras' views these seeds seem to be pure qualities without any quantity at all; in others they seem to be quantitative infinitesimals, perhaps following Zeno's assumption of real infinite divisibility; and sometimes they seem to have very small size. These seeds, like Empedocles' roots and Parmenides' Being, lack temporal beginning and end and lack internal change. But each seed is unlike Parmenides' Being in the fact that it is in motion and has either no size at all or only a very small size; however, Parmenides' position implies, as Melissus saw, that his Being has no size. Here the tables are turned on Parmenides' dictum that thought and being are identical and on Zeno's assumption that what is divisible in thought is divisible in reality, for Anaxagoras accepts both propositions, at least tacitly, and yet accepts the consequence rejected by Parmenides and Zeno that there is in reality an infinity of infinitesimal entities. Is it logically possible to derive from these unextended seeds the extended things that make up the world? Zeno, with his paradox of the millet seeds, argues "No." If no single millet seed makes any sound when it is dropped, then a handful of millet seeds cannot make any sound. Getting extension from nonextension looks, in short, like getting something from nothing.

The agency which causes the motion of the seeds, according to Anaxagoras, is reason or mind *(nous)*. But it is an element as well as the agency, for Anaxagoras speaks of reason seeds as the finest of all. Reason seeds are distributed with the other seeds throughout all things, and thus reason also functions as a principle of unity and intelligibility. As agent, however, reason is pure and homogeneous, and it is the only thing which is entirely of one kind.

Change is simply the rearrangement of the seeds by reason. Is this a change of place? Anaxagoras seems to think so; he agrees with Empedocles in having motion without a void. But if the seeds are themselves unextended, seemingly a change of place cannot occur nor any quantitative change at all.

Democritus (born about 460 B.C.) developed a theory of atomism whose essential ideas were probably derived from Leucippus, about whom very little is known. The basic principles are the full and the empty, being and nonbeing; and the elements composing being or the full, he calls atoms—undivided and indivisible particles (from a = not and *tomein* = to cut). As its name implies, each atom has a definite size, even though it is too small to be visible; and it is not divisible into any smaller parts or more basic elements. Zeno had argued that change and multiplicity logically require infinitesimals, because extended continua are infinitely divisible in thought and what is divisible in thought is divisible in reality. Anaxagoras also seemed to accept this position implicitly, and this created the problem of getting extended things out of unextended components. But Democritus rejects this position, holding that while things are infinitely divisible in thought they are not infinitely divisible in reality. He thus avoids Anaxagoras' problem: things can be extended because the elements composing them are extended. This position marks the beginning of a break from the rationalism of the Eleatics from the view that thought and reality are identical, and it also marks the beginning of another distinction in the originally undifferentiated, hylozoistic whole of reality— a distinction between subjective thought and objective reality. This distinction will not be made absolute until modern times, however; and it will become the essence of modern philosophy.

According to Democritus, the atoms possess only quantitative characteristics such as size, shape, position, and motion. Qualitative characteristics like color, sound, and odor arise only in our perception of the gross objects that are compounded out of the atoms. This distinction between objective quantitative and subjective qualitative characteristics is another manifestation of the distinction between the mind and its objects which will be seen to grow to an extreme in modern philosophy. Like everything else, our subjective experiences are by hypothesis composed of quantitative, nonqualitative atoms. How can these qualities possibly be obtained from something that has no qualities? Here Democritus only reverses rather than solves Anaxagoras' problem. Anaxagoras believed that quantity and extension are derived from what is nonquantitative and extensionless (the seeds), and Democritus believes that qualities come from what is without qualities (the atoms). Each seems to be a case of getting something from nothing, and thus a failure to meet Parmenides.

Democritus' void is another case of a solution to one problem creating a new problem. The existence of a void is necessary to account for the possibility of motion; here Democritus agrees with Melissus and disagrees with Empedocles and Anaxagoras. However, Democritus disagrees with Melissus' conclusion that therefore there cannot be any motion. It is indeed difficult to see how a thing can move from one place to another when there is no empty place for it to move into. But it is also difficult to see how a place can exist which is totally empty of everything whatsoever. Melissus had argued that the very idea of a totally empty place is self-contradictory, for it is a nothing which is also something. For a thing to move into a place that place must be empty. If it is empty, then there is nothing between the bounding bodies. But if nothing is between the bounding bodies, they are together, and if they are together there is no empty space. Yet motion apparently requires empty space. This situation is similar to that in Anaximander's indeterminate. Just as the indeterminate had to be both indeterminate and determinate, so Democritus' void has to be both nothing and something. A clear resolution of this problem will not be achieved until Plato (Ch. 3-2.1.).

The agency of motion and change is just the atoms themselves, according to Democritus. There is no distinct principle of agency and none is necessary, he argues, because motion is an inherent property of the atoms themselves and therefore is as everlasting as they are. As William of Ockham and others said much later, entities should not be multiplied beyond necessity. Whether change requires any outside explanation and agency is a question which will divide philosophers all through history. For Democritus, however, change is simply the unending rearrangement of atoms in the void. Everything is mechanically determined; there is no chance and no purpose—a view which will be revived in the atomistic, mechanistic materialism of Hobbes and early modern science (Ch. 7-3). And all change is change of place, all change is quantitative. Whether qualitative changes can be reduced to such locomotion is a corollary of the problem of whether quality can be derived from quantity.

1-5. *Summary*

The Pluralists, and especially Democritus, conclude the story of the Cosmological Period of ancient Greek philosophy. The guiding theme of that story is the nature of the ultimate stuff of which all things are made and its change into all particular things. Such a stuff must be absolutely universal, and it should be as simple or unitary as possible. Thales' water and Anaximenes' air are too restricted, and Anaximander maintained that the world stuff must be completely indefinite. But this created the problem of deriving the definite things of the world out of something which lacks all definiteness. The Pythagoreans solved this problem by adding to the indeterminate a second principle, one of determinateness; to the Unlimited is added the Limit, and all things are begotten from this cosmic mother and father. Such begetting, such change, was to Heraclitus essentially an identity of opposites. But the idea of opposites being identical seemed self-contradictory to Parmenides and his Eleatic followers, so they concluded that change, and along with it multiplicity, must be merely illusory appearance. How can the reality of change and multiplicity be preserved in the face of Eleatic logic? By pluralizing the Eleatic Being, the Pluralists answered, with change as the rearrangement of these basic, immutable beings. For Empedocles these basic, immutable beings are the qualitative-quantitative elements fire, air, water, and earth; and they are moved by love and hate. For Anaxagoras they are qualitative seeds of all possible kinds, and they are moved by the finest of all seeds, those of reason. For Democritus the basic, immutable beings are purely quantitative atoms possessing motion as an intrinsic property, and all change is the motion of these particles in empty space. Reality is both many and one, both changing and unchanging, though in different respects.

This conclusion of the story of substance and change is only temporary, however, for in the Systematic Period this ending becomes part of the beginning of a new story. While the Pluralists saved the appearances, keeping a world of multiplicity and change, their solution seems not to satisfy the demands of reason, for it contains conceptual difficulties which later philosophers will note and try to remove. First, the Pluralists have not really analyzed the concept of being in such a way as to avoid the arguments of the Eleatics. How can there be more than one atom? Any second atom, Parmenides argued, would be other than the first one, and if the first one is real, the second one would have to be other than what is real. But to be other than what is real, is to be unreal. Hence it would appear that logically there cannot be two beings—whether atoms or seeds or roots. This argument is not met by the Pluralists; their concept of being is merely ad hoc. Second and correlatively, Democritus has not analyzed the concept of nonbeing or the void in such a way as to avoid the arguments of the Eleatics. How can nonbeing be? Is this not a contradiction in terms? How can space be empty of *everything?* Third, as a consequence of the first two points, the problem of change is still unsettled. Does change require an identity of opposites, as Heraclitus said? Is this notion self-contradictory, as the Eleatics thought? A more adequate and sophisticated analysis of the concepts of being and nonbeing upon which these questions are based must await Plato and Aristotle.

SUGGESTED READINGS

The extant fragments of the writings of the philosophers of this period. The standard edition is Diels, H. *Fragmente der Versokratiker,* ed. W. Kranz. 3 vols. 5th and later eds. Berlin: Weidmann, 1935–54. The following English translations are recommended.

Freeman, K. *Ancilla to the Pre-Socratic Philosophers.* Cambridge: Harvard University Press, 1948.

————. *The Pre-Socratic Philosophers: A Companion to Diels.* Oxford: Blackwell, 1949. Freeman's two books constitute a translation and adaptation of Diels.

Burnet, J. *Early Greek Philosophy.* 4th ed. London: A. and C. Black, 1930; paperback ed. New York: Meridian Books, 1960. A standard study with most of the extant fragments.

Kirk, G. S. and J. E. Raven. *Pre-Socratic Philosophy.* New York: Cambridge, 1957, 1960. Excellent, though it has fewer fragments than Burnet. Good bibliography on pp. 446–49.

Nahm, M. C. *Selections from Early Greek Philosophy.* 4th ed. New York: Crofts, 1965. Some of the fragments with introductions.

For bibliography, see:

Guthrie, W. K. C. *The Earlier Pre-Socratics and the Pythagoreans,* Vol. I of *A History of Greek Philosophy.* Cambridge University Press, 1962. Pp. 493–503.

Chapter 2

The Anthropological Philosophers

In addition to their concern with substance and change, the Cosmological philosophers gradually began to pay attention to man and increasingly developed a psychology, epistemology, and even an ethics. Thus another aspect of the originally un-differentiated whole of experienced reality gradually began to be distinguished. Empedocles had a distinct theory of conscious-ness and perception according to which tiny replicas or effluxes of things enter percipient pores in the body of the conscious person; each pore or sense organ is receptive to effluxes which are like itself. Anaxagoras held a similar theory, except that in it each sense organ perceives its opposite. Democritus also held an efflux theory of perception, but he developed it much more fully to distinguish sensation from rational knowledge and to formulate a theory of error. Illusion and error are due partly to differences among the various sense organs and partly to damages suffered by the effluxes en route from the object to the perceiving person. Rational knowledge escapes this sensory distortion to a certain extent, because in rational knowledge the effluxes by-pass the sense organs and travel directly to the soul atoms. The soul consists of the finest, roundest, smoothest, most mobile atoms (note the similarity to Anaxagoras' reason seeds); and they are inhaled like Anaximenes' air and spread throughout the entire body. Consciousness is the motion of these soul atoms, and death is the loss of all soul atoms from the body and their dispersion back into the universe at large, carrying with them an impersonal immortality. Democritus even developed an ethical theory, though almost no knowledge of it remains today.

This concern with man becomes the dominant motif of the Anthropological Period; the human part of reality is extracted and focused upon, and everything else is viewed in relation to man. Furthermore, not only is man as a whole concentrated upon, but the withdrawal from the whole of reality also tends to be a withdrawal even to the individual person. This emphasis becomes a growing individualism and relativism, an outlook which tends to conclude from the contradictions in and among the earlier philosophers that human intelligence is incapable of grasping any universal or abiding truths. While this whole Anthrological Period is a withdrawal from the whole of being to the human part of it, this period also includes a withdrawal and a return: the Sophists' withdrawal to the opinions of the individual at the moment and the return of Socrates to man as a whole and his relation to the world.

2-1. *The Sophists*

The word "sophist" is related to the word for wisdom, and the Sophists were so called because they were regarded as wise men and as teachers of wisdom; the word "sophist" did not at first have any pejorative connotation. The philosophy of the Sophists is relativistic and individualistic in two main ways.

First, the Sophists maintain a relativism and individualism in their theories of knowledge and reality. The best expression of these is the famous dictum of Protagoras (born about 490 B.C.): "Man is the measure of all things, of things that are that they are, and of things that are not that they are not." Truth is what is perceived true by man, and being is seeming. The individual person, not man as such, is the final measure of truth and reality; and furthermore, ultimately the individual person's experience of the moment is the measure and determinant of all things—at least it is as Plato depicts Protagoras. "Truth" and "reality" are only the flux of momentary individual sensations. Protagoras thus presents the subjective corollary of Heraclitus' famous dictum that everything flows.

This skeptical relativism is carried even further by Gorgias, the nihilist, in his famous three sentences: Nothing exists. If anything did exist, it would be unknowable. And if anything did exist and were knowable, the knowledge of it could not be communicated to others. His arguments (which contain the particularly unjustified premise that whatever is nowhere does not exist) are quite similar to those of the Eleatics, though his conclusions are quite opposed to theirs. However, Gorgias' arguments are also Heraclitean: everything was or will be or is becoming, but never actually is; and things change before they can be known and communicated. Reality is just what it seems to be to the individual at a moment; it is only a flux of sensation.

Second, the Sophists maintain an ethical and social relativism and individualism. Callicles, who is known only through Plato's *Gorgias,* believes that conventional morality is wholly relative to particular social conditions; it is unnatural and therefore bad. Natural or real morality for him is the will of the stronger. Thrasymachus holds with greater consistency that there is no such natural morality, and hence no morality, no right or wrong, at all. "Right" is simply a word used to designate what is in the interest of the stronger. Right and wrong, like truth and error, existence and nonexistence, are basically the momentary impressions and desires of the individual.

2-2. Socrates

While Socrates (469–399 B.C.) seems in his early life to have been interested in Cosmological philosophy and especially attracted to Anaxagoras, his major concern, like that of the Sophists, is man. Unlike the Sophists, however, he is concerned with man as essentially and naturally social and as possessing, at least potentially, universal and stable truths. While the Sophists are the subjective counterpart of Heraclitus, Socrates is the subjective counterpart of Parmenides: truth is unchanging and the same for all. With Socrates the withdrawal to the individual person is followed by the beginning of a return to society and to the world of which the individual is a part and to which he is essentially related.

Socrates the man, seeker for truth and martyr of philosophy, is well depicted in Plato's dramatic trilogy, the *Apology, Crito,* and *Phaedo,* presenting the trial, imprisonment, and execution of Socrates on the charges of impiety and corrupting the youth. Socrates' speeches in his own defence which are reported in the *Apology,* as well as his activities throughout Plato's dialogues, reveal his character as a paradox involving seemingly conflicting roles.[1] On the one side Socrates played negative roles. Socrates the agnostic claimed that he had no knowledge, and the oracle's intention in saying that no one was wiser than Socrates must have been that only Socrates knew that he was ignorant and that human wisdom is of little worth. Socrates the destructive critic relentlessly exposed and destroyed the claims to knowledge made by others. He was like a gadfly sent to sting awake the great steed of Athens. On the other side Socrates played positive roles. Socrates the preacher preached that the soul is more important than the body and that the Athenians should therefore spend less time on material things and more on their souls. Socrates the teacher taught that knowledge is the only way to save the soul, that no one does wrong willingly but only because of ignorance.

These opposed roles are integrated and the paradox of Socrates' character resolved, however, by a fifth and more basic role, that of the searcher or inquirer. Socrates preached, not a system of detailed doctrines, but that each person must discover the truth for himself; and Socrates taught, not doctrines, but a method of discovering the good and the true. As a critic Socrates exposed unexamined pretensions to knowledge, and he was agnostic concerning any final, infallible knowledge. While each person should find for himself justifiable beliefs, even giving his life for them if necessary as Socrates himself did, every belief is open to question, and Socrates was always the first to submit even his deepest convictions to re-examination, as he does in the *Crito*. This method which Socrates used and taught has been so influential that even today it usually bears his name: the Socratic method. It is also known as the maieutic method, the method of intellectual midwifery: Socrates is the midwife who delivers the ideas and convictions of others. He does this by a process of continual questioning which reveals the implications of the questioned belief. These implications are then examined, the belief is revised in the light of this examination, the revised belief is questioned, and so on. The unexamined life, Socrates taught, is not worth living.

Since Socrates wrote nothing, so far as it is known, since he taught very few specific doctrines, and since he never clearly defined the nature of the good the knowledge of which he was seeking, one would expect that his followers would define that good variously and that the spirit of Socrates would be expressed in quite different ways by his many disciples. The major Socratic, the most gifted and influential of Socrates' followers, was Plato. But there were also lesser Socratics, the other less gifted and less influential philosophers who were enthralled by Socrates and who tried to discover and formulate the wisdom and the good which he had sought.

2-3. *The Megarians*

One group of Socrates' disciples was led by Euclid of the Greek city of Megara (not to be confused with Euclid, the Alexandrian geometer). Euclid the Megarian's early training had been in Eleatic philosophy (Ch. 1-3.2.), but he was also a devoted follower of Socrates—perhaps one of his earliest disciples—and he was present at Socrates' execution. With this dual background, naturally Euclid would see Parmenides' and Socrates' similarities: the Good sought by Socrates but never clearly defined is the same as the one Being which was central to Eleatic philosophy. Like Parmenides' Being, Socrates' Good is one and unchanging; it is the same for all men in all times and places, and it is the unchanging essence of which the various specific virtues are but particular manifestations. Since Parmenides' Being and

Socrates' Good thus have the same characteristics, they are, Euclid and his school concluded, one and the same thing. Ultimate reality is thus distinctly of human concern rather than a bare, valueless, neutral world of mere facts; and, conversely, human values are rooted in ultimate reality and are not merely artificial or conventional. The Megarian philosophers' method of proving these conclusions was, not surprisingly, the indirect or *reductio ad absurdum* method of Zeno, Parmenides' follower; and in practicing this method they added to the stock of paradoxes established by Zeno. Such a conceiving of ultimate reality in terms of value will reach its peak in Plato's identification of the source of all things with the Good and Aristotle's identification of the Good with full actuality; but, since it is a central theme of Socratic philosophy, it is also expressed by the other lesser Socratic philosophers.

2-4. *The Cynics*

The Cynics probably received their name from the fact that Antisthenes (born about 444 B.C.), the founder of their movement, taught in a gymnasium outside Athens called Cynosarges, although someone has suggested that it was because the Cynics lived a dog's life (*kynos* = doglike). The present-day meaning of the word "cynic," while traceable to this school, is only partially applicable to it. According to Antisthenes virtue is knowledge, as Socrates had claimed; and pleasure-seeking is a positive impediment to the acquisition of virtue. "I would rather be mad than glad," Antisthenes is supposed to have said. Much of the essential character of the Cynic comes out in Antisthenes' colorful follower, Diogenes, whose living in a tub was apparently one of the main sights in pleasure-loving Corinth. His cynicism is evident in the need he felt for a lantern when searching for an honest man in the searing sun of Greece, and also in the response he is said to have given Alexander the Great when that ruler of the world asked Diogenes what he could do for him. "Get out of my light," was the answer; and after that according to the legend Alexander said that if he were not Alexander he would want to be Diogenes, for, perhaps, each was a king, though Diogenes was a king only over his own soul. Another legend indicative of Diogenes' cynicism (though perhaps not of that of Antisthenes who was more dialectically inclined) concerns his response to a long and careful exposition of Zeno's arguments for the impossibility of motion. Diogenes silently arose and walked across the street.

Civilization in most of its forms is what the Cynics were cynical about, but they were cynical about it because there was something else about which they were not cynical. Their conviction was that virtue means inner strength, spiritual ruggedness, self-sufficiency; and in comparison with this ideal they condemned the moral weakness of civilization. They believed that all forms of society are corrupt because they rob the individual of his self-sufficiency. The ideal is a return to nature, especially to that true and uncorrupted nature or soul within the individual person. The theoretical foundations for this ethical individualism were supplied, especially by Antisthenes, in a corresponding logical individualism or nominalism—universals are only names *(nomina)*. There are no common or universal properties; only the unique individual is real. Hence only judgments of identity are possible; one cannot say that "A cow is white" because a cow is just a cow and white is just white. Thus the Cynics emphasized Socrates' concern for the individual at the expense of his concern for universal definitions and truths.

2-5. *The Cyrenaics*

The Cyrenaics were so named because they lived in the city of Cyrene on the Mediterranean coast of Africa. Contrary to the Cynics, the Cyrenaics emphasized the convivial side of Socrates' personality; and in their hedonism they at first seem to be diametrically opposed to the Cynics who held pleasure in contempt. The story of the development of the philosophy of the Cyrenaics, however, reveals a strong similarity between these two movements.

The story opens with Aristippus' (born about 435 B.C.) advocating a relatively simple, straight-forward hedonism. The good is the greatest amount of intense and enduring pleasure. All pleasures are equal in value; pinball is as good as poetry if the pleasures arising from it are as intense and enduring, and in point of fact the sensual or so-called bodily pleasures are ordinarily the most intense ones. The second stage of the story, which is conjectured and only implicit in what is known of the Cyrenaics, is the discovery of a paradox, the paradox that pleasure-seeking (at least in the case of sensual or bodily pleasures) involves its opposite, pain-seeking, because the enjoyment of bodily pleasures involves antecedent and subsequent pains. In order to get the greatest amount of pleasure out of a banquet, for example, a person should build up the greatest possible appetite, a state of privation in which he even experiences pangs of hunger. After getting the greatest amount of pleasure out of the banquet, he has indigestion and a hang-over. Thus arises the paradox that the greater the amount of bodily pleasure, the greater the amount of bodily privation and pain, and that pleasure-seeking is therefore also pain-seeking. Hence in the third stage of the story the conclusion is drawn that one should seek mental rather than bodily or sensual pleasures because the former are freer of pain and more enduring. Indeed, sensual pleasures are even to be avoided because they are ephemeral, mixed with pain, and disturbing to the mind and its pleasures. But in the fourth stage the discovery is made that mental pleasures also suffer from the paradox of involving their opposites, although to a lesser extent than bodily pleasures do. The saying, "Absence makes the heart grow fonder," implies that anything can be tiring after a time. Therefore, in the fifth stage Theodorus concludes that the particular pleasure is unimportant and that the good life is rather an abiding, steady state of cheerfulness. But what is cheerfulness, and how is it to be attained? By "the avoidance of trouble," says Hegesias in the sixth and final stage of the story; this is the most we can hope to achieve, and Hegesias is said even to have recommended suicide; perhaps he did so in the belief that death would bring the avoidance of all trouble. Anniceris the Younger later returned to a theory of positive pleasure, but he so attenuated it that it had little of the simplicity and robustness of Aristippus' hedonism.

Thus robust pleasure-seeking turns into a quietistic, negative avoidance of pain and trouble; and the ending of the story of the Cyrenaics will be the beginning of the story of the Epicureans (Ch. 5-2). Hence the philosophy of the Cyrenaics ultimately is not as different from that of the Cynics as it initially seems to be. The Cynic seeks tranquillity through an independence of and contempt for pleasure and pain, and the Cyrenaic seeks it through the control of pleasure and the avoidance of pain and trouble.

2-6. Summary

The philosophers of the Anthropological Period turn their attention to the part of reality that is most interesting and important to man, namely man himself; and they see the rest of reality from this perspective. The Sophists withdraw even to the individual's sensations of the moment; and Socrates and his followers, while still primarily concerned with the individual, begin the return from the individual sensations of the moment to the whole life of the individual, and even toward society and the world as a whole. This return to the Cosmological philosophers' concern with the whole of reality but with a vision of man's place in it will now be brought to its culmination in the two great philosophers of the Systematic Period, Plato and Aristotle.

SUGGESTED READINGS

2-1. The sections on the Sophists in either Freeman or Nahm:
   Freeman, K. *Ancilla to the Pre-Socratic Philosophers*. Cambridge, Mass.: Harvard University Press, 1948.
   ————. *The Pre-Socratic Philosophers: A Companion to Diels*. Oxford, Eng.: Blackwell, 1949.
   Nahm, M. C. *Selections from Early Greek Philosophy*. 4th ed. New York: Appleton-Century-Crofts, 1965.
2-2. Plato *Euthyphro; Apology; Crito; Phaedo*, the beginning to 63E and 115A to end; and *Symposium* 215A to the end.
   For different pictures of Socrates see:
   Xenophon. *Memorabilia*.
   Aristophanes. *Clouds*.

2-3, 4, 5. Zeller, E. *Socrates and the Socratic Schools,* trans. O. J. Reichel, 3rd ed. New York: Russell & Russell, 1962. Chs. 3-10 and 12-14.

For Bibliographies, see:

Guthrie, W. K. C. *The Earlier Pre-Socratics and the Pythagoreans,* Vol. I of *A History of Greek Philosophy.* Cambridge, Eng.: Cambridge University Press, 1962, Pp. 493–503.

Owens, J. *A History of Ancient Western Philosophy.* New York: Appleton-Century-Crofts, 1965. Pp. 184–86, 377.

Chapter 3

Plato

The basic philosophical task that confronted Plato of Athens (428/7–348/7 B.C.) was to find a way to purify and synthesize the main ideas of his predecessors. These are generally and basically the ideas of stability and change, unity and multiplicity, form and flux, reason and experience. The Eleatics recognized a principle of form, a principle of stability and determinateness, and Socrates depicted and exemplified the rational process leading to its discovery and its effect upon man. Heraclitus recognized a principle of flux, a principle of change and indeterminateness, and the Sophists stressed its subjective corollary of sense experience. These two principles, and the rational and experiential cognitions of them, seem incompatible with each other; and yet they cannot really be since they are both true. How, then, can they be combined and reconciled? By developing the basic insight of the Pythagoreans that two opposed yet harmonized principles exist in the world: the principles of the Limit and the Unlimited, of definiteness and indefiniteness.

Plato's development of this Pythagorean insight into a synthesis of form and flux occurs in two fairly distinct stages, that of the so called middle dialogues and that of the later dialogues. Even if Plato actually rewrote earlier dialogues in the light of later ones to make them all contemporaneous and thus not properly arrangeable in a chronological order,[1] their internal characteristics make them fall fairly naturally into three groups. The "early" or Socratic dialogues—such as the *Euthyphro, Crito, Charmides,* and *Lysis*—tend to be inconclusive, with Socrates seeking a truth he has apparently not yet found. The "middle" dialogues—such as the *Phaedo, Symposium, Republic,* and *Phaedrus*—present the Plato best known to the general public; in them Socrates advocates a systematic hierarchical dualism of Ideas and particulars, souls and bodies. In the "later" dialogues —such as the *Parmenides, Sophist, Philebus,* and *Timaeus*—the Socrates of the early and middle dialogues tends to fade into the background in favor of a view which though less clear and explicit is more integrated and dynamic than the Form-Flux dualism of the middle dialogues.

3-1. *The Middle Dialogues*

3-1.1. *The Realm of Forms*

The most fundamental concept in the philosophy of the middle dialogues is the realm of Forms or Ideas. By "Idea" or "Form" Plato does not mean a mental idea in anyone's mind; the traditional translation of *idea* as "Idea" is very misleading and is now, happily, being abandoned. A Platonic Idea is not a mental seeing but rather that which is seen by the mind (*idein* = to see), the *object* of an idea or concept. Thus the Forms are not mental, but neither are they physical; they are independent of and prior to both the physical world and the mind. Hence Plato's Idea-ism is not the metaphysical idealism or mentalism which will arise only in the modern period. The Forms are unique or *sui generis;* they have their own, peculiar, formal kind of being, a special realm of their own quite distinct from that of bodies and minds. They are archetypes, exemplars, essences, or "whats"—such things as manness, goodness, and happiness.

Why should Plato—or any one else, for that matter—accept such a doctrine of Forms? What are the reasons for believing in a realm of Forms, and what are the reasons for believing that they are prior to sensed particulars? Fundamentally three such reasons, three main lines of argument, lead to the conclusion that a special realm of Forms exists.[2]

The first reason is an *epistemological* one: the realm of Forms is necessary in order to account for the facts of human knowledge. On the one hand, the sensory world is composed of ever-changing particular things; this conviction Plato derived from Heraclitus and the Sophists, largely through an early teacher named Cratylus who was supposed to have gone Heraclitus one better by insisting that it is impossible to step into the same river even once, since the first stepping takes time during which the river has changed and thus is not the same. (Cratylus was also supposed to have refused to speak on the Heraclitean ground that the meaning of his words could not stay the same long enough for another person to grasp it.) Knowledge, on the other hand, is always of unchanging universals; this conviction Plato derived from Parmenides and Socrates. The chemical composition of sugar, unlike a particular lump of sugar, remains always the same. These two premises— that the world of the senses is changing and particular and that the objects of knowledge are unchanging and universal—lead to the conclusion that knowledge cannot be about the sensory world. Hence, it follows either that knowledge is impossible, or else that there is a nonsensory world which contains the objects of knowledge. Plato eliminates the former alternative without giving explicit reasons and leaves the latter, a world composed of unchanging, universal characteristics or forms which are what we know whenever we know anything. We *sense* the changing particulars of the physical world, but we *know* the unchanging universals of the formal world. Furthermore, these unchanging, universal forms are inescapably used to characterize the changing, particular things which we sense: a particular, melting lump of sugar is white, granular, sweet, and melting. Thus sensed things can be apprehended only as instances of forms. Hence the forms are, with respect to knowledge, prior to the changing particulars and thus properly Forms, with a capital *F*.

The second reason for believing in a realm of Forms is *axiological:* the realm of Forms is necessary to account for values and for moral, religious, and esthetic aspiration. Human aspiration or action is essentially a striving for unrealized goals. One aspires toward what does not yet exist; one acts to bring into existence that which is as yet unrealized. Where or how do these unrealized goals exist? They must exist somehow, for if they did not exist in any sense, they couldn't exist as goals of action; and our action toward them could not exist either. These unrealized goals cannot exist in the sensory world, for everything in it is already actually realized. For example, the education you seek, symbolized perhaps by a college diploma, does not yet exist actually in the world of nature. Nor can these unrealized goals exist merely in the mind; of course, the knowledge of them does exist in the mind, but the goals themselves are not at all subjective. Your mental picture of a college education is not what you are striving to realize but rather the college education itself; that which you picture, not your picture of it, needs to be explained. Where can these unrealized goals exist if not in the physical world or the mind? There must be a third domain, a third way of existing, peculiar to these unrealized goals—a world of ideals. Furthermore, these ideals or unrealized goals are *prior* to the actions which we actually perform in the world of nature. While the *realized* goal of receiving your diploma comes after the striving toward it, the *un*realized goal of receiving your diploma comes before the striving toward it as the cause of that striving and as a critical standard by which to judge that striving. Hence these ideals are truly Ideals, with a capital *I*. Finally, these unrealized goals or Ideals which determine and evaluate human action do so only insofar as they are known. A person cannot aspire toward something without having some idea of it, however vague. Therefore these Ideals are also Ideas or Forms.

The third reason for believing in a realm of Forms is an

ontological one: the realm of Forms is necessary to account for the facts about being or reality. Being itself cannot change, for, as Parmenides argued, the only thing it could change into is nonbeing. But the sensory world does inevitably change, just as Heraclitus insisted. Form these two premises the conclusion follows that being itself cannot be found in the sensory world, that genuine reality must lie in another realm. Furthermore, there *is* a sensory world only to the extent that it mirrors or participates in being, so the realm of being is prior to the sensory world as its cause. It is therefore a realm of Being, with a capital *B*. Finally, Being must also be both the object of true knowledge and the goal of action. True knowledge consists in apprehending what is, what exists. Action is for the sake of realizing something in the natural world that is already real as an Ideal. Hence Being lies in the realm of Ideas-Ideals, in the realm of Forms. As the plural of the words "Ideas," "Ideals," and "Forms" indicates, however, this Being is pluralistic as it was for the Pluralist philosophers rather than monistic as it was for the Eleatics.

These three reasons for believing in the realm of Forms are somewhat conflicting, however, in their indications as to just exactly what counts as a Form. The third reason, to account for being, implies that every Form is a positive being, and the second reason, to account for ideals, implies that every Form is a positive value. According to the third reason, therefore, negative or privative Forms, such as void or nonbeing, should not exist and according to the second reason no disvalue Forms, such as evil and ugliness, would exist. However, according to the first, epistemological reason, such negative and disvalue Forms must exist since they are objects of knowledge and since we conceive them. Negative and disvalue Forms have a place in Plato's later dialogues, but whether they remain truly Forms is not clear.

3-1.2. *The Ladder of Life*

From this doctrine of Forms Plato develops a comprehensive theory of the structure of the world and of man's relation to it, and nowhere does he do this more clearly and vividly than in the myth of the cave and the corresponding figure of the divided line which he presents in Books VI and VII of the *Republic:*

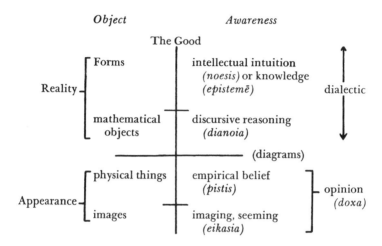

The verticality of the line indicates that reality and the awareness of it are higher and truer than appearance and the opinions about it, and the greater length of the higher segment of each main division of the line indicates the same thing.[3]

The images at the bottom of the line are analogous to the shadows on the wall and the echoes reverberating inside the cave, and the imaging or seeming of these images is analogous to the prisoners' seeing the shadows and hearing the echoes. What Plato has in mind is a state of consciousness, concerning both cognition and action, which is purely sensory and immediate, which is wholly absorbed in present appearances and impulses. The physical things at the next higher level on the line are analogous to the puppets and the fire inside the cave, and the corresponding empirical belief is analogous to the prisoners' awareness of them. This state of mind commonsense would call true knowledge of the physical world; it is physical knowledge in contrast to the metaphysical knowledge above the major division of the line. It includes not only commonsense knowledge of the world but also knowledge gained through natural science insofar as it is sensory rather than mathematical. It includes not only the immediate sensations of the lowest part of the line but also sensory memories and images which are added to immediate sensations to produce three-dimensional and enduring perceptions. This state of mind represents the purely physical attitude toward life, both in awareness and in action. It is only belief and not knowledge; together with imaging it is only opinion and not knowledge because it is only sensory and because the objects of sensation are not true beings but only particular fluctuating becomings.

The mathematical objects at the next higher level of the line are analogous to the shadows and reflections on the surface of the earth which are the first things the prisoner just out of the cave can discern, and discursive reasoning is analogous to the released prisoner's seeing of them. Here Plato is referring to conceptual knowledge which is discursive and deductive and which moves entirely on the plane of concepts from initial assumptions to deduced conclusions. The best example of this kind of knowledge is mathematics; but it also includes modern science in so far as it is conceptual and deductive, and, indeed, all purely deductive reasoning and the active attitudes based on it. The mathematical objects are forms yet not the same as the Forms, and Plato does not make their relation to the Forms entirely clear. The epistemological reason for believing in the Forms would indicate that mathematical objects are Forms, but the axiological and ontological reasons would indicate that they are not. While mathematical objects are, like the Forms, the objects of universal concepts, unlike the Forms they abstract from true reality and true value. They abstract from true reality because they are only possibilities and not actualities. Mathematical systems—and all deductively formulated sciences—possess in themselves only validity and not objective truth. A deductive conclusion is true if the postulates from which it is validly derived are true, but within the deductive system itself those postulates are only assumed and are not known to be true in themselves. Thus the truth or reality of a mathematical system requires reference to something outside it. Mathematical objects and deductive systems also do not consider values. A deductive system is concerned with what is good or beautiful or holy only if it is considered in terms of something outside it which is independently regarded as good or beautiful or holy. When the question of the truth or value of a mathematical or deductive system arises, we must, therefore, go beyond it to another realm.

This conclusion supplies the clue to the necessity of the highest part of the divided line, for the Forms are the absolute truths and values to which mathematical systems are relative and on which they are contingent. The Forms are analogous to the living beings seen by the released prisoners on the surface of the earth, and also, perhaps, to the stars and moon; and the intellectual intuition of the Forms is analogous to the released prisoner's vision of these things. The process which Plato calls dialectic in Book VII of the *Republic,* which is close to what is later called metaphysics, is analogous to the process of passing from the shadows and reflections to the real things from which they are derived. It is the process of mounting up from the hypothetical, relative, contingent, derived truths of discursive reasoning to the axiomatic, absolute, necessary, underived truths upon which the former depend. Dialectic or metaphysics is the search for the underlying absolute truths which give reality and value to all derivative truths. When these absolute truths and values (the Forms) are intellectually seen, and when the relative and hypothetical propositions of discursive reasoning are viewed as deriving from them, those relative and hypothetical propositions take on truth as well as logical validity and value as well as neutral factuality. While Plato attaches the name dialectic to the grasp of mathematical objects and Forms, this relation of dependency of the derived upon the underived extends also to the relation of sensory particulars, the things inside the cave, to the mathematical objects and Forms outside the cave. Everything lower depends upon the higher for its reality and value. Thus the Forms give reality and value not only to the mathematical objects but also, and a fortiori, to physical things and sensuous appearances. The return from the Forms to the mathematical objects must be continued in a return to the puppets and shadows inside the cave.

The Forms are not quite absolute, however, unless the Good

be counted as a Form; and here lies a problem. The Good, according to the *Republic,* is the single ultimate source of all things, both things known and the knowing of them. Like the sun in the myth of the cave, it is the source of all life and light, of all being and intelligibility; but as their source it transcends all being and intelligibility. One cannot gaze steadily at the unveiled sun but can glimpse it only briefly and know steadily that it is there only obliquely through the things which it illuminates; in the same manner one can never know the Good itself, the Absolute, more than momentarily but can know it steadily only indirectly through the things which it causes and makes intelligible. The Good itself seems not to be properly a Form, therefore, although Plato sometimes calls it a Form. It is rather the absolute source of the Forms and, through them, of everything else, and it is equally the absolute source of the awareness of all things. In the figure of the divided line the Good therefore properly belongs over both sides of the line equally, not just on the side of the objects. The Good is thus the ultimate unifying principle of Plato's system—explicitly in the middle dialogues and implicitly in the later dialogues. It is the God of the philosophy of Plato's middle dialogues, although what will be called God in the later dialogues is slightly different (Ch. 3-2.2). Perhaps it is also the ultimate good which Socrates sought but was never able to formulate, and which the Megarians identified with being (Ch. 2-3).

The relation between the world of Forms and the world of apparent particulars is the central problem of the philosophy of the middle dialogues. The bridge between the correlative types of awareness of these two worlds is supplied in Plato's theory of "secondary" education by mathematical diagrams, though they do not explicitly appear in the account of the divided line. As visual patterns diagrams are sensory, but as representing abstract forms they are conceptual. Thus they have one foot in each world; they bridge the gap between sensory awareness of particulars and conceptual awareness of mathematical objects and the Forms. But how can a concrete, particular, sensory object possibly represent an abstract, universal, conceptual object? If the Forms and particulars are related by similarity, there must be another Form, a "third man," by virtue of which the Form and the particular are similar. But then there would have to be still another Form to ground that similarity, and so on ad infinitum. So goes the famous "third man argument" which Aristotle used against the doctrine of Forms and which Plato himself offered as a criticism in his later dialogue, the *Parmenides.* This problem of the relation of Forms and particulars will be partially solved in the middle dialogues by the principle of the soul as a mediating agent (Ch. 3-1.6), and it will be more fully solved in the later dialogues (Ch. 3-2.2).

3-1.3. *Knowing as Recollecting*

Plato's famous theory of reminiscence *(anamnesis),* that all knowing is remembering what we already knew before birth, may seem like a poetic fancy; but powerful systematic reasons support it.

The epistemological reason for believing in the realm of Forms, that the Forms are necessary to account for knowledge because sensed objects are utterly unstable and particular, logically entails that knowing, as distinct from sensing and imagining, is a nonempirical activity, that the objects of knowledge, the Forms, are not intellectually abstracted from sense experience. The epistemological reason for believing in the priority of the Forms over sensory particulars—that a particular lump of sugar, for example, can be known to be what it is only because it "participates" in the Forms of sugar, white, sweet, etc.—logically entails that this nonsensuous knowledge of the Forms must occur *logically prior,* and apparently also *chronologically* prior, to the exercise of sensory recognition. If sensory recognition *(re-cognition)* begins with birth, knowledge of the Forms used to characterize those sensed particulars must have existed prior to birth. Therefore, assuming that sensory recognition begins, although of course in an extremely primitive form, with biological conception (Plato does not say this.), then prior to conception, prior to the existence of a body, a soul must already possess knowledge of the Forms which are used in the earliest sensory discrimination. Thus one obtains Plato's theory of a preexistent soul whose knowledge is forgotten when it is entombed in a body at birth (Plato here puns on *soma* = body, *sema* = tomb.) and which must, therefore, be laboriously recalled in the process ordinarily called learning. Logically, this preexistent soul also must be omniscient; it must know *all* the Forms, for the simple reason that there is no limit to what can or might be learned or remembered. Thus Plato writes in the *Phaedrus* that the soul —at least those of humans and gods—originally witnessed all things by virtue of a complete revolution of the spheres.

While knowledge is not empirical in the usual sense of being sensory, however, knowledge is empirical in the sense that it is acquired through a nonsensuous, incorporeal experience: the disembodied soul experiences the Forms. Furthermore, while the objects of knowledge are not found in and abstracted from sense experience, sense experience is absolutely necessary as a stimulus for the recollection of the objects of knowledge. While Meno's slave boy does not (supposedly) learn the Pythagorean theorem *from* Socrates' questioning, he does recall it by *means* of that questioning. This example also illustrates, as an important corollary, that which things are learned (i.e., recollected) depends on the individual's social and natural environment. Thus the *Republic,* concerned as it most obviously is with the best form of society and the best type of education, hardly mentions the theory of recollection; only in the concluding myth of Er is any reference to it made. While learning is itself a process of remembering the knowledge acquired before the soul took on a body, every learner needs a Socrates to deliver him of the knowledge with which he is pregnant, hence also the use Plato makes of the Socratic, maieutic method of questioning to bring out the knowledge the person already possesses.

While the *Republic*'s myth of the cave and the figure of the divided line tend to stress the theoretical, cognitive dimension of Plato's view of the ladder of life, the correlative and equally important practical or conative dimension of this view is emphasized in the *Symposium* and *Phaedrus.* In love and aspiration one tries to scale the levels of reality to recall and relate to the ultimate values once encountered directly by the disembodied soul that now lie forgotten in the cave-tomb-womb of the body; the highest and final stage in this process is the famous

Platonic love. Once again, however, such recollection and relation require as extrinsic necessary conditions the support and encouragement of friends and society.

3-1.4. *The Soul*

The word "soul" is a translation of the Greek word *psychē;* and the term *psychē,* related to the verb *psycho,* to breathe, basically connotes life and motion. *Anima,* the Latin translation of *psychē,* carries this meaning better than the English word "soul"; it is the animating principle of animate beings, it is that which distinguishes the quick from the dead. Therefore we must guard against assuming any associations of the word "soul" which are not intended by the ancient Greek philosophers. Plato uses the term *psychē* or *soul* at two levels: at the macrocosmic level as an ultimate principle of reality and at the microcosmic level as the nature of man. Let us consider these separately.

In the *Phaedo* one of the main arguments given by Plato (by the persona Socrates) for the immortality of the soul is that the essence of the soul is life (remember that the primary meaning of *psychē* is life), and that it is therefore self-contradictory for the soul to die. While Socrates is talking primarily about the immortality of the individual soul, this argument, as well as some of his other arguments, really concerns soul in general, soul as the principle of life everywhere. Likewise just before presenting the myth of the charioteer in the *Phaedrus,* Plato declares that the soul is self-moving motion that has the care of inanimate being everywhere. It is the activity which is the source of all other activity, and thus the soul is without beginning or end; it is immortal. Is the idea of self-moving motion self-contradictory? Aristotle will argue that it is and that the first mover must lack motion (Ch. 4-3).

In Plato's middle dialogues, the soul is thus the ultimate agency, the first principle of all life and motion. Just as Empedocles saw love and hate and Anaxagoras saw reason or mind as the ultimate agencies or moving principles, thus Plato sees soul. If Plato's Forms are counted as the principle of determinateness and his sensed particulars as the principle of indeterminateness, parallel respectively to the Limit and the Unlimited of the

Pythagoreans, then with his account of the soul as a cosmic principle Plato joins Empedocles and Anaxagoras in adding a third principle, a determining principle of movement, which mediates between the principle of determinateness (the Forms) and the principle of indeterminateness (the particulars). Plato presents this solution to the problem of the relation between forms and particulars in the middle dialogues, and the solution he gives in the later dialogues is only slightly different. His solution to the correlative problem of the relation between the awareness of Forms and the awareness of particulars will be considered later (Ch. 3-1.6). A substantial part, but not the whole, of what Plato is doing with his arguments for the immortality of the soul is therefore a specifying of the soul as the ultimate source of vitality and movement, for an ultimate is of course immortal by definition.

Plato sometimes contrasts the soul of man with the body, but at other times he identifies the soul with the whole nature of man. The former is the case in the *Phaedo*. In it the soul excludes all bodily functions and is radically opposed to the body. The famous "practicing death" *(meletē thanatou)* advocated in the *Phaedo* as the way of the true lover of wisdom refers to the death of bodily and mortal concerns that impede the life of intellectual and immortal concerns. Thus the life of the soul involves the death of the body, and the life of the body involves the death of the soul. When the crass materialist regards the philosopher as already as good as dead, he is right in this important sense: it is essential that the philosopher reject the life of the crass materialist, the life of the body, because only in so doing can he achieve true life, the life of the soul.

In the *Phaedrus* and the *Republic* the soul includes the bodily functions, and thus the soul is identified with the whole nature of man. Just what is left for the word "body" to signify in these dialogues is hard to say. Something is left, as is perhaps symbolized by the chariot in the parable of the charioteer in the *Phaedrus* and by what is left behind in bodily death, but this something which is the body seems to be only an amorphous status rather than something with definite characteristics, the status of being removed from full reality—a view which Aristotle will develop into his theory that the body is only amorphous potentiality for the soul (Ch. 4-4.1). All the specific faculties and activities of man are included, in these dialogues, under the word "soul". The soul, thus considered, has three parts: reason, the spirited element, and the sensory (bodily) appetites. Every human society, just because it is human, also has the same three parts; "Where else can they have come from?"[4] Plato presents the nature and interrelation of these three parts of the soul concretely as well as abstractly in a number of different but parallel accounts:

Individual	*Phaedrus*	*Republic*			*Timaeus*	Social
Reason	Charioteer	Gold	Man	Outside cave	Head	Rulers
Spirited element	Noble horse	Silver	Lion	Diagrams	Chest	Auxiliaries
Sense appetites	Ignoble horse	Iron	Monster	Inside cave	Belly	Economic groups

The nature of man has two basic sides—as does every other sentient being, for that matter—cognitive and conative, awareness and action, knowing and doing (*logos* and *ergon*), seeing and seeking. Since these two phases are basic to human nature, they are also basic to each part of human nature, to each of the three parts of the soul.

First of the three parts of the soul have three modes of awareness, one for each part, and they differ from each other according to their range of awareness and the reality of their objects. Reason possesses the longest range of awareness and its objects are the most real; reason grasps the Forms, invisible to the physical eye, which determine all lesser things. The spirited element possesses an intermediate range of awareness, and its objects are intermediate in reality; this fact is indicated by Plato's whole theory of the mediating role of the spirited element. A central theme of Plato's moral philosophy is that reason is to rule the appetites through the spirited element; the rulers are to govern the citizens by means of the auxiliaries. The primary stage of the education presented in the *Republic* is a training of the spirited element and its social counterpart, the auxiliaries, to view life in terms of such works of art as poems and stories which are imaginative representations of the intangible truths which the future ruler will later learn by means of his higher education in mathematics and dialectic. This awareness characteristic of the spirited element may perhaps be conveyed by the word "imagination," though this must be sharply contrasted with mere imaging or having sense impressions, a characteristic of the sense appetite part of the soul. Imagination is like imaging in being sensuous and clothed in the materials of the here and now, but imagination is radically unlike imaging in not being restricted to the here and now. With imagination the spirited element goes beyond what is presently sensed, and it can use sensuous materials to stand for what cannot be sensed at all. The sensory appetites, finally, possess a short-range awareness, and their objects are least real of all. They are the particular, changing, always becoming but never being, things of the here and now—a visual impression of this man now, not an image of what the ideal man looks like nor a concept or definition of the ideal man.

Second, action follows vision, so the three parts of the soul also have three modes of action, each of which must correspond to one of the three modes of awareness; each mode of action differs from the others according to the range of its seeking and the reality of its objective. Rational action, whether in the wise individual or in the ruling group, is the longest in range; it extends to the ultimate ideals of life which possess the highest degree of reality as the determinants of all intermediate and short-range goals, both individual and social. The imaginative action of the spirited element, whether in the individual courageous man or in the auxiliary class, is intermediate in range and extends to the intermediate goals, which are not yet present but which can be pictured as steps toward the ultimate goals laid down by reason or the ruling class. Since they are dependent upon those ultimate goals, they have a lesser, an intermediate, degree of reality. Finally, the sensory appetites, whether in a single man or in the mass of citizens, are the shortest in range and have the least real objectives. They are concerned with the present and immediate future and with what is only of very transient value—a drink to quench a present thirst, food to satisfy a present hunger. You apprehend and strive toward the ultimate goal of a rich and happy life, for example, a goal which you cannot adequately imagine. But you strive toward this ultimate, abstract, rationally conceived goal through intermediate goals which you can picture in your imagination—goals such as receiving a college diploma and seeing your name and title on an office door. Such imaginatively grasped goals, which are distant yet picturable, can elicit an enduring, powerful ambition. Thus Plato refers to the spirited element as ambition and as the honor-seeking element; it is the power element of the soul, just as the noble horse in the myth of the charioteer supplies most of the driving power to the chariot. The achievement of such an imagined, ambitioned goal (and through it the achievement of the ultimate, rationally apprehended goal) requires, however, the achievement of many immediate sensed goals, the satisfaction of the sensory appetites, as present steps toward the intermediate and ultimate goals. Thus the achievement of a particular ambition (and through it the achievement of an ultimate ideal) requires the satisfaction of daily needs in such a way that they do not conflict with each other or with the intermediate or ultimate goal. In order for the chariot to reach its ultimate objective, each of the three elements—the charioteer, the noble horse, and the ignoble horse—must be satisfied, but they must be satisfied harmoniously so that they work togeher. This, however, is the topic of ethics and politics.

3-1.5. *The Perfection of Man*

For Plato the central concept of ethics and politics is that of human virtue, both individual and civic. But what is human virtue? And first of all, what does the word "virtue" mean? For Plato virtue (*aretē*) means excellence of functioning. Everything has a special function to perform or job to do, and it is virtuous or excellent when it performs that function properly, when it does that job well. The function of a knife is cutting, and thus a virtuous or excellent knife is one that cuts well. The job of eyes is to see, so good eyes are ones that see well. By the same token human virtue is excellence of human functioning, doing well the job of being human. But what is the job of being human? What is the function of man? Human functioning, the job of being human—as we have seen in our consideration of the three parts of the soul—involves three modes of awareness and action: rational, imaginative, and sensuous. Human virtue, then, is the excellence of this tripartite functioning which is definitive of human nature. To use a Latin pun, virtue is manliness—acting like a human by performing excellently these three essential functions of man. But what should be the relation of these three functions; what is the proper order of the three parts of the soul? The answer to this question is the heart of Plato's ethics and politics.

The three parts of human nature and their corresponding functions are, according to Plato, *really* and *naturally* interrelated in a certain *ideal* way. The natures of the three parts make them fall into a natural order, but the fact that this order is natural means that it is also ideal since goodness is natural functioning. As we saw in the axiological approach to Plato's realm of Forms, human actions are essentially determined by unrealized goals; and these goals are prior to the actions in the sense that they elicit and specify them. A corollary of this is that a more ultimate or remote goal has priority over a less ultimate one, since the latter exists for the sake of the former. As we have seen, the goal of the rational part of the soul is most ultimate, the goals of the sensory appetites least ultimate, and the goal of the spirited element intermediate. Therefore the rational part of the soul has priority over the sensory appetites with the spirited element falling in between. The natural functioning of man is not merely the functioning of the three parts of man separately, nor their functioning in just any order; it is, on the contrary, the functioning of these three parts of man in this order: reason, spirited element, sensory appetites. This order is just as much a part of the nature of man, just as natural as the three parts themselves. The nature of the three parts requires that reason rule, that aspiration strive ambitiously and spiritedly toward the imaginatively clothed vision of reason, and that the sensory appetites be satisfied harmoniously among themselves and with reason and the spirited element in order to supply the needs of the whole under the rule of reason and its spirited auxiliary. Phi Beta Kappa: *philosophia biou kybernetes:* Philosophy is the guide of life.

The myth of the charioteer which Plato presents in the *Phaedrus* illustrates this natural order of the three parts of human nature. Note especially the station, the job, and the behavior of each of the three components. The charioteer holds the reins guiding the progress of the two horses and the chariot because he alone knows the ultimate destination of the chariot and how the goals of the two horses relate to it. The charioteer must command and the horses must obey. One of the horses is white and on the right; he is the righteous horse and dextrous *(dexios, dexter)*. His head is erect, he has clear eyes, and his vision is steadfast. He responds to the pressure of the charioteer's reins and drives powerfully forward toward a distant goal in line with the charioteer's vision of the ultimate destination. The other horse is dark and is on the left; this is the sinister horse *(aristeros, sinister)*. His head is down, his eyes are bleary and bloodshot, and his vision veers from one near object to another. So he tries to dash gauchely back and forth, heedless of the steady pull of the dextrous horse and the ultimate destination seen by the charioteer. He cares only for the satisfaction of immediate, random desires. If the control of the chariot is left to this sinister horse, the chariot will surely be wrecked, the destination of the charioteer and the righteous horse will not be reached, and even the sinister horse himself will founder on his fodder in the ditch. Hence the sinister horse must obey the command of the charioteer as translated into power by the dextrous horse, and the sinister horse must do this for his own good as well as for the good of the righteous horse, the charioteer, and the whole ensemble.

When all three components are working harmoniously one can almost see the flow of energy from the ultimate destination to the eyes of the charioteer through his arms and along the reins through the bit of the dextrous horse and his powerful body and through his harness into the body of the gauche horse thus checking his erratic motions and bringing him into line with the vision of the charioteer. This natural order is the order of excellent functioning, the order of virtue, the righteous life. When this natural order is destroyed the flow of energy is reversed; it passes from a bit of grass at the side of the road through the eyes of the sinister horse to turn his body toward it, then through the harness to pull the righteous horse away from his path, and finally, to jerk the reins from the hands of the charioteer and his eyes from the destination. A moment later a different clump of grass reverses the sinister horse and thus the whole chariot, and then still another clump, and the chariot swerves one way and then another until, finally, the whole ensemble is wrecked. This unnatural, inverted order is the order of improper functioning, the order of vice, the unrighteous, upside-down life.

The virtuous life is thus the life of excellent human functioning, of acting in accordance with human nature, of being truly human. The structure of the virtuous life, at the level of both individual and society, is the natural, hierarchical order of the three basic parts of human nature. The main dimensions of this natural order are Plato's four virtues:

Individual faculties	*Virtues* (Justice)	*Social groups*
Reason	Wisdom	Rulers
Spirited element	Courage	Auxiliaries
Sensory appetites	(Temperance / Justice)	Economic groups

Justice (*dikaiosynē*) in the broad sense of rightness or righteousness is simply virtue in general, the excellent functioning of the whole nature of man. Such justice or virtue in general has four inseparable, though distinguishable, parts: each of them requires each of the others, and the absence of any one of them involves the absence of the rest. Wisdom is the aspect of virtue which is special to the rational part of man; it is the excellence of rational knowing and willing. Courage is the aspect of virtue which is special to the spirited part of man; it is the excellence of imaginative vision and spirited and honorable striving. The other two aspects of virtue—temperance and justice—are not peculiar to any of the three parts of man; rather, they are virtues peculiar to the relations among these three parts. Virtue in general involves a harmony of the soul, and a harmony of the soul involves both the integration and the differentiation of its three parts. Temperance is the integration of the three parts of man; it binds them together in harmony, it is the cement in the social fabric. In so far as there must also be an integration and harmony of all of the various sensory appetites with each other, however, temperance concerns the sensory appetites more than it does the other two parts of the soul. It is the harmonious integration of the various appetites with each other and with the spirited element and reason by means of the subordination of all sensory appetites to the rule of reason through the commands of its auxiliary, the spirited element. Finally justice, as a specific aspect of virtue distinct from justice as righteousness in general, is the differentiation of the three parts of man. It is the fact of each part's minding its own business: reason rules, the spirited element ambitiously executes the rule of reason, and the sensory appetites submit to the spirited element's execution of the rule of reason so that all parts of man, the sensory appetites as well as the spirited element and reason, may be satisfied as fully as possible.

The structure of vice, the improper and unnatural functioning of man, is the opposite of this structure of virtue. When any one of the parts of a human individual or society fails to perform its natural function, the natural chain of command is disrupted and the cement of personal integration and social harmony is dissolved. In the parable of the ship of state at the beginning of Book VI of the *Republic,* when the navigator (reason, the philosopher-king) is regarded as a mere star-gazer and the sailors (the sensory appetites, *hoi polloi*) drug the master of the ship (the man as a whole, the state as a whole) and fight among themselves to take the wheel, the inevitable result is vacillation and the eventual wreck of the ship of individual and social life.

While only one virtuous, upright, natural way of life exists, the vicious, inverted, unnatural life involves various logical stages of increasing degeneration which Plato depicts as a temporal history.[5] Aristocracy (which literally means rule by the best) is the life of virtue just examined; this is life lived for the sake of truth, beauty, and goodness. Timocracy (literally rule by honor) appears when reason fails to mind its business of knowing and ruling and when control therefore passes to the spirited element, the auxiliaries. A timocrat lives solely for the sake of ambition, honor, status, prestige; he is the status-seeker. Oligarchy (rule by the few) is really plutocracy (rule by the wealthy); it appears when control passes from the spirited element to appetite as a whole, to sensual satisfaction and the money which buys it. In an oligarchy "reason" and "knowledge" are defined in terms of know-how, and honor is an accompaniment of material success. Democracy (rule by the people, by the mob according to Plato) appears when control passes from appetite as a whole to the various particular appetites at random. Since everyone is in control, no one is in control; therefore democracy is anarchy or chaos in individual and social life. Reason and knowledge, honor and ambition, and even material success are sacrificed to the particular pleasure of the moment, to the loudest vested interest. Since this democratic or anarchical way of life is chaotic and unstable, it must pass into another and final stage, tyranny. Tyranny appears when some one sensory appetite, some one vested interest, bests the others and forces its way upon them. At this final stage of degeneration to a completely vicious, perverted, unnatural, evil life, some one lust rules the life of one man, the tyrant or dictator; some one lust of some one person rules reason (the philosopher-kings) through the spirited element (the auxiliaries), and thus rules the whole society. This state has unity and order as had the virtuous, aristocratic life, but it is an inverted, unnatural, destructive order. Tyranny, the worst possible life, resembles aristocracy, the best possible life, as the wolf resembles the dog.

Which of these two lives is the happier? The virtuous, aristocratic life, of course, but why? Plato answers with a rigorous and compelling proof.[6] Actually doing anything entails being able to do it; if a person is not able to do a certain thing, then he is not actually doing it. Now happiness *(eudaimonia)* is actually functioning or living well, and virtue is that which enables a person to function or live well. Hence, happiness entails virtue: if a person is happy he is virtuous, and if he is not virtuous he is not happy. Note however that it does not follow that if a person is virtuous, he is happy, nor that if he is unhappy, he is not virtuous—although Plato does not embrace this logical truth as clearly and explicitly as Aristotle does. In any case, the most happy life is also the most virtuous one, the aristocratic life; and the most vicious life, the tyrannical life, is also the most miserable. The happy life is one in which the head rules the belly through the chest.

Plato's ethical and political theory thus amounts to a theory of natural moral law. Moral goodness is psychic health and moral evil is psychic disease. Virtue is to the soul what health is to the body; each is the proper and excellent functioning of one's nature. As Heraclitus indicated with his *logos,* the laws of nature are not merely descriptive of what does as a matter of fact happen; they are also prescriptive of what should happen, of what must happen if nature, or the nature of a particular thing, is to continue to exist. Such a natural law theory of ethics and politics reduces basically to two propositions. First, "good" (or some other value term) is defined as acting in accordance with one's nature. Second, one's nature is declared to have a certain structure, such as the three parts in Plato's theory. The first is a value proposition, the second a factual one, and the rest of the propositions constituting the natural law theory follow from these two.

Plato identifies the natural individual and social functions of man with natural social classes. The rational social function is to be performed by only one particular class of citizens, not by all, and likewise with the executive and industrial social functions. But Plato's functional theory is logically independent of his class theory, so the acceptance of the former does not commit one to the acceptance of the latter. One may believe that the rational, spirited, and appetitive functions are natural and indispensable to every society, and also that the order of priority from rational to spirited to appetitive is natural and right, without thereby being obliged to agree with Plato that people are divided into three natural (and pre-ordained, according to the myth of the metals) classes of people each with only one of these three functions. Put differently, democracy in the modern sense is not incompatible with aristocracy in Plato's sense. While Plato's social theory is a class theory, contrary to the usual criticism it is not organismic or totalitarian in any significant sense of those terms. Plato did not consider the individual secondary to the state. On the contrary, he avers that the individual is prior to the state both in existence (A state derives its characteristics from its individual citizens; "Where else can they have come from?")[7] and in value. (The state exists for the sake of the individuals, in order to satisfy their natural human needs.)[8] The state is the individual writ large; the individual is not the state writ small.

Where does immortality fit into this picture of the soul and its perfection? We have seen that the soul as a cosmic principle, as the ultimate agency or principle of determination, of course, is immortal, and that Plato's arguments for immortality partly reduce to this idea. But this is not all. For Plato the individual soul is also in some sense immortal, but in what sense?

As the pure life of the *Phaedo* and the self-moving motion of the *Phaedrus,* such an immortal soul is not an individual one; it is not your soul or mine. Plato certainly seems to maintain in the middle dialogues that all three parts of each individual person are immortal; after bodily death this tripartite individual soul is reborn in another body selected by the soul partly on the basis of its past life and partly by chance, and such reincarnation continues until the soul gains, with its rational part, enough wisdom to break free from the body and dwell forever in the realm of Forms. Only the rational part of the soul can dwell in the realm of Forms, however, for the Forms are the objects of reason alone. Furthermore, the sensory appetites involve bodily functions in their definition, and so, indirectly by way of sensuous images, does the spirited element. Seemingly only the rational part of the soul can be truly immortal. We have already seen that the rational part is what is meant by "soul" in the *Phaedo,* and this same meaning of "soul" is implied by many of Plato's other arguments for immortality. Plato's belief that the Forms must be separate from and prior to sensed particulars entails his theory of recollection which in turn entails the pre-existence of the soul. However, the preexistent soul required by the theory of recollection is purely rational; it is that which has already apprehended the Forms. In like manner Plato argues for the postexistence of the soul by means of the eternality of the soul's proper objects, the Forms; but once again only the rational part of the soul—which, after all, is the distinctively human part of man—is truly immortal. But this rational part of the soul, pure reason, seems to be impersonal. It is not my reason or yours but reason as such which is immortal to the extent that it performs its function of apprehending the Forms.

3-1.6 *Summary*

With his realm of Forms Plato preserves the insight of his predecessors into a principle of determinateness, stability, or form, and in his world of changing particulars he also preserves the insight of his predecessors into a principle of indeterminateness, instability, or flux. The world of Forms explains knowledge, action, and being; and the world of particulars is reported by our sensory experience. Corresponding to these two realms as their respective apprehensions are reason and sensation; reason grasps the Forms and sensation grasps the particulars. The theory that a moral life consists of ordering and subordinating all sensed particulars to the rationally apprehended and willed Forms also corresponds to the Forms and particulars and to reason and sensation.

How are the principles of determinateness and indeterminateness bound together to form a single world? At the microcosmic level, the level of man, form and flux seem bound together by that middle part of the soul which Plato calls the spirited element. Like the diagrams which introduce the student from sensory perceptions to mathematics by representing abstract conceptual forms in concrete sensory guise, the imagination of the spirited element represents to the ephemeral sensations and cravings of the appetites the universal Forms apprehended and willed by reason. At the macrosmic level form and flux are synthesized, apparently, by the soul in its cosmic sense. As the spirited element mediates between reason and appetite, the soul mediates between Forms and particulars. Thus Plato preserves the third type of principle discovered by his predecessors: the principle of agency identified by Empedocles with love and hate and by Anaxagoras with reason. As self-moving motion the soul has the care of inanimate being everywhere. But *how* the soul cares for all things, how it mediates between form and flux, how the soul is the ultimate agency behind all particular things becomes clear only in the later dialogues.

3-2. *The Later Dialogues*

The solution to this problem of the relation of form and flux which Plato develops in the later dialogues involves, first, a new conception of being and, second, the utilization of this new conception of being to frame a set of principles which can explain and unify the whole world.

3-2.1. *Being as Power*

Plato approaches his new conception of being through self-criticism and exploration of possible hypotheses. The main thing which he subjects to self-criticism is his identification of being with the many Forms united under the one Good and his identification of nonbeing with the many changing particulars. This theory implies that being is both one and many, many because there are many Forms and one because they are united by the Good into one realm of Forms; this we may call the problem of being. The philosophy of the middle dialogues also implies that nonbeing exists, for fluctuating particulars do exist and yet they are identified with nonbeing; this we may call the problem of nonbeing. Plato tries to solve these two correlative problems in the *Sophist*.

The problem of being involves both the number of beings and the nature of being. In solving the problem of the number of beings (the problem of the one and the many), Plato criticizes both pluralism and monism. His criticism of pluralism, which is at once a criticism of the Pluralist philosophers and of Plato's own theory, is essentially the same as that put forth by Parmenides. However, the monistic conclusion which Parmenides drew from this criticism is also subjected to criticism. Being cannot be one, for if being is one the implication is that there are two beings, "being" and "one." Even the formulation of monism is thus a commitment to pluralism. The world is further plurified by the monist when he cites other characteristics of this one being, such as being identical with thought or like a well-rounded sphere. From these criticisms we must conclude that being cannot be merely one or merely many. Unlike beings or things, Being itself cannot be counted as one or two. Just as Anaximander criticized Thales for identifying Being with a being thing (water) and insisted that the ultimate Being cannot be any determinate thing, so also Plato's criticisms imply that monists and pluralists are alike mistaken in tacitly identifying Being with a being thing or things. Being must be a relational unity which binds together a plurality.

In solving the problem of the nature of being Plato criticizes the materialists or fluxists who, like Democritus, identify reality with fluctuating, material particulars, but he also criticizes the Formists or idealists or "friends of the Forms" who identify being with the Forms. To identify being with changing particulars is absurd, for even to express this thesis is to grant the existence of such stable, intellectually apprehended Forms as "being," "change," and "particular." Thus being must be broadened to include the stable Formal objects of reason, and also to include reason and the soul which apprehend these objects. But Formism is likewise subjected to criticism. Being cannot be wholly identified with the stable and static Forms; being must also be active for otherwise it cannot include knowing, and it must also be passive, must include being acted upon, for otherwise it could not be known. These criticisms of materialism and Formism show that being must include both activity and passivity, both stability and change, both form and flux—and, indeed, that being must of course include everything whatsoever. What conception of being is broad enough to include all this and still be a meaningful unity in itself?

The new conception of being Plato offers in the *Sophist* is *power*. Whether Plato himself actually endorses this idea is not entirely clear; but he does put it forth at least tentatively, he never retracts it, and it fits in well with the increased dynamism that importantly characterizes his later dialogues. The conception of being as power *(dynamis)* also fits the conclusions drawn from the criticisms just discussed under the problem of being. First, being as power includes both activity and passivity, for power is both active and passive and necessarily so, since the idea of either requires the idea of the other: passive power implies something which can act upon it and active power implies something to be acted upon. Being as active and passive power thus includes both Forms and particulars, and both mind and matter, the Forms and mind being active powers and particulars and matter being passive powers. Second, the conception of being as power solves the problem of the one and the many. Power is relational, since power is necessarily power *to,* power *over,* power *for,* etc. It is therefore both one and many: one as one relational complex and many as involving a relation and at least two terms. Hence if being is identical with power, being is also both one and many, neither simply one nor simply many. Thus the claims of both monism and pluralism are justified and reconciled.

Third, the conception of being as power solves the problem of nonbeing. Particulars are nonbeing, Plato had held in his middle dialogues. But how can nonbeing *be?* Earlier Parmenides had declared this expression self-contradictory, yet the philosophy of Plato's middle dialogues requires that nonbeing in some sense *is.* Plato now solves this problem of the being of nonbeing by the analysis and application of the conception of being as power. Plato agrees with Parmenides that absolute nonbeing, complete nothingness, is impossible and nonexistent in every way. (Then is this discussion about it, one might ask?) Contrary to Parmenides, however, a relative nonbeing does indeed exist, and it is basically *otherness.* Being as power implies motion and rest (activity and passivity); and motion and rest, activity and passivity, all share in being. Motion is, rest is, activity is, and passivity is. Thus they are bound together by the common bond of being. Moreover, each is the *same* as itself; motion is the same as motion, and rest is the same as rest, etc. And finally, each is also *different,* not from itself, but from each of the others; motion, rest, and being are all different from each other. Hence there are three universal modes *(genē)* of being: being, same, and other. Everything whatsoever—Forms, particulars; mind, matter; permanence, change; unity, multiplicity; good, bad; positive, negative; being, nonbeing; etc.—is a *being,* is the *same* as itself, and is *other* than every other being. The property of otherness is the root of the relative nonbeing which can and must be allowed to exist. For *x* to be other than *y* is for *x* not to be *y*. Hence everything whatsoever is both a being and a non-being (relatively): it is (itself) and is not (anything else). Fluctu-ating particulars are no more nonbeing than the Forms are ex-cept in the sense that the particulars are other than the funda-mental principles, in the sense that they are derived. Thus the problem of nonbeing is solved by means of the relativity or re-lationality inherent in the conception of being as power, and thus is Plato enabled to frame a conception of reality which will include everything whatsoever within one unified world.

Plato thus sustains the dualisms of the middle dialogues by embracing them within a larger framework, the framework of being as power. The dualisms of Forms and particulars, perma-nence and flux, soul and body, reason and appetite are retained; but the bridging of these dualisms—which in the middle dia-logues was unclear, tenuous, and metaphorical—is made clear, strong, and conceptual by the notion of being as power. For the first time, contrary to Parmenides' claim but consistent with his logic, *many beings and many nonbeings may be within one uni-verse of being,* many universal archetypes and many particular copies, many stable and many changing beings, many souls and many bodies, many active causes and many passive effects. Here at last is the analysis of the concepts of being and nonbeing which the Pluralists failed to provide and the lack of which rendered their pluralism merely ad hoc (Ch. 1-5). At last a con-ceptual analysis justifies our saying that we live in a universe.

3-2.2. *The Four Principles*

How does being as power manifest itself to originate and ac-count for the world we experience? This question is considered, especially in the *Timaeus,* on the basis of Plato's new analysis of being and nonbeing. His answer to the question is a theory of the originative and explanatory principles of the world.

These principles advanced in the later dialogues grow out of insights captured in the middle dialogues. In the middle dialogues Plato had expressed a principle of determinateness, the Forms, which is a modification of the Pythagorean principle of the Limit, of the element of determinateness in the Being of the Eleatics, and of the beings of the Pluralists. Plato also preserved in his changing world of particulars the principle of indeterminateness formulated by Anaximander and the Pythagoreans as the Unlimited or indeterminate, by Empedocles and Anaxagoras as the primordial undifferentiated state, and by Democritus as the void or nonbeing. A third ultimate which emerged in the middle dialogues is the Good, the source of all being and intelligibility. Finally, the middle dialogues also presented (though unclearly and metaphorically) the soul as a fourth principle, a principle of agency suggested by Empedocles' love and hate and by Anaxagoras' reason.

Of these four the principle of determinateness, the Forms, seems clearest and most adequate, perhaps because it was the first to be grasped by Plato's predecessors, beginning with Thales' concept of water, and perhaps this happened in turn because determinateness is most easily grasped by reason. The changing world of sensed particulars is not so much itself a *principle* or explanation of indeterminateness (like those of Anaximander, the Pythagoreans, and Democritus) as it is an *area* especially inhabited by this principle; the principle still remains to be abstracted from its home ground. Moreover, the exact manner in which the Good functions as a principle is never completely clear in the middle dialogues; nor is the soul, the fourth principle, made clear.

Just how does the soul exercise its function of mediating between the realm of Forms and the world of particulars? Exactly how does it transfer the determinateness of the Forms to the indeterminateness of the particulars? These are the main questions to be answered by Plato's later account of the principles and of the origin of the world from them. The principles enunciated in the later dialogues are the same as the four expressed in the middle dialogues; but in the later dialogues they are clarified, systematized, and expressed more literally.

This more adequate statement of these four principles occurs more abstractly and literally in the *Philebus,* though not explicitly as principles of the world, and more concretely and metaphorically in the *Timaeus* where they are explicitly regarded as the principles of the origin of the world:

Philebus (the four classes)	*Timaeus* (the origin of the world)
The Principles	
the limited, the finite	the Forms, the pattern, the determinate
the unlimited, the infinite	the Receptacle, space, the indeterminate
the cause	the divine Craftsman, the determining
(measure)	(the Good), the motive
The Originated World	
the mixed	the particular things in nature

The concept of measure is placed in parentheses because measure is not one of the four classes in the *Philebus,* but it is introduced near the end of that dialogue as the highest form of the Good. And the concept of the Good is placed in parentheses because it does not clearly emerge as a separate factor in the *Timaeus* but operates rather as a part of (the motive of) the divine Craftsman. Though the Good is not separate from the divine Craftsman in the *Timaeus,* it is logically distinct from it and equally primordial. The identification in the *Philebus* of measure or proportion with the highest essence of goodness justifies the analogy between it and the goodness of the divine Craftsman in the *Timaeus.*

In the *Timaeus* the Craftsman (demiurge, *demiourgos*) whose motive is goodness molds the chaos of the Receptacle or empty space into imperfect and changing copies of the perfect and changeless patterns or Forms. The Forms appear in the *Timaeus* much the same as they do in the middle dialogues, except that their earlier role as archetypal causes can now be justified by their implicit transformation into active powers by the new conception of being as power. They are the pattern, the determinate; they form the class of the limited or finite, in the sense of being definite and the source of the definiteness and stability in the world. They are the world-builder's blueprints.

At the other extreme is the material, the Receptacle, the space in which the copies of the Forms or patterns are received. In itself and prior to the origin of the world, it lacks all forms and is indefinite—or at least almost entirely so. Plato speaks of it as containing random motions which are to be arranged in the production of the world. The Receptacle is the class of the unlimited, infinite, or indefinite; it is the mother and nurse of the world waiting to be informed by the divine father, earth waiting to be fertilized by sky. (Plato uses the metaphor of procreation side by side with that of fabrication.) It is the matter, the matrix, the mother of the world. Plato had not yet expressed this principle of indeterminacy in the middle dialogues, but it was implicit in them as the root of the world of particulars. Why did he not explicate this principle earlier? Perhaps because it is, by its very nature, so difficult to grasp. Whatever we frame a concept of seems necessarily to be something definite, so the Receptacle, as the indefinite which is something and yet not anything, is apprehended, Plato tells us, only by "a bastard kind" of knowledge.

Thus form and matter wait to be brought together to form a world. What brings them together is the third principle, the Demiurge or Craftsman who is also called God. It is also a new expression of the cosmic soul of the middle dialogues: The ultimate agent, the first mover, the mediator between the realm of Forms and the realm of matter, is now called God and Craftsman. But the change is not great for the divine Craftsman necessarily possesses reason and soul—how else could he see the Forms, and how else could he move matter to copy them?—and is even the very highest and first expression of soul. The divine Craftsman is the cause mentioned in the *Philebus,* the love and hate of Empedocles, and the reason of Anaxagoras. He makes the indefinite become definite, the unlimited, limited. He is the father of the world who impregnates the mother, matter, matrix of the world, the Receptacle, with the stable pattern of the Forms.

What makes God make the world? The goodness of the Forms and the goodness of God. Cosmos is better than chaos, order is better than disorder; and the divine Craftsman is motivated solely by the Good. Here we have the fourth and final principle, the principle of purpose or goal, the motive of the world. This principle is expressed in the *Philebus* as measure, proportion, order, harmony—the very essence of goodness. It shows the way in which the Good of the *Republic* is the source of all being and intelligibility, namely as its purpose or reason. The goodness of God, the father, causes him to make the world, the child, out of the material of the Receptacle, the mother, in the light of the perfect pattern of the Forms. Here, then, is Plato's set of four interrelated principles to account for the world: determinateness, indeterminacy, determination, and purpose.

The origin of the world from these four primordial principles is a process of fabrication out of preexistent matter, a process which should be carefully distinguished from three other conceptions of world-origination. One is the process of *emanation* of the world out of the substance of the ultimate or God. This conception of emanation is close to that apparently entertained in the *Republic* when Plato speaks of the Good as the source of all being and intelligibility, and it will be Plotinus' conception of world-origination (Ch. 5-5). A second conception of world-origination is one of *elicitation* or attraction of a preexistent matter to the ultimate or God. This will be Aristotle's conception, and seeds of it are found in Plato's writings about matter copying and imitating the perfect Forms and the goodness of God. The third alternative conception is the most familiar; it is the Judaeo-Christian conception of *creation* of the world out of nothing at all—neither out of a preexistent matter nor out of God's own being. This conception we will examine when we come to medieval philosophy (Ch. 6-1, 4), but it is not the conception of Plato.

Plato presents a "likely story" of the process of the fabrication of the world in the *Timaeus*. The four ultimate, originative principles are the eternals; they are timeless because time is made with the world as a concomitant of change and as "the moving image of eternity." Though no products of the four originative factors are thus eternal, some of them are everlasting—temporal but without temporal beginning or end. Chief among these is the world animal, the universe, which is composed of a soul and a body. Its soul, the world soul, is made first, since the ruler should be the elder; and it is made by the divine Craftsman out of two elements and their mixture, one element immutable and indivisible and the other element mutable and divisible, the first anchored in the realm of Forms and the second in the realm of matter. Thus the intermediate and mediating status of the cosmic soul of the middle dialogues is accounted for. While the divine Craftsman is the ultimate projection of the principle of the soul as agency and while he contains soul, according to Plato, he is on the side of the ultimates and thus needs something to mediate between those ultimates and the about to be generated particular things.

After the world animal is formed, the souls of individual animate beings are made; and each of these souls, as we have learned from the *Phaedrus* and the *Republic,* has three parts. One part, seated in the head, has the same composition as the world soul. This is reason, and it is by virtue of its immutable, indivisible part that we can have knowledge of the immutable, indivisible Forms; and by virtue of its mutable, divisible part we are aware of mutable, divisible, sensible particulars. The second part of the soul, situated in the chest, is the spirited element; and the third part, situated in the belly, consists of the sensory appetites. In the *Timaeus* only the rational part of the soul is immortal for it alone is akin to the everlasting world soul and the eternal ultimates. As we saw before, this also seems to be the implication of the doctrine of the middle dialogues, although in the *Phaedrus,* and to a lesser extent in the *Republic,* all three of these parts of the soul are declared to be immortal. The multiplication of mediating triads begun in the *Timaeus* is later expanded in Neoplatonism: the spirited element mediates between the sensory appetites and reason, the mixed element in reason mediates between the mutable and the immutable elements, the world soul mediates between the world body and the divine Craftsman, the mixed element in the world soul mediates between its mutable and immutable elements, and the divine Craftsman mediates between the Receptacle and the Forms.

Why, then, does the world exist? Because *God* saw that it was *good* to *order* the *disordered*. Everything is explained in terms of these four principles.

3-3. *Summary of Plato*

In the middle dialogues the principles of form and flux discovered by Plato's predecessors are brought together with a realm of Forms above and prior to a realm of changing particulars. Since the changing particulars do not themselves contain the Forms, and since it is the Forms which are the objects of knowledge, it follows that knowledge is nonempirical, and, with the added assumption that the mind cannot initially obtain this nonempirical knowledge while it is entombed in a body, it also follows that knowledge is a recollection of what was learned by a previous unembodied soul. That knowledge is recollection in turn entails the preexistence of the soul, and the achievement of permanent possession of knowledge of the Forms entails its full immortality. This soul as a principle mediates between the Forms and the particulars as the spirited element of the soul mediates between reason and appetite.

This world view requires, however, a conception of being that will be broad enough to include all three of these levels yet sufficiently strong to bind them all together. This conception which Plato forges in his later dialogues is of being as power, and thus as both active and passive, one and many, Formal and material. This central bond of being as power manifests itself in four dynamic ways. The Forms are power as active patterns, the Receptacle is power as passive potentiality, the divine Craftsman is power as active agent, and the Good is power as his active motive. Even the fluctuating particular things that make up the manufactured world exist as powers—artifacted powers which are, though only derivatively, both active and passive. Thus *everything* is a being as a manifestation of power, and everything is also a nonbeing as other than every other being-power. The only sense in which the fluctuating particulars are *especially* nonbeing is that they are other than the originative principles, in the sense that they are derived.

Plato has thus effected a creative synthesis of the fundamental discoveries of his predecessors. By means of an agency governed by a motive or purpose, he has rejoined as the whole of being its most fundamental parts: man and nature, form and flux, and reason and experience. Plato's principle of Form or determinateness was clearly expressed by the Pythagoreans and Eleatics; his principle of the indeterminate Receptacle by Anaximander, the Pythagoreans, and Democritus; his principle of the divine agent was anticipated in Empedocles' love and hate and in Anaxagoras' reason; and his principle of goodness as purpose was the central concern of Socrates. But Plato has clarified these concepts, greatly purified their meanings, and systematized them into one coherent whole. Thus, he enriched a heritage from which Aristotle, his student for twenty years, has much to learn in constructing his own more literal, less metaphorical, more scientific, and more exact formulation of this synthesis.

SUGGESTED READINGS

3-1.1. *Phaedo* 72E–80C, 100B–106E.
3-1.2. *Republic* 507A to end of Bk. VII.
3-1.3. *Phaedo* 72E–77B.
       Meno 81B–86C.
       Phaedrus 249A–253B.
3-1.4. *Phaedo* especially 63E–68C, 78D–81E, 100B–106E.
       Symposium 199C–212C.
       Phaedrus 245C–256E.
       Republic 434E–441C, preferably from Cornford, Francis Mac-
          Donald, ed. and trans. *The Republic of Plato*. London and
          New York: Oxford University Press, 1941. Pp. 129–38.
3-1.5. *Republic* 441B–445B, 427C–434D, 352E–354B, 576B to end of
          Bk. IX, preferably from Cornford.

3-2.1. *Sophist* 242B–260B.
3-2.2. *Philebus* 23B–31A, 61A to end.
      Timaeus 27C–34D, 48E–53C.

For bibliography, see:
Brumbaugh, Robert S. *Plato for the Modern Age.* New York: Crowell-
   Collier, 1962. Pp. 237–52.

Chapter 4

Aristotle

4-1. *Introduction*

4-1.1. *Aristotle and His Predecessors*

Aristotle (384–322 B.C.) conceives his philosophy as an inductive yet creative synthesis of both present experience and the past. The experience which he wants his philosophy to explain is that of his philosophical predecessors as well as his own; therefore, a schematic, synoptic view of all previous ancient Greek philosophy is a good introduction to Aristotle. The accompanying chart is a representation of the major themes in the story of ancient Greek philosophy when the philosophy of Aristotle is regarded as its culmination, although Aristotle's own statements occasionally are at variance with this chart.[1] The principal theme in that story is the gradual discovery of the determining principles of reality, of what Aristotle will call the four causes. These are the principle of the indeterminate (Aristotle's material cause), the principle of determinateness (Aristotle's formal cause), the principle of agency (Aristotle's efficient cause), and the principle of purpose or goal (Aristotle's final cause). Subsidiary to this central theme, but closely related to it, are two others: the problem of change and the problem of man, his nature and his good. While each of the earlier philosophers contributed to only some of these themes, Plato contributes to all of them and so does Aristotle as he critically develops Plato's synthesis into a more literal and exact system.

Aristotle's relation to Plato is ambivalent. On the one side he is quite critical of Plato, his basic criticism being that Plato does not do justice to nature; and this criticism lies behind Aristotle's enormous and painstaking attention to nature. Plato cannot explain nature, Aristotle argues, because Plato's ultimates exist separately from nature. This basic criticism is certainly less applicable to Plato's later dialogues than to his middle ones; yet even in the later dialogues the Forms—and also the Receptacle and the Craftsman-God—are further removed from nature in their own eternal realm than Aristotle thinks they can be if they are to explain the characteristics and changes of natural things. Neither can the Forms explain knowledge of natural things, according to Aristotle, because they are separate from them. In "knowing" natural things, according to Plato, the natural things themselves are not really known but rather the Forms of which they are copies. From these criticisms Aristotle concludes that Plato's ultimate realities must be brought down to earth and made into explanatory principles of natural things. The Forms, the Receptacle, and the divine Craftsman and his goodness must be made to involve each other in their very meaning. The Forms must become formal causes; the Receptacle, the material cause; the divine Craftsman, the efficient cause, and his goodness, the final cause—of natural things.

While Aristotle is critical of the *status* of Plato's ultimates, he thus accepts their essential *content*. For this reason the popular opposition of Plato and Aristotle as idealist and realist, rationalist and empiricist, poet and scientist is more one of temperament and procedure than of philosophical position. After all, Aristotle studied with Plato for twenty years; and during this long period "the soul of the school," as Aristotle reputedly was called by Plato, cannot help but have acquired much from his master, and perhaps he also gave much in return, for the difference between Aristotle's philosophy and Plato's later dialogues is not much greater than the difference between the later dia-

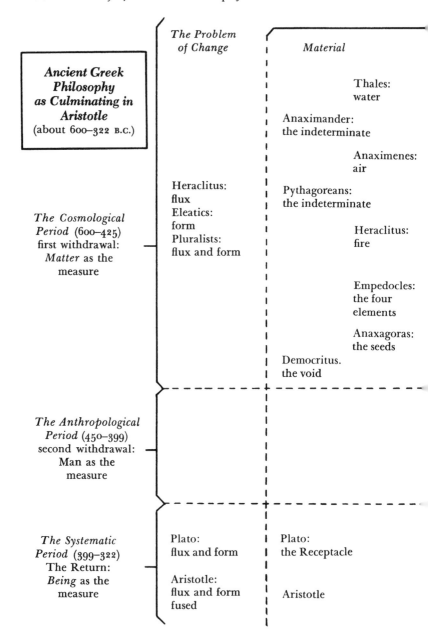

	The Problem of Change	*Material*
Ancient Greek Philosophy as Culminating in Aristotle (about 600–322 B.C.)		Thales: water Anaximander: the indeterminate Anaximenes: air
The Cosmological Period (600–425) first withdrawal: *Matter* as the measure	Heraclitus: flux Eleatics: form Pluralists: flux and form	Pythagoreans: the indeterminate Heraclitus: fire Empedocles: the four elements Anaxagoras: the seeds Democritus. the void
The Anthropological Period (450–399) second withdrawal: Man as the measure		
The Systematic Period (399–322) The Return: *Being* as the measure	Plato: flux and form Aristotle: flux and form fused	Plato: the Receptacle Aristotle

The Discovery of the Causes

Formal	Efficient	Final	The Problem of Man
	Pythagoreans: the determinate		
Eleatics: Being			
	Empedocles: love and hate		
	Anaxagoras: reason		
	Democritus: the atoms		
		Socrates: the Good	Sophists Socrates Megarians Cynics Cyrenaics
Plato: the Forms	Plato: the divine Craftsman	Plato: the Good	Plato
Aristotle	Aristotle	Aristotle	Aristotle

logues and the middle ones, though Aristotle's procedure is more prosaic, literal, empirical, and cautious.

4-1.2. *Method and Branches of Philosophy*

Aristotle's methodology is expressible in a formula which is carried throughout his entire philosophy: What is first in the order of knowing is last in the order of being, and what is first in the order of being is last in the order of knowing. The way of wisdom proceeds by abstracting from what is initially more familiar to or knowable by us humans—the particular things in the world which we sense around us—to what is initially less familiar but more knowable or intelligible in reality—the principles of being, which explain the initial particulars. The procedure is from particular facts to self-evident principles and back to particular facts now explained, just as the physician goes from symptoms to causes and back to symptoms. The rungs in this ladder of abstraction are similar to those depicted in Plato's myth of the cave and diagram of the divided line. The procedure begins with an initial sense experience, which itself is not a rung on the ladder but is comparable to the imaging at the bottom of Plato's divided line. The first rung of Aristotle's ladder of abstraction is philosophy of nature analogous to the "belief" at the second level of Plato's divided line. The second rung of Aristotle's ladder of abstraction is mathematics, whose proper objects can be conceived but cannot exist apart from matter; this rung is comparable to the mathematics and discursive reasoning at the third level of Plato's divided line. And the third rung of Aristotle's ladder of abstraction is ontology (the science of being) or first philosophy or metaphysics whose proper objects can be conceived and can also exist apart from matter; this stage is analogous to the intellectual intuition at the fourth level of Plato's divided line.

The major divisions of Aristotle's philosophy reflect his methodology though they also include it, for the first major division is logic and methodology itself, the second major division is theoretical philosophy which is an ascent up the three rungs of the ladder of abstraction, and the third major division or practical philosophy is a return down the ladder from principles to particular things to be done and made. Aristotle's logical and methodological treatises were later grouped together under the title, *Organon,* for they present the instruments or tools for the acquisition of knowledge rather than that knowledge itself. Theoretical philosophy is concerned with knowing what already is and must be the case; it is concerned with reality as fixed and unchangeable by human beings. This theoretical philosophy has three divisions corresponding to the three levels of abstraction on the way of wisdom. Philosophy of nature is concerned first with nature generally as the domain of change; with the structure, causes, and types of change; and with the categories of changing things; second, with the ultimate cause of change, God; and third with the nature of man. Mathematics is concerned with quantity and quantitative relations, according to Aristotle, and ontology, first philosophy, or metaphysics is concerned with the nature of being in general, and as theology, with the nature of the only purely actual being, God. Practical philosophy has doing and making rather than knowing as its goal; it is concerned with reality as fluid and changeable by human beings. Such change is either human action, the domain of ethics and politics, or human making, which is the domain of the arts. The remainder of this chapter is devoted to Aristotle's theories of nature, God, man, and being; consideration of his other theories—including his logic, mathematics and esthetics—is omitted from this study.

4-2. *Nature*

Aristotle maintains that we must assume the existence of nature, of the world of change. Although it is neither logically demonstrable nor logically self-evident, the world of change is evident to our senses, from which we cannot escape even if we should try. Nature and change are inextricably bound together, even by definition, for Aristotle defines *nature* as that whose principle of change is internal to it (though not wholly internal, as we shall see). Thus a plant or an animal changes itself and is

therefore natural, whereas a saw or a hammer is changed by
something else and hence is artificial. So the problem of nature
is essentially the problem of change.

4-2.1. *Change*

The problem of change, as examined in connection with
Heraclitus and the Eleatics (Ch. 1-3), may be expressed as a
riddle: How can a thing change and yet remain the same? For
something to change is for it both to *change* and also to remain
the *same* something throughout that change. How is this possible? Heraclitus and the Eleatics agreed that it is not possible.
For Heraclitus only change exists (except for the law of change),
and for the Eleatics only stability exists. The important element
in the stands taken by Heraclitus and the Eleatics is that both
are based on an all-or-none presupposition. This assumption
that a thing changes in toto or not at all involves the further assumption that a changing thing has only one level, at which it is
either changing or not and cannot be both changing and not
changing.

This single level at which the change occurs consists of two
components: that from which and that to which the change
proceeds. Viewed at this single level, an autumn leaf changing
from green to yellow involves only the factors of green and yellow—or, perhaps better, the green leaf and the yellow leaf.
Heraclitus and other earlier philosophers regarded change as
entirely analyzable into these two determinate states both of
which occur at the same level; thus a one-level, two-factor analysis of change is maintained; change is essentially a "pair of
opposites." This one-level, two-factor view of change, as illus-
trated in the dialectic between Heraclitus and the Eleatics, involves either a contradiction of reason or a contradiction of sensation; it involves either a logical contradiction or a denial of
the sensory experience of change. If change is regarded as continuous and as involving only the pair of determinate opposites
(for example the green leaf and the yellow leaf), then because of
the continuity of change these opposites must be identical, a
logical contradiction. However, if this contradictory identity of
opposites is denied, the first state remains unchanged until it is

annihilated and followed by the second state created *ex nihilo* which also remains unchanged so that there is no change at all, which contradicts our sense experience. How are we to avoid thus contradicting either our reason or our sense experience of continuously changing things? How is the problem of change to be solved?

Aristotle's solution arises from his conviction that the one-level, two-factor analysis of the earlier philosophers is overly simple, and his solution therefore recognizes in change a second level, which is also a third factor. This second level—third factor is the *stuff, substrate,* or *matter underlying* the change. In analyzing the leaf's changing from green to yellow, we must recognize the leaf as a third factor, distinct from and on a deeper level than the green and the yellow. After all, the change involves not just green leaf and yellow leaf, but a leaf changing from green to yellow, and the leaf remains the same leaf throughout the change. By adding this second, underlying level or third factor, we can now say that a thing both changes and yet remains the same, thus solving the riddle of change. It changes with respect to its characteristics, its properties; but it remains the same with respect to its matter, its substrate. The leaf changes in color but remains the same in substance. We need no longer contradict ourselves by making the two opposite characteristics identical, for the *thing which changes,* the substructure, accounts for the continuity, while the superstructure accounts for the discontinuity. Thus we retain both the continuity and the discontinuity experienced in change, and thus also both reason and sensation are satisfied.

This solution to the problem of change introduces two principles which will increasingly be seen to be the most fundamental ones in Aristotle's philosophy: the principles of form and matter. Form is the principle of determinateness, of definiteness, of the actual character of a changing thing. It is the Pythagoreans' Limit and Plato's Forms—except that it is made immanent in each natural, changing thing as its form. The actual, definite colors of the leaf are forms it acquires in the process of natural change. Matter is the principle of indeterminateness, of indefiniteness, of the potential character of changing things. It is the indeterminate or Unlimited of Anaximander and the Pythagoreans and the Receptacle of Plato—except that it is immanent in each changing thing as its very matter. Thus form and matter are both adjectival rather than substantival; they are not themselves things but rather the formal and material aspects of things. For this reason one must guard against thinking of matter, as Aristotle conceives it, as extended corporeal substance. Aristotle thinks that matter is sometimes but not necessarily corporeal. Some of the examples he gives of the material factor[2] are the bronze of a statue, the silver of a bowl, the genus of which bronze and silver are species, the premises of a syllogism, and the letters of a syllable. While the first two examples are clearly corporeal and extended, the next two are certainly not and the last one is only dubiously so. However, each of them is truly material for something, potential with respect to something. The bronze is the material for the statue, and the premises are the material for the syllogistic conclusion. Thus everything in nature, whether corporeal and extended or not, has both a now being and a not yet being, both an actual, determinate form and a potential, indeterminate matter. It is both now what it is actually and formally and also not yet actually what it is potentially or materially. Form and matter, like the Limit and the Unlimited, sky and earth, are the father and mother of natural things.

The leaf, you will already have noted, however, is not always and unchangingly a leaf. It, too, changes from a bud to mold to peat to coal to diamond. The material, potential substructure of any particular change is also itself a formal, actual thing that is in the process of changing into something else. Hence it, too, like the leaf's change from green to yellow, must be analyzed into form and matter; its forms supply the discontinuity in its change and its matter supplies the continuity. Furthermore, this matter underlying the leaf-change, let us say a cellulose compound, is also itself changing, so it too must be composed of a formal superstructure and a material substructure; and this substructure is also changing, so it too must be composed of form and matter, and so on, indefinitely. In fact, everything in nature is constantly changing; nature is the realm of change; so everything in nature must be composed of matter and form. Everything, that is, except matter and form themselves, for they are not themselves *things* but rather the constitutive and explanatory *principles* of things. Hence the world of nature ranges from pure, indeterminate potentiality (which Aristotle calls primary matter and which by definition never actually exists alone at all) through a hierarchy of hylomorphic (material-formal), potential-actual, indeterminate-determinate, changing things up to pure, determinate actuality or form which is not in nature because, lacking matter or potentiality, it cannot change.

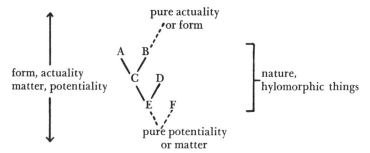

The thing at each lower level is the matter or potentiality for the thing at each higher level, and the thing at each higher level is the form or actuality of the thing at each lower level. Thus form and matter, actuality and potentiality, appear at every level of nature as the constitutive and explanatory principles of all natural, changing things. In nature no form exists without matter and no matter without form.

The definition of change which Aristotle draws from this solution to the problem of change in terms of the principles of form and matter, actuality and potentiality, may now be stated: *Change is the actualizing of what is potential insofar as it is potential.*[3] It is the forming of a material thing insofar as it is material. Only by virtue of its matter or potentiality or capability is a thing able to change, and only by virtue of the forming of this matter, the actualizing of this potentiality, does it actually change.

4-2.2. *Causes and Categories*

The four causes of change, already noted in connection with Aristotle's relation to his predecessors, also emerge from this analysis and definition of change. The question answered by Aristotle's four causes is the why of changing, natural things. What types of factors must be cited to explain adequately why a thing is the way it is? Aristotle holds that there are four such types of factors, and we have already noted two of them: matter and form or potentiality and actuality. The *material cause* is simply the material of which the thing is composed, the potential energy captured in its present form. The *formal cause* is the form or structure given to that material, the present actuality of that potential energy. A thing is the way it is because of its matter and its form. But what is the cause of the imposition of that particular form on that particular matter, the actualization of that potentiality? The answer to this question yields the other two of the four causes. The *efficient cause* is the force which imposes that form upon that matter, the agency which actualizes that potential energy in this particular, determinate way. But what caused the efficient cause to exercise its force in the particular way in which it did? This is the *final cause* or purposive factor which directs the agency or efficient cause to actualize the indeterminate potentiality of matter in some specific way. What types of factors must be cited to explain an acorn, for example? The material of which it is composed, the form or structure of that material, the forces which gave the material this structure, and the end or goal toward which these forces are moving.

Aristotle's theory is a more literal and less metaphorical, a more interfused and less separated, version of Plato's four principles. The material cause is a conceptual version of Plato's Receptacle, the formal cause a naturalistic expression of Plato's Forms, the efficient cause a literal version of Plato's metaphorical divine Craftsman, and the final cause a more factual equivalent of Plato's Good. The final cause is final in two different senses. It is the final cause in being the end or goal cause (*finis* = end); in this sense it is less misleading to call it the *telic cause* (from the Greek word *telos* = end or goal), but it is also the final cause in being the ultimate cause, the most basic of the causes. It is the cause of the exercise of the causality of the other three causes—it is the cause of causes—because from it the causation begins; it is the final cause which is the reason why everything else is done. The final cause need not be, though sometimes it is, a purpose in the sense of a conscious aim. It is a purpose in the case of the causal actions of conscious beings, but in a non-sentient thing the telic cause is simply the objective end toward which the thing unconsciously moves.

Each of the four causes may be more proximate to or more remote from the changing thing being caused by it. In the diagram on page 89 we can see that the material cause and the formal cause can range from the immediate situation all the way to primary matter and pure actuality, respectively. This diagram also shows that the same proximity-remoteness series holds for the final or telic cause too, for the goal of every natural thing is the actualization of its potentiality, and this actualization is a matter of degree. Thus the ultimate goal-cause or actuality of an acorn is to be an oak tree; but the accomplishment of this end requires more immediate goals, more proximate stages of actualization. Finally, this proximity-remoteness series holds true of the efficient causes, too, for they range from the most immediate to the most remote ones. Thus, for example, the president moves his secretary who moves the vice-president who moves his secretary who moves the office manager who moves his secretary who moves the plumber to turn the valve. For want of a nail a kingdom was lost, but not *merely* for want of a nail, we should note, for other causal factors are necessary, also.

Aristotle's four types of causes manifest only two fundamental principles, however, for three of the four causes—formal, efficient, and final—are manifestations of the principle of form or actuality. The material cause is the efficacy of the principle of matter or potentiality, and the formal cause is the efficacy of the principle of form or actuality. But the formal cause (say the shape of a statue) is the final cause as realized in the changing thing; it is the *de facto* actuality which *de jure* is the goal sought. The efficient cause also is the same in kind or species as the formal cause, Aristotle says, for the efficient cause's own form, at least in part, is what it imprints on the matter as its form and end (man begets man, for example). So formal, efficient, and final causes are all expressions of the principle of form or actuality. Only the material cause expresses, in the yielding passivity which it alone can offer, the principle of matter or potentiality. While Aristotle has four causal factors, his two complementary principles of actuality and potentiality, therefore, remain ultimate.

The *categories* are the major kinds into which all natural, changing things and their characteristics fall. While we want the smallest number of categories or classes, the number must be large enough to include all natural things and properties. Aristotle has eight categories with one or two others sometimes added to make nine or ten:

The Categories

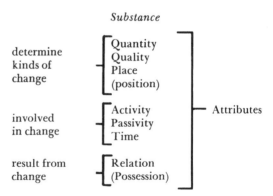

The main division of the categories is into substance and the seven (or nine) attributes or "accidents." Primary substance is that which exists in itself, for example, an individual like you, and the only sure examples of Aristotelian substances are living organisms. Secondary substance is the essence or definition of a primary substance—your human nature, for example. The attributes are classes of characteristics of substances; they are what exist not in themselves but in something else, like your size (quantity), philosophical knowledge (quality), place or position, your activity of learning, your passivity in being taught, your birthdate, your being a son or daughter, or your manner of dress. The first five of these categories determine the different kinds of change. Substantial change, or generation and destruction, is the coming into being or passing away of a substance, for example, the conception or death of an individual human being. Quantitative change and qualitative change are, respectively, changes in the quantity and quality of a substance; and locomotion is the change of place or position. Relations and possessions result from change; and activity, passivity, and time are involved in change, rather than determining specific kinds of change. Activity is the exercise of the actual, formal element and passivity the exercise of the potential, material element in change; time is the measure or number of change, and all change is temporal.

Purpose, necessity, and *accident* in nature all follow from Aristotle's theory of the four causes. They therefore are not, as we often think of them today, three alternative incompatible theories about nature. Instead of thinking that nature is either purposive or deterministic or purely a matter of chance, Aristotle holds that nature is all three, that purposiveness, mechanical determinism, and chance are all present in nature. The purposiveness of every natural thing and of nature as a whole is supplied by the final or telic cause. *Purpose* means an end or goal toward which a thing is moving, and this end is its fullest possible actuality, its final cause. This end or final cause of a thing may or may not be present in the consciousness of the thing; the thing which is moving toward an end may or may not be aware of the end toward which it is moving or of the fact that it is moving toward an end. A child is, an acorn is not. Thus purpose does not imply consciousness, and Aristotle's view that all nature is purposive does not imply any variety of panpsychism or metaphysical idealism.

Necessity or mechanical determinism in nature is, for Aristotle, always conditional. If a natural event must occur, it must occur *if,* and only if, something else occurs. This something else is some temporally prior event, and *it* also must occur if and only if some other temporally prior event occurs, and so on, ad infinitum. The world of nature is for Aristotle without temporal beginning or end; it is everlasting. Thus necessity in nature involves an endless series of antecedent events. But necessity in nature also involves, according to Aristotle, an end or goal which is *to be* realized. If a natural event must occur, it must occur if, and only if, something else occurs; and this something else is not only some antecedent state of affairs, the efficient cause, it is also the end toward which the thing is moving, its purpose or final cause. If the thing is to move toward this end, then it must do so in a certain way. Rationally conscious human beings, who are rationally aware of their purpose or final cause, have, at least in most cases, a choice from among alternative means toward the end; however, the alternative means toward the end are restricted in number, and some one of them must be chosen and performed if the end is to be realized. The final cause, as we saw before, is the cause of causes; it is that which moves the efficient cause to realize its efficacy in some certain way to imbue some matter with some certain form. Thus necessity or mechanical determinism does not preclude but actually requires purposiveness in nature.

Chance or accident is also necessarily present in nature; and this is not a contradiction in terms since only the occurrence of some chance events or others is necessary, not the particular chance events which do occur. *Accident* is, according to Aristotle, the material coincidence of two or more independently necessitated effects. Even the coincidence, the accidentality itself, is caused, though it is caused by a wholly indeterminate cause, matter or potentiality. Since matter is in itself wholly indeterminate and completely lacking in form, it may receive any form at all and thus even wholly unconnected ones. Thus accident in nature is traceable to the material cause. When the accidental event is such that it might have been purposefully sought or avoided by an intelligent, human being (such as a chance meeting of some one who owes you money in a store where you went only to shop), it is called luck, either good luck or bad luck. When the accidental event is not of this kind, it is called chance. Thus the fact that everything in nature is what it is because of the four causes means that everything in nature involves necessity, purpose, and accident. Necessity is traceable to the efficient cause, purpose to the final and formal causes, and accident to the material cause.

4-3. *God*

God is necessarily involved in the very fact of change as its first cause. For this reason Aristotle, perhaps to our surprise, discusses God in a treatise on physics, as well as in the *Metaphysics*. There are changing things; this premise, while not logically demonstrable, is the formulation of what is inescapable to the senses. Change is the actualizing of what is potential insofar as it is potential; this is Aristotle's definition of change arrived at through his solution of the problem of change.

The first thing to note in seeing the necessity of a first cause of change is that nothing can actualize itself. Insofar as a thing is actual*ized* it must first be potential, and insofar as it actual*izes* it must first be actual; and nothing can be both actual and potential at the same time and in the same respect. Of course *composite* things often do change or actualize themselves, but when this happens the potential which is actualized is a *different aspect* of the whole than the actual aspect which actualizes it. One single aspect of a thing cannot be at the same time both actual and potential; this would be a contradiction. Hence the actualizer or cause must be distinct from the actualized or effect.

The second and most difficult thing to see in recognizing the necessity of a first cause of change is that the series of *causes* cannot *regress* to infinity. While one may argue that the series of *effects* may *progress* to infinity on the ground that the existence of the cause does not depend upon a completed series of effects, the existence of the effect, by definition of "effect," depends upon the completion of the series of the actually existent causes of it. This is a tautology. However, the completed causal series is not a *temporal* series for two reasons. First, according to Aristotle, there cannot be a first moment of time. As we have seen, Aristotle holds that the world of nature is everlasting, without beginning and without end, for the very idea of a first or last moment of time is self-contradictory. "Time is the measure of change with respect to the before and after";[4] time is a movement from past to future, from what is earlier to what is later. Everything temporal must have both a past and a future. If the "first moment" were a moment and hence itself something temporal, it would have to follow something earlier and thus not be first at all, and if the "last moment" were a moment and hence itself something temporal, it would have to precede something later and thus not be last at all. Thus there cannot be any *temporally* first or last event. Second, even if there could be and were a temporally first event, it could not be a cause of, it could not account for, a present changing thing because since it is past, it is no longer even in existence. Therefore the first cause of a presently changing thing cannot occur at a first moment of time; it must rather be something now existing, something copresent with the changing thing whose cause and explanation it is. Hence, the conclusion follows that there is and must be a cause of change which is first in a completed logical and ontological series of causes every member of which is copresent with the changing thing which is their effect. Such a first cause cannot be escaped by making this completed series a circle, for a causal circle involves the contradiction that each simple item in it is both before and after itself, existent both before and after it is existent, since it is both the cause and the effect of itself.

This first cause or mover must itself be uncaused or unmoved simply by virtue of its firstness. If it were caused or moved or changed, it would have to be so by some other cause; and this other cause would then be more "first" than the first cause, which is a contradiction. Thus the first cause of change is the Unmoved Mover. Furthermore, the first cause must even be unmoveable or unchangeable, for if it were able to be changed, even though not actually changed, it would have some other cause prior to it to prevent the realization of the first cause's capacity for change and to hold it in a stable state.

From this unchangeability follows the essential nature of the first cause or Unmoved Mover: pure actuality or pure form. Unlike the hylomorphic things of nature, the first cause must be purely actual, purely form, for if it were partly potential, partly material, it would be able to be changed and therefore would not be the first cause. From the pure actuality of the first cause follows the fact that it is not a part of nature, for the realm of nature is the realm of change and therefore the realm of the potential, the material. The first cause is the cause of all natural things, but it is not itself a natural thing. The ultimate cause of nature transcends nature.

The absolute firstness of the first cause implies that it is a final or telic cause, for among the four causes the telic cause is first. The telic cause is the cause of causes, so the first cause of nature is a telic cause. The first cause, the Unmoved Mover, God, moves things as does the object of desire, Aristotle says, just as the Venus de Milo moves the viewer while itself remaining unmoved. God thus causes and moves all things not by creating them out of nothing but by attracting them toward Himself. He does this because He is actuality pure and simple, for actuality is the goal of all natural things, the terminal of every process of change (change is the actualizing of the potential). Insofar as the final cause often coincides with the formal and efficient causes, Aristotle's God might also be the formal and efficient cause of nature. From this point of view Aristotle's God would combine the originative function of Plato's Forms with that of the divine Craftsman and his goodness. But since it is as object of desire that God is said to move things, and since the final cause, the goal or end of goodness, is the ultimate cause, the cause of the exercise of the causality of the other causes, Aristotle's God is at least primarily if not merely a telic or final cause, and thus most like the goodness of Plato's divine Craftsman. Hence His name is most properly, as Aristotle saw, the Unmoved Mover.

Since the Unmoved Mover is pure actuality and thus not subject to any kind of change and since time is the concomitant of change, the Unmoved Mover is also timeless or eternal. Nature is everlasting, because it is the realm of change and time and because time itself cannot have a beginning or an end. Nature also is everlasting and everchanging for a deeper reason: it is the domain of primary matter or pure potentiality which is infinite and inexhaustible in its actualizability. Having in itself no form whatever, primary matter can take on an infinity of forms in an endless process of temporal change. The first cause of this everlasting process of natural change is God, the Unmoved Mover; but God is eternal rather than everlasting, for God contains no potentiality for change. In the *Metaphysics* Aristotle writes that God is also *living* and has a life of endless duration.[5] This cannot consistently mean that God is everlasting for the reasons just noted; perhaps it means that God is eternal or timeless. And God cannot be said to be living in the sense in which Aristotle defines life as the life of a body (Ch. 4-4.1); perhaps, therefore, this is only an analogous sense of "life" meaning literally actuality and activity. In the same place Aristotle also says that God is self-thinking thought, thinking about thinking *(noesis noeseos)*. If God is to think about anything at all, he must think about that which is most perfect, most real, true, and good—and this is Himself. But why must God think about anything at all? What is the reason for saying that pure actuality is thought? The answer to this question will be considered in Aristotle's theory of mind and thought: Since thought in itself lacks all matter or potentiality, it is more purely actual than anything else we experience.

4-4. *Man*

We shall first examine Aristotle's theory of human nature and then his theory of the perfection of that nature, since the latter is based on the former.

4-4.1. *Man's Nature*

The soul or *psychē* is the most basic concept in Aristotle's theory of human nature. We have noted that the Greek concept of soul is closely tied to the concept of life, and in Aristotle's theory of the soul this tie is especially tight. Aristotle defines *soul* as *the first actuality of an organic body*.[6] Actuality is form as before, and an organic body is living matter. Hence the soul is the form of living matter. Every living thing is also a natural thing and is therefore hylomorphic—material-formal, potential-actual. The matter or potentiality of a living thing is its body, and the form or actuality of a living thing is its soul or *psychē*. Just like form and matter or actuality and potentiality, soul and body are not themselves things but rather the constitutive principles by which things are what they are. The soul is not a thing or substance which has some unknown, dubious relation to the body. Rather it is the very form or actuality of the living body; the definition of the soul includes the body. Consequently a disembodied immortal soul is logically impossible, although Aristotle does maintain a type of immortality which we shall consider shortly. By the soul's being the *first* actuality of an organic body, Aristotle means that the soul is the very *life* of the living body. The soul is the being alive of a living organism in contrast to the second actualities of the organism which are its particular ways of *acting* alive. These second actualities or activities are manifestations of the various levels and powers of the soul.

Aristotle divides the soul into three parts, which are similar to, though more biologically oriented than, the three parts into which Plato divided the soul. The vegetative level of the soul is common to all living things and is the only level of the soul in plant life. The sensitive level of the soul presupposes the vegetative level and is found in animals; this form of being alive is sensitive to the environment. The rational level of the soul presupposes the sensitive and vegetative levels and is peculiar to human beings; this form of being alive is aware of the stable and universal traits of things. This successive presupposition of one level by another means that the three phases of the soul are arranged in an hierarchical order similar to that in Plato's account (Ch. 3-1.4, 5), and this hierarchy is determined by the degree of actualization of potentiality, by the forming of matter, and therefore by the degree of independence from bodily states. This hints at a conclusion to be drawn later, that the highest level of the soul, the rational level, is in some sense completely actual and hence independent of mortal and bodily conditions. Each of these three levels of soul or modes of life normally gives rise to a corresponding faculty of the soul, a power of acting alive in a specific manner. Nutrition and reproduction are the faculties of the vegetative level of soul; sensation, sensory appetite, and locomotion are the faculties of the sensitive level of the soul; and reason and will (or wish) are the faculties of the rational level of the soul.

Cognition occurs at the two higher levels of the soul, the sensitive and the rational. The objects of sensory cognition are changing particulars, and the objects of rational cognition are unchanging forms, just as they were for Plato. Contrary to Plato, however, these rationally cognized forms are immanent in the sensed particulars of nature and are psychologically posterior to them. While Plato held that sensed particulars are prior to the recollection of the Forms in the present bodily state of the soul, he insisted that the earliest cognitive state is an intellectual apprehension of the Forms with no antecedent sensory experience at all, an apprehension possessed by an unembodied soul in an earlier life (Ch. 3-1.3). For Aristotle soul entails body, so there cannot be any unembodied soul; and this means that rational cognition cannot occur apart from sensory cognition, although, as we shall shortly see, immortal reason can contemplate its proper objects once it has derived them from the senses. The forms, which are the proper objects of rational cognition, are *in* the objects of the senses, but they are not apparent *to* the senses. The proper object of sense is the changing particular, as such. The proper object of reason is the unchanging formal structure of a particular changing thing grasped by sense. This again is a manifestation of Aristotle's desire to tighten the relation between Plato's two worlds: no form without matter, no soul without body, and no conceptual forms without sensory particulars.

In accordance with his general principles Aristotle holds that the faculty of reason has a material or potential aspect as well as a formal or actual aspect, a passive reason as well as an active reason. His fundamental justification is simply that the mind is able to know before it actually does, so this ability is its potential or material aspect. This does not mean that Aristotle was a materialist or behaviorist in the modern sense of making the mind corporeal and extended for Aristotle's concept of matter is broader than extended body and means "material *for*" or potentiality. Of course the material or potentiality for many things, such as the bronze of a statue, does indeed result in an individual, extended, corporeal thing, *e.g.* the statue. But the material aspect of the mind or the potentiality of knowing is not itself the same as but is only analogous to corporeal potentiality, so the result of the material aspect of the mind is not an individual corporeal thing but rather a noncorporeal knowledge of something, such as an individual corporeal thing. As Aristotle says, the known stone itself is not in the mind, but rather its form.

Aristotle restricts immortality to the active reason, to reason in its active and actual aspect. The vegetative and sensitive levels of the soul and their corresponding faculties involve body and therefore mortality, and the potential or passive reason does not exist at all actually but only potentially. I am not immortal, but the active reason in me is immortal to the degree to which it is actual and active. This is an unequivocal statement of the view of immortality which was implicit but unclear in Plato. (See p. 66.) The soul is the form of the body and therefore partakes of bodily mortality; any immortality that it may achieve must come from the principle of form, from stable, nontemporal actuality. But only the rational part of the soul can participate in the immortality of this principle of form, and that only insofar as it actually knows and contemplates the forms, so only the active reason can be immortal. The achievement of this immortality through rational attachment to the principle of form we have already seen as the ultimate goal of man in Plato's ethics and we shall shortly see it again in Aristotle's ethics.

What is the relation of this immortal active reason in man to the self-thinking thought which is the Unmoved Mover or God? As we shall shortly see, the ultimate object of the active reason is God himself, and since God is self-thinking thought the active reason would seem in the last analysis to be the thinking of thinking of thinking. This description is very close to the description of God himself, yet the active reason is clearly in man. Aristotle's own view on this much disputed point is not at all clear; he refers to the active reason sometimes as the divine part of man and sometimes as that in man which is most nearly like God.

4-4.2. Man's Perfection

". . . the good has rightly been declared to be that at which all things aim"; thus Aristotle begins his *Nicomachean Ethics.* What is it at which all things aim? The answer to this question has been given in Aristotle's philosophy of nature. That at which all things aim is their own actuality, for natural things are changing and change is the actualizing of the potential. Every natural thing is an aiming at and yearning for its own actuality, the realization of its potentiality. Hence, the good of anything is its full actuality, and good*ness* is the same as God, the Unmoved Mover (though Aristotle doesn't say so), for God is pure actuality. Here we should note the similarity of Aristotle's view that good means the actuality of potentiality to Plato's view that virtue means the excellent functioning of a thing, and we should also note that Aristotle's ethical theory, like Plato's, is a natural law theory, one that regards the good as acting and being in accordance with nature. Now the meaning of human goodness follows immediately from the meaning of goodness in general. Human goodness is the full actuality of human nature at which human beings as potential necessarily aim. Since man is the rational animal, and as animal also vegetable, human goodness is the full actuality of man's vegetable, animal, and rational potentialities.

This deductive definition is, by itself, too abstract and general, however, so Aristotle proceeds to derive a more concrete picture of the nature of human goodness by an induction from the facts of human experience and belief. According to Aristotle, it is generally agreed that the human good is happiness; this is more plausible in Greek than in English, for *eudaimonia* means objective well-being as well as the subjective sense of its possession, which is more nearly what our word "happiness" means. Yet on the nature of happiness people often disagree, so Aristotle surveys a number of important traits of happiness upon which at least most people agree. Happiness is the final good, not an instrumental one, the end and not merely a means. The happy life is also the complete and self-sufficient one; happiness leaves nothing to be desired. So also happiness includes both pleasure and virtue, and since human beings are physical beings living in a material world, it also requires material possessions, not as ends in themselves but as necessary means to human self-realization. Furthermore nearly everyone agrees that happiness is something permanent and stable: "One swallow does not make a summer,"[7] nor does a fleeting joy suffice to make a man happy. So never count a man happy until you see him dead, the Greeks used to say, for then you can see the whole of his life. Moreover, happiness is something prized rather than praised, and this means again that happiness is the end and not a means. Finally, happiness is an activity, not just a state or disposition; it is an active being and doing and not a passive, inert holiday or vacation.

These various traits of happiness, these generally accepted criteria of human goodness, Aristotle concludes, are best included in and explained by the previously deduced view that the good is rational activity, the actuality of man as the rational animal. Nothing can be more ultimate and final, more complete and self-sufficient, or more prized than the end at which man's nature aims, his own full well-being. Such a life of rich well-being also requires both virtue or character and a certain amount of material possessions, and it also yields pleasure. Of course, it is also an active life, since actuality is activity. Hence Aristotle concludes that happiness or the good of man. "is an activity of the soul in accordance with virtue, or, if there be more than one virtue [as indeed there is], in accordance with the best and most perfect of them [which is the virtue of the rational part]. And we must add, in a complete life."[8]

Saying that the good is virtue, etc., seems rather like saying that the good is the good, unless "virtue" can be given some clear, independent meaning. What is virtue *(aretē)?* The first and most basic thing to note about virtue, and also vice, is that for Aristotle it is a *habit* or character-structure or disposition *(hexis).* Thus ethics has fundamentally to do with character *(ethos).* As habits or character-structures, virtues and vices are acquired rather than innate, they make up our second nature rather than our first nature. The innate or first nature of man, the soul with its levels, is only potential with respect to its later actualizations. Virtue is the actualization of this first nature as an acquired disposition to continue to act in accordance with the soul and its faculties, especially reason; vice is the acquired second nature or habit of tending to act in conflict with the inborn nature of the individual. Virtues are thus habits of acting to realize and express one's nature, and vices are habits of acting to inhibit one's nature. In brief, virtues are simply good habits and vices are simply bad habits.

Since man's inborn nature is complex, he has many different virtues and corresponding vices. Aristotle's main division of the virtues is into intellectual and moral ones. The intellectual virtues are habits of acting in such a way as to realize man's capacity for knowledge, both theoretical and practical. The moral virtues are habits of acting in such a way as to use this knowledge for the actualization of one's whole nature with its many aspects in harmony with each other. The famous but widely misunderstood doctrine of the golden mean applies to the moral virtues alone. The reason the moral virtues are means is two-fold: their subject-matter is subject to degrees, and the extremes are detrimental to the agent's self-realization. Thus temperance, for example, is concerned with the *degree* to which we should satisfy our love of pleasure, from the one extreme of no satisfaction at all to the other extreme of total satisfaction. Temperance is a mean between these two extremes because both no pleasure and nothing but pleasure inhibit the development of some part of our nature. The love of pleasure is a natural, inborn, capacity in man and as such it should be satisfied, but the exclusive satisfaction of this love of pleasure with no thought for anything else means the frustration of other parts of our nature. Aristotle thus avoids the extremes both of Puritanism and of hedonism. Yet he is closer to Puritanism because our pleasure-loving tendencies ordinarily need no encouragement whereas our self-control certainly does.

This analysis of temperance applies also to the other moral virtues; each is a golden mean between two extremes, which are vices, but the mean lies closer to the extreme involving strength of mind and will. For example, the golden mean of courage is closer to rashness than to cowardice because our fear of pain normally needs no encouragement whereas our endurance of pain for worthwhile ends definitely does. Just as the navigator or pilot turns his craft into a wind which tends to blow him off course, so also does the moral man lean his life against the forces of his passions, which tend to divert him from his ultimate end of self-realization and happiness. The golden mean in each case is relative not to our opinions but to the objective facts of the matter; the mean is not subjectively but objectively relative. The realization of a person's potentialities in the situation in which he lives calls objectively for a certain degree of abandon and a certain degree of restraint, no matter what he would like to think about the matter. Not only is the mean not subjective; in one important sense it is not even a mean but rather an extreme. "In respect of its essence and according to the definition of its basic nature, virtue is a state of moderation," Aristotle tells us, "but regarded in its relation to what is best and right, it is an extreme . . . for the proper mean is, in its own way, an extreme."[9]

The virtues are thus habits of tending to act so as to realize human potentialities, and happiness is the active possession and exercise of these good habits. Yet Aristotle adds, " . . . if there be more than one virtue, [then happiness is activity] in accordance with the best and most perfect of them."[10] Now more than one virtue exists, we have seen; but which is the best and most perfect of them? For a human being, distinguished as he is by his rationality, the highest of the virtues is the virtue of wisdom, the habit of actualizing one's rational powers. According to Aristotle, therefore, the highest and most distinctively human part of happiness is a life of wisdom, and the life of wisdom, at least in its highest phase, is identified with the contemplative life. The peculiarly human happiness, and the acme of happiness of man as a rational animal, is thus the life of contemplation. But why contemplation?

The specific and defining difference of human nature is its rationality. Now the function of rationality is to understand, to gain wisdom; and once such wisdom is possessed there is no further to go. Hence the final fulfillment of human nature as rational is a dwelling in the wisdom gained and contemplating the world as rationally understood. This much Aristotle clearly holds; but (as his medieval followers realized) his philosophy seems to imply something more which Aristotle himself does not explicitly affirm, that the ultimate object of contemplation is God. To understand means to know the causes of things. Hence the complete actuality of reason involves knowing the first cause, God, as the fundamental cause of all things. Understanding, the satisfaction of one's rational striving, is not complete short of this point. Upon attaining the knowledge of God as the first cause of all things, however, there is no further for reason to go. Hence the ultimate good or actuality of man as a rational being can only be a resting in contemplation of God as the first cause of all things. This way of wisdom is destined for man in so far as he is man, in so far as he is rational, and in this life of contemplation man's life merges with that of God who is in Himself pure contemplation, self-thinking thought. "He who leads such a life will do so not in his strictly human capacity," Aristotle writes, "but only so far as there is in him an element of the divine."[11]

The good is thus self-realization, in which the self to be realized is rational as well as animal, but it is also social as well as individual, for man is "the political animal." It is not merely my nature or yours which is to be realized, though it is this; it is also the universal human nature embodied in you and in me which is to be realized, and this fact that all human beings share a common nature is the fundamental cause of the sociality of man. While the contemplative life is the highest of which man is capable, it does not by any means exclude a life of active participation in social and political affairs.

The best summary of Aristotle's moral philosophy is one which he himself states: "Whatever is proper to the nature of each thing is best and pleasantest for that thing. Since it is reason that is most truly man, a life according to reason must be at once best and pleasantest for man. Such a life, therefore, will be most truly happy."[12]

4-5. *Being*

Philosophy is, both etymologically and according to Aristotle, the love of wisdom; and wisdom is the knowledge of the ultimate causes of all things. Now what is most ultimate in things is their being, their reality, and from this it follows that wisdom is the knowledge of the nature and principles of being. Thus, in the first two chapters of his treatise titled, *Metaphysics,* Aristotle introduces us to the nature of that division of philosophy which he believes to be pedagogically last and yet logically first. Aristotle himself does not call this discipline metaphysics as do most philosophers today; he calls it first philosophy because it deals with what is first in reality or theology, because what is absolutely first in reality is God. The word "metaphysics" is an historical accident, a label later pinned on this untitled treatise in order to indicate that it belongs after *(meta)* Aristotle's treatise, *Physics.*

According to Aristotle's definition of this discipline, however, it might better be called *ontology,* the science of being. "There is a science which investigates being as being and the attributes which belong to this in virtue of its own nature," writes Aristotle in opening Book IV of his *Metaphysics.* "Now this is not the same as any of the so-called special sciences; for none of these others treats universally of being as being. They cut off a part of being and investigate the attribute of this part . . . ." The object of ontology or first philosophy, being as being, can exist as well as be conceived apart from matter; and in this sense the title *Metaphysics,* in spite of its accidental origin, does have a significance which is justified by the subject-matter: it is concerned with what is beyond (another meaning of *meta*) physics and physical reality.

An immediate result of this definition of "metaphysics" as the science of being as being is that its principles must possess absolute certainty and universal validity. Principles of being are, first, absolutely certain because, as principles of all being, they cannot have any possible exceptions. There *cannot be* anything whatsoever to which a principle of *being* does not apply. Hence, second, ontological principles, truths about being as such, have universal applicability; they are necessarily true of all possible ways of existing and of all possible modes of knowledge simply because they are true of the being which any possible thing or knowledge must have. The prime example of this absolute certainty and universal applicability of an ontological principle is the law of noncontradiction. "Being must be." "Being cannot not be." These absolutely general expressions are inescapably true just by virtue of the idea of being. By making this abstract truth more specific we have its necessary application to everything whatever: "No being can be other than it is, hence a being cannot both be and not be a certain thing at the same time and in the same respect." This last expression is roughly the principle of noncontradiction as Aristotle gives it[13] and as we understand it today. One of Aristotle's greatest contributions is that he saw clearly the nature and power of ontological truths, completely universal and necessary propositions, though not until modern times has the possibility of such ontological truth been given its profoundest scrutiny.

The problem of the one and the many, which so occupied Aristotle's predecessors, is a basic problem confronting the discipline of ontology, and Aristotle's treatment of this problem follows the relational solution of Plato. The most basic plurality or distinction in being is that of potentiality and actuality, as we have seen; and here is Aristotle's reflection of Plato's division of being into active and passive power. Potentiality and actuality are different modes of being, thus justifying pluralism, but they are both modes of *being* and thus bound into a single universe. Potentiality is the ability-to-be-actual and is, as such, relative to actuality both in itself and in our conception of it. A thing can't be able or potential just simply; it must rather be able to be *something*, be potentially some *actuality*. Actuality is actual-being, full, perfect, and complete. As such it is not in itself relative to potentiality nor does the concept of actuality logically entail the concept of potentiality, although our recognition of actuality is psychologically derived from and relative to our experience of potential things. Since pure actuality is, for Aristotle, identical with God, the Unmoved Mover, it follows that all potential or natural things are relative to God, both for their being and for the understanding of them, while God as pure actuality is independent of and not relative to natural, potential things. God thus thinks only of himself and not of the world. Aristotle's identification of God with pure actuality plus the priority of actuality over potentiality makes God the ultimate object of ontology so that it is finally theology.

With his theory of the unity and multiplicity of being Aristotle lays the foundation for the medieval doctrine of the analogy of being *(analogia entis)* (p. 153). Over and over Aristotle writes, "Being is said in many senses" (pluralism) rather than as a proper name as Parmenides seemed to think, though these many senses are related by sharing a single basic reference to that most fundamental principle, active actuality (monism). Among its many important consequences, this doctrine of the analogy of being permits us to accept ethical relativity without being condemned to ethical relativism. The good of anything is its full, actual being. Since there are many, diverse beings, there are also many, diverse goods; what is good for a man need not be good for a child, and what is good for people in one time and place need not be good for people in a different time and place. Yet all these relative and diverse goods have this in common: each is the actualized being, or conducive to the actualized being, of the specific thing or situation in question. This common reference or meaning of goodness is a universal principle which binds all ethical relativity together into one ethical universal.

4-6. *The Ancient Greek Story Reviewed*

With that prodigious care and sanity so characteristic of him, Aristotle sifts the sayings of his predecessors, weighs them against each other and against his own experience and reflection, and welds his findings together into a rich and coherent picture of man's life in the world. Aristotle's originality lies not so much in his basic insights as in the systematic clarity and the universal scope which he bestows upon these insights, a way of seeing the world we now call classical. The world is a hierarchy of existences, a great chain of being as A. O. Lovejoy called it, ranging from the asymptote of purely potential, primary matter through the various levels of hylomorphic, natural things—especially plants, animals, and men—to the supreme perfection or pure actuality of God. This world was not created; it did not come into being in time and it will not pass away in time; it is everlasting. The becoming of the world is unceasing, and it is driven by the endless yearning of the stuff of existence for its own realization in the pure actuality of God. Since man is a being in this world, his stuff, too, is driven ceaselessly by its desire for its own full actuality; and since man himself is already the highest level of the self-actualization of nature, his self-realization brings him into contact with that full reality which is God. This individual self-realization occurs not in isolation, however, but in social concert with fellowmen and in natural concert with the whole of nature. This goal of life, perfect self-realization, may be experienced concretely in the dynamic tranquillity, the active serenity, of classical Greek sculpture and architecture. The full being, truth, goodness, beauty, and even holiness of each thing lies in that actual perfection of inner form which is the latent nature of each thing and its reason for being. "Whatever is proper to the nature of each thing is best and pleasantest for that thing. Since it is reason that is most truly man, a life according to reason must be at once best and pleasantest for man. Such a life, therefore, will be most truly happy."[14]

Aristotle thus provides the final chapter in the story of the Greek period of ancient philosophy. It is the story of a halting yet persistent search for an understanding of the ultimate principles of man's world and for man's self-perfection by means of that understanding. The search proceeds from that which is first in the order of knowing and initially more familiar to us human beings (the Milesians' changing world of the senses) to what is first in the order of being and hence more intelligible in itself (Plato's and Aristotle's unchanging principles graspable by reason). The search begins with the hope that everything whatever can be understood in terms of some one principle (the Milesians and Eleatics), it continues with the concession that more than one principle is needed (the Pythagoreans and Pluralists), and it concludes that the understanding of all things requires reference to four principles: indeterminacy, determinacy, agency, and purpose (Plato and Aristotle). Yet the priority of one of these four, the principle of purpose (Plato's Good and Aristotle's Unmoved Mover), fulfills at last the original hope of understanding all things in terms of one single principle—that ultimate purpose which, as the full actuality of the potential being of all natural things, magnetizes them into a great chain of being ranging from the pure potentiality of primary matter through hylomorphic plants, animals, and men to its own divine pure actuality.

Stated in the broader and more general terms sketched in the Prologue, finally, the story of the Greek period of ancient philosophy is the story of the withdrawal from the undifferentiated whole of experienced reality in which philosophy originated and a return to that whole viewed as a system of parts. In the Cosmological Period there is a withdrawal from the whole of reality to its material part; matter is the measure of all things. In the Anthropological Period there is a further withdrawal to the human part of reality, and man is the measure of all things. Plato and especially Aristotle, however, bring philosophy to the third stage of the three-stage sequence, a rejoining of subjective man and objective nature in one systematic whole-of-parts. Man is fused with nature, then man is delivered free, then man is reunited with nature. Objective whole, subjective part, and systematic whole-of-parts, these three stages in the ontogenetic development of the individual are abstractly recapitulated in the three stages of the Greek period of ancient philosophy.

SUGGESTED READINGS

4-1.1. *Metaphysics.* Bk. I.
4-2. *Physics.* Bk. I; Bk. II, Chs. 1–3, 7; Bk. III, Ch. 1.
   Categories. 1a21–2b22.
4-3. *Physics.* Bk. VIII, Chs. 1, 3–7, 9–10.
   Metaphysics. Bk. XII, Chs. 6–7, 9.
4-4.1. *De Anima.* Bk. II, Chs. 1–6, 12; Bk. III, Chs. 1–7.

4-4.2. *Nicomachean Ethics.* Bk. I, Chs. 1–8, 12–13; Bk. II; Bk. VI, Chs. 3, 6–7; Bk. X, Chs. 4–9.

Politics. Bk. I, Chs. 1–2; Bk. VII, Chs. 1–3.

4-5. *Metaphysics.* Bk. I, Chs. 1–2; Bk. IV, Chs. 1–4, 7; Bk. VI, Chs. 1–2; Bk. IX, Chs. 3, 6, 8–10.

For bibliography, see:

Ross, W. D. *Aristotle,* New York: Meridian Books, 1959. Pp. 281–87.

Chapter 5

Hellenistic
and
Roman
Philosophy

In relation to the philosophies of their predecessors the philosophies of Plato and especially of Aristotle represent the third stage in the natural three-stage movement from objective whole to subjective part to systematic whole-of-parts. In relation to their successors, however, Plato and Aristotle provide a new statement of the first stage of the objective union of man with nature; and the remainder of ancient philosophy, the Hellenistic and Roman period, will be seen to complete this new statement of the three-stage sequence. The second stage in this new statement will be supplied by the Skeptics, the Epicureans, and the Stoics with their return to the Anthropological Period's emphasis upon man; and the third and final stage of this new statement of the sequence will be presented by Neoplatonism, especially by Plotinus, in a new and heavily Platonic and Aristotelian union of man and the world. This Hellenistic (Greco-Roman) and Roman period is marked geographically, as its name indicates, by a gradual westward movement of the center of philosophical (and political and cultural) activity. Its dates may be fixed somewhat arbitrarily from the death of Aristotle in 322 B.C. to the closing of the schools in Athens in 529 A.D.; however, these dates make the ancient and medieval periods

overlap since medieval philosophy was well under way long before 529 A.D.; St. Augustine, for example, died in 430 A.D.

5-1. *Skepticism*

Skepticism formed an important tendency from about 350 B.C.
to about 250 A.D., though its influence varied within this period.
Quite reminiscent of the Sophists in the Anthropological Period
(Ch. 2-1), the Skeptics of the Hellenistic and Roman Period may
perhaps be counted as starting with Pyrrho of Elis (about 360–
270 B.C.) from whose name comes a synonym for Skepticism:
Pyrrhonism. Pyrrho maintained that both sensation and reason
are illusory and relative and that consequently any certain or
universal truth cannot exist. Like the Sophists before him,
Pyrrho espoused the implied ethical relativism and drew the
moral that one should suspend judgment and conform to local
mores; apparently he did not see that his conclusion itself seems
to be a nonrelative, absolute standard.[1] Skepticism also dominated the Academy of Athens (founded by Plato) during its
so-called middle period. After Plato's death the interests of the
Academy became increasingly mathematical and Pythagorean
in what is called the Early or Old Academy, and the Late or
New Academy (the Academy during its final years prior to being
closed in 529 A.D.) was mainly Stoic in character. The Middle
Academy, however, saw the rise of two great Skeptics, Arcesilaus
(about 315–241 B.C.) and Carneades (about 214–129 B.C.), who
differed from Pyrrho and the other early Skeptics most importantly in stressing probability and in laying the foundations for
a theory of probability. Carneades distinguished three degrees of
probability and began to develop a theory of the objective criteria of each of them. Both thinkers apparently agreed with
Pyrrho in accepting an ethic of tolerance and moderation.

Insubordination arose within the ranks of the Skeptics a little
later, however, when Antiochus of Ascalon (about 125–70 B.C.)
criticized Carneades' theory of degrees of probability on the
ground that it is incompatible with his Skepticism. To say that
something is probable to a certain degree implies some standard
of absolute certainty, Antiochus argued, yet such a standard is
precisely what Carneades and his fellows had denied. How can

one know that anything is probable unless one knows that something else is certain? Is the degree of probability that proposition *p* has certain, or is this too only probable? Is the probability that *p* has that degree of probability certain, or is *that* also only probable, and so on? The point of Antiochus' criticism is that the meaning of probability is relative to evidence, and to say that something else is probable in relation to *it* seems to make no sense unless one is at one point, sooner or later, certain of some piece of evidence. If nothing at all is certain, then nothing can be even probable; if everything whatsoever is only probable, then nothing whatsoever is probable. Finally, the Skeptic cannot of course consistently be skeptical of his Skepticism itself or doubt that he doubts. Clearly, then, Skepticism must have a limit. This argument of Antiochus later received its most famous formulation by the seventeenth century philosopher Descartes, both as a general point on which to lay the foundation of his system (Ch. 8-2.1) and as a specific point in claiming the possession of a standard of perfection (Ch. 8-2.2).

The Alexandrian Skeptic Aenesidemus, who probably lived at about the beginning of the Christian era, is interesting especially because of his skeptical critique of causation anticipating the famous one by the eighteenth century philosopher Hume (Ch. 10-3.2), although Aenesidemus' arguments seem not to be the same as Hume's basic argument. Ancient Skepticism may perhaps be reckoned as ending with Sextus Empiricus, a physician who flourished about 200 A.D. He did not himself add much that was new, but we are indebted to him for much of the little knowledge of ancient Skepticism extant. No matter how skeptical the ancients got, however, whether the Sophists or the Hellenistic and Roman thinkers, they always stopped short of the subjectivistic and solipsistic Skepticism which we shall see arise in modern times, a skepticism concerning the existence of any world outside consciousness.

5-2. *Epicureanism*

The name of this movement is taken from that of its founder, Epicurus (342–270 B.C.), who came from the Aegean island of Samos and founded a famous school in Athens. The later, Roman period of Epicureanism is marked by Lucretius, the author of the classic *De Rerum Natura,* who lived in the first half of the first century b.c.

Epicurus divides philosophy into three parts: logic or canonic, physics (including metaphysics), and ethics. He regards his logic or canonic as an introduction to ethics and physics, and it is concerned with the criteria of truth rather than with formal logic. The criteria of truth are direct perceptions in the case of factual truth, and they are feelings of pleasure and pain in the case of ethical truth. These perceptions and feelings are infallibly true, and so are the ideas or representations which are the memory images of them. An opinion or belief is true when it corresponds to a perception or feeling and false when it does not. Thus the Epicurean theory of knowledge is a straightforward empiricism closely anticipating the more famous one of the eighteenth century Scottish philosopher, David Hume (Ch. 10-3.1).

Ethics was the primary interest of the Epicureans, however. They were mainly interested in philosophy as a way of life—no doubt a basic reason for the wide popular appeal enjoyed by their teachings—although they were careful to consider the theoretical justification of that way of life. The main historical origin of Epicurean ethics is the teaching of the Cyrenaic philosophers. While Epicurus is alleged to have proclaimed that the greatest pleasure is that of a good digestion—thus founding the modern meanings of the words "epicure" and "epicurean"—his teaching picks up the Cyrenaic story at its end rather than at its beginning; it presents Hegesias' ideal of an untroubled life rather than the robust, sensuous hedonism of Aristippus. Epicurus and his followers taught that the good is *ataraxia* (no trouble or disturbance), an "absence of pain in the body and trouble in the soul," a "health of body and tranquility *(ataraxia)* of mind." Note that the ideal life is conceived negatively; it is the absence of pain rather than the presence of pleasure. "Every pleasure . . . is good, yet not every pleasure is to be chosen,"[2] Epicurus writes. His reason seems to be that many, if not all, pleasures involve corresponding pains; here again the story of hedonism in the Cyrenaic movement should be recalled (Ch.

2-5). Hence the ethical ideal is a neutral and quiet state quite unlike the present-day image of the epicurean life.

The metaphysical theory of the Epicureans, their theory of the nature of reality, is a justification of their ethics and of their attitude toward life. The best symbol of this attitude is the famed walled garden of Epicurus. Just as Epicurus and his followers withdrew from the active life of their society to the tranquillity of their walled garden, so also does the Epicurean *ataraxia* call for a theoretical neutralizing of all human troubles from which physical withdrawal is impossible. Chief among these troubles and anxieties to which human flesh is heir are death, divine intervention, and fate.

Anxiety about death is one fundamental obstacle in the way of a tranquil, trouble-free life. Since no man can escape death, however, the fear of death must be removed by a true understanding of death as something of no concern to man. This true understanding of death is effected by the Epicureans primarily by means of a metaphysical materialism which they inherited with only a few changes from Democritus. All things, including the human soul, are composed of material atoms; and death is the dispersal of the soul atoms (and then the body atoms) of which a human person is composed. From this it immediately follows that "so long as we exist, death is not with us; but when death comes, then we do not exist. It does not then concern either the living or the dead, since for the former it is not, and the latter are no more."[3] While this argument is put in the context of metaphysical materialism, it is quite independent of materialism, and of every other metaphysical theory, for that matter, because it is purely logical in character. No matter what may be the nature of the soul and body and no matter whether a person be mortal or immortal, if a person dies he ceases to exist; this is the meaning of dying. Now if a person ceases to exist, either at the time of bodily death or later, then of course he does not exist to suffer any trouble. On the other hand, if a person does not die, does not cease to exist, why then of course his death does not exist for him to suffer. In either case death cannot logically concern him.

Fear that the divine, especially the many contending and ca-

pricious Greco-Roman gods, may at any time interfere with human life for no humanly intelligible reason is a second main
hindrance to the pursuit of *ataraxia,* a life of tranquillity. The
Epicureans attempt to remove this fear by understanding the
nature of the gods in terms of the Epicurean ideal. The gods,
who do indeed exist, must, of course, live a life of blessedness;
if they did not, they would not be gods. That blessedness is un-
troubledness *(ataraxia)* has been established in the ethical theory. Since human life is certainly troubled and troubling, it
follows that the gods in their untroubled life cannot have anything to do with human life, and they thus leave the Epicurean
free to pursue a god-like life of tranquillity. This argument is
quite independent of the Epicurean idea of goodness as *ataraxia,* though it does involve the assumption that by "god" one
means a being which is perfectly good. A being which is perfectly good cannot experience or be concerned with evil. Human
life is evil, at least partially; therefore, a god cannot experience
or be concerned with human life. This still leaves open the
question whether a devil, whose definition certainly does not
exclude concern for evil, might intervene in human affairs, but
it does seem to prevent a god from doing so. This theory provides a more mundane (and polytheistic) reflection of Aristotle's
theory that God is oblivious of the world and also an anticipation of the problems which will confront the medieval Christian
philosophers in their attempts to talk consistently about God
(Ch. 6-4).

A third barrier to the pursuit of Epicurean tranquillity is the
fear of fate *(moira),* retribution *(nemesis),* and determinism
(ananke). Implacable fate can determine a person's destiny ir-
respective of his own efforts, so what is the point of seeking
ataraxia? This fear of fate the Epicureans endeavor to remove
by means of a metaphysical tychism or "chance-ism" *(tyche =*
chance). Every event in the world is the outcome of collisions of
the atoms; on this the Epicureans agree with Democritus, but
they reject Democritus' determinism in favor of the view that
any atom may at any time deviate from its previous path spontaneously and without cause. Hence the atoms of which a person is composed, especially his soul atoms, may also deviate

spontaneously from their previous paths, thus crippling fate and establishing the freedom of the will—a view curiously like that of certain scientists and philosophers in the 1920's and 1930's who clutched at the uncertainty principle of physics as a vindication of free will.

Thus men's fears are quelled, both by a physical and social withdrawal from those disturbances from which man is free to withdraw and by a proper philosophical understanding of things which are beyond man's control.

5-3. *Stoicism*

The name of this movement, and hence also of the attitude which this movement has bequeathed to us, comes from the fact that the first Stoics, Zeno of Citium on Cyprus (about 340–265 B.C.) and his followers, were accustomed to meet at a certain *stoa* or arcade in Athens. Perhaps their name means also that they were concerned with the pillars or first principles (*stoicheia*) of knowledge and culture. Stoicism was a tremendously influential movement; it counted among its converts Seneca, the first century A.D. Latin essayist, and the Roman emperor Marcus Aurelius (who reigned 161–180 A.D.), and it deeply affected Christian philosophy especially in its doctrines of the *logos* or divine word and the brotherhood of man.

Ethics or ethico-religion was for the Stoics as for the Epicureans the primary concern; logic and metaphysics were subsidiary, and their definition of the good life is also like that of the Epicureans in being essentially negative. The good, the Stoics declare, is *apatheia;* but this is not to be identified with what "apathy" means today. For the Stoics *apatheia* (*a* = not, *pathē* = passion, suffering, vicissitude) means an independence from and indifference to whatever happens to one, a rugged strength of mind which brings peace of mind or tranquillity. In this fundamental notion and in the whole of their ethics the Stoics are thus heirs to the doctrine of spiritual ruggedness taught and practised by the Cynics (Ch. 2-4).

This Stoic contempt for the vicissitudes of life arises from the conviction that they are beyond the individual's control and

that it is, therefore, irrational or foolish to worry about them.
Apatheia means freedom from passion, and this requires that we
follow the dictates of reason. But what does reason dictate? That
some things are within our control and that others are not, and
that we should be concerned only with what is within our control. But what is within our control and what is not? Not within
our control are our bodies, health, property, wealth, reputation,
status in life, and apparently, everything even partially conditioned by external physical and social forces. Within our control
is only the rational judgment which we pass upon the things
which are beyond our control. Emotions or passions are thus
mistaken evaluations; they are treatments of outward things as
within our control when in fact they are not. In short, it is not
what happens to you but how you take what happens to you
which is of ethical and psychological importance, and the way
to take it is to "Take it!" "Everything has two handles," writes
Epictetus, "one by which you can carry it and one by which you
cannot."[4] The handle by which you cannot bear it is that it is a
misfortune; the handle by which you can bear it is that it is
beyond your power and must not be allowed to overwhelm you.
The tendency today is to applaud this attitude when the misfortune is one's own but to be a little shocked when the Stoic
consistently extends this attitude to the misfortunes of others.
Epictetus says:

> When you see a man shedding tears in sorrow for a child abroad or
> dead, beware that you are not carried away by the impression that it
> is outward ills that make him miserable. Keep this thought by you:
> "What distresses him is not the event, for that does not distress an-
> other, but his judgment on the event." Therefore do not hesitate to
> sympathize with him so far as words go, and if it so chance, even to
> groan with him; but take heed that you do not also groan in your
> inner being.[5]

Stoicism, unlike Epicureanism, thus meant for its founders
pretty much what it means today. That Stoicism is even quite
alive today can be seen in the popularity of the many "peace of
mind" books of recent years; whether they are placed in the
context of religion or of psychiatry or of good common sense,
they all reflect our Stoic heritage. "If you are fond of a jug, say

you are fond of a jug; then you will not be disturbed if it be broken. If you kiss your child or your wife, say to yourself that you are kissing a human being, for then if death strikes it you will not be disturbed."[6]

The metaphysics of the Stoics, their view of the nature of reality, like that of the Epicureans, is a clear justification of their ethical attitude. The goodness of *apatheia,* of the power of the mind over life's misfortunes, requires the belief that emotion is mistaken evaluation, that it is foolish to let things upset one. This in turn requires the belief that it is reasonable and good to accept everything that happens; and this belief requires, finally, the further belief that it is reasonable and good for everything to happen as it does. Upon being told that his son had just died, a legendary Stoic replied that he had never thought that he had given birth to an immortal. Since it is right that things happen as they do, the world must be governed by a divine providence or *logos,* which is immanent in the world and everything in it, although it does not also transcend the world. Especially in this doctrine of the *logos,* though in their metaphysical views generally, the Stoics were indebted primarily to Heraclitus. Everything in the world passes away except the determining providence itself, the *logos,* which destines that and how everything shall pass away. The *logos* is not only the intelligible law behind all things in nature; it is also the *logos* or reason in the minds of men, from which the later Stoics derived the doctrine of the brotherhood of man. Hence the Stoic's reason which judges and accepts whatever happens is the divine reason or God himself. Epictetus says:

> You are a principal work, a fragment of God himself, you have in yourself a part of Him. Will you not remember, when you eat, who you are that eat, and whom you are feeding, and the same in your relations with women? When you take part in society, or training, or conversation, do you not know that it is God you are nourishing and training? You bear God about with you, you poor wretch, and know it not.[7]

Hence God's in his earth and all's right with the world. So no evil can befall the good man, the man who knows and accepts this fact.

5-4. *Epicureanism and Stoicism Compared*

Psychologically and ethically Epicureanism and Stoicism are much more similar than the modern meanings of their names would indicate. Both are attempts to achieve tranquillity by withdrawing from the troubles of the world. Yet their withdrawals are quite different in kind. The Epicurean withdrawal is partly physical and social as well as psychological and spiritual. While of course not all Epicureans lived within a walled garden, the walled garden of Epicurus is symbolic of the essential Epicurean tendency to withdraw from society. The Stoic withdrawal from the world's misfortunes is not a physical or social withdrawal, but it is a withdrawal in a psychological and spiritual sense. While Epicurus lived within his walled garden, Marcus Aurelius was an emperor of Rome and battlefield commander who withdrew only into his own meditations, the silent ones of his mind and the ones he wrote in his tent at night. While the ideal Epicurean is one who experiences no pain or trouble at all, the ideal Stoic is one who experiences all the pains and troubles attendant upon his station and its duties but whose interior life is thereby unimpaired. Hence the Epicurean avoids pain and trouble while the Stoic endures it. Hence the Epicurean tends to be "out of this world" while the Stoic tends to be "in but not of the world." Moreover, the Epicurean withdrawal is a withdrawal to just the individual himself rather than to anything transcending him. The Stoic withdrawal, on the other hand, is a withdrawal not merely to the individual self but rather to a divine principle, the *logos,* which transcends the individual and is ultimate in nature, though it is also within the individual self. This emphasis upon the presence in man of something greater than himself upon which he can lean and from which he can draw moral courage seems to indicate that Stoicism has greater psychological strength and vitality than Epicureanism.

Logically and systematically, however, the Epicurean philosophy seems the stronger. While no major logical weaknesses appear in the Epicurean system, the Stoic system contains three glaring paradoxes. First, the rational part of every person must be naturally immortal for the Stoics, since it is an expression of and fundamentally identical with the divine *logos*. Yet apparently only the Stoic sage is immortal, since immortality is an ethical prize to be won rather than a given fact and since only the Stoic sage is truly ethical. Second, there cannot really be any evil at all, not even moral evil, according to the Stoic position, since everything whatever is due to the divine *logos* which is itself good. Yet on the other hand failure to be a Stoic is a moral evil; if this were not maintained, the ethical force of Stoicism would vanish. Finally, everything whatever is determined by the divine *logos,* according to the Stoic, so each man's rational decisions must likewise be determined. Yet it is essential that every person be free to become a Stoic or not to do so; if this were not the case the Stoic's exhortations would be pointless. Later in the Stoic Period the attempt was made to remove these paradoxes, especially the paradoxes of evil and freedom, by limiting the power of God (the *logos*) by means of a separate principle of matter and evil. Thus God is responsible only for the good, evil results from the principle of matter, and each person is free to ally himself with either of these powers. This modified position does permit the existence of evil, of freedom, and of immortality as a prize to be won; but it does so at the high cost of destroying the justification for the Stoic ethics of acceptance. If not everything that happens is for the best because it comes from God and if some things which happen are evil because they come from matter, why should we tranquilly accept everything that happens?

5-5. *The Neoplatonism of Plotinus*

The last major movement of the Hellenistic-Roman Period is Neoplatonism. Whereas the Skeptics, the Epicureans, and the Stoics all turned to philosophers of the Anthropological Period for their main inspiration and followed them in focusing upon man, Neoplatonism draws on Plato, as its name indicates—though also on Aristotle—and in so doing it follows the Systematic Period of Greek philosophy in presenting the third stage in a three-stage sequence, in trying to effect a reunion of man and the world. While Neoplatonism is represented by a number of important philosophers, especially Philo (born about 20 B.C.) and Proclus (about 410–485 A.D.), we shall examine only the philosophy of the greatest of them, Plotinus (205–270 A.D.).

As the name "Neoplatonist" suggests, Plotinus' view of the nature of man's world is fundamentally Platonic. Life proceeds from an initial union with ultimate reality through a fall to mortal existence toward a reunion with ultimate reality, a cosmic drama beautifully depicted in Plato's *Phaedrus*. The ladder of love in Socrates' speech in Plato's *Symposium* and the allegory of the cave in his *Republic* are vivid depictions of the reunion part of the sequence, the part with which this life is concerned. The original part of the sequence—the withdrawal or fall or emanation—Plato presents in the *Republic* in the idea of the Good as the source of all being and intelligibility just as the sun is the source of all life and light, in the *Sophist* in the definition of being as power, and in the *Timaeus* in the notion that the divine Craftsman ·makes the world because he must share his goodness. Plato's dualisms—of Form and matter, of soul and body, of good and evil—must have seemed congenial to the religious experience of Plotinus; yet Plotinus agreed with Plato and with Aristotle (by whom he was also influenced) that these dualisms needed to be bridged. Just as a wide chasm may be bridged more easily if it is broken up into a number of narrower chasms, Plotinus attempted to bridge the chasm between Plato's two realms by inserting a number of intermediate levels of existence. These intermediate levels of existence are expressed in the emanation of the world from the primordial reality.

The emanation of the world, which is the metaphysical or theoretical dimension of Plotinus' system, may be understood in terms of Plato's image, which Plotinus also frequently uses, of the sun radiating all light and life. The sun itself, the original and supreme reality, Plotinus calls the One or the Good and sometimes God. As the source of all being and intelligibility, the One of Plotinus, like the Good of Plato, is itself beyond all being and intelligibility. Since it is absolute unity or simplicity, nothing can properly be predicated of the One, not even being or existence, not because the One is beneath or less than these predicates but rather because it is above and more. To say even, "the One exists" would be to make the One into two: unity and existence—a point which Plato made against absolute monism (Ch. 3-2.1). This means that the supreme reality is absolutely ineffable and can be grasped only in mystical experience. Here in its simplest and purest form is the basic problem of the very possibility of a theology, of a thinking or speaking or writing *(logos)* about God *(theos),* a problem which will become central to medieval Christian philosophy (Ch. 6-3). Since thinking, speaking, and writing seem inevitably to involve distinctions and thus multiplicity, how can they truly be about a God who transcends them by being utterly simple or completely one? Apparently they can't, and Plotinus accepts this conclusion by insisting that God is ineffable; yet he also says a good bit about God or the One.

Although the One is in itself absolutely simple, its nature and goodness are too rich to remain encapsuled in pure simplicity, so it must overflow and plurify itself in a process of the emanation of the world. This emanation arises from the necessity of the One's own nature; it is not a matter of choice. Here we should keep quite distinct four different theories of the origin of the world (Ch. 3-2.2.). One theory is that the world is *made* or *fabricated* by God out of matter (space or the Receptacle) where God is an efficient cause or agency; Plato presents this theory in the *Timaeus.* A second theory is that the world is *elicited* out of matter or potentiality by the magnetic, telic causality of the absolute purpose or pure actuality which is God; this is Aristotle's view. A third theory is that the world is emanated out of God's own substance and by the necessity of his nature; this is Plotinus' view and it is also the view expressed in Book VI of Plato's *Republic*. The fourth theory is that the world is *created* by God out of nothing at all, neither out of matter nor out of His own substance; this is the medieval Christian view which we will consider later.

Reason *(nous)* is the first emanation from the One or God, according to Plotinus; and hence Reason is the *logos,* the statement or expression, of the One. Here the infinite richness of reality, which in the One is fused into utter simplicity, is plurified into an infinity of distinct Ideas. Reason is thus Plato's realm of Forms taken together with the thoughts of them, the realm of Ideas in the dual sense of "idea" (thought and object of thought), except that Reason also apparently includes, unlike Plato's realm of Forms, the ideas of individuals as well as of universals. Reason is also like Aristotle's God or Unmoved Mover in being self-thinking thought. Whereas primal reality, the One, transcends the distinctions that are necessary to thought (fundamentally the subject-object distinction), its first expression is to think itself in all its infinite richness.

Soul *(psyche)* is the second emanation from the One and thus the *logos,* the statement, of Reason. At this level the infinite richness of reality, which in the One is fused in simplicity and in Reason is plurified logically and nontemporally, becomes plurified temporally. The One is eternal simplicity, Reason is eternal multiplicity, and Soul is everlasting, temporal multiplicity. Hence consciousness at the level of the One is mystical, at the level of Reason intuitive, and at the level of Soul discursive. An analogy may perhaps help clarify this relation between the One, Reason, and Soul. When a movie is made of the many aspects of a single object and then projected on a screen, the same object is present at three different levels. First, in the object itself its many aspects are fused together into a single thing. Second, the many different frames composing the movie film are each of some aspect of the object, and all of them together express the object as a multiplicity of phases present in the film at the same time. Finally, when the film is projected on a screen, these many phases of the unitary object are spread out temporally, each following another in time. Thus the same reality is present as a nontemporal unity (the object, the One), as a nontemporal multiplicity (the frames of the film, Reason), and as a temporally projected, moving multiplicity (the moving scene on the screen, Soul).

While Reason is in itself still and eternal, Soul brings movement and time into the world, just as Plato held. Furthermore, just as soul mediates between the Forms and the particulars for Plato, so it also does this for Plotinus, and thus Soul is present in two contexts or relations. Soul in its transcendent aspect is with Reason, the realm of Ideas; and Soul in its immanent aspect is with the next emanation, Body, as the vitality or animating principle of organic bodies. These two uses are a reflection of the two uses of "soul" in Plato—as cosmic principle and as the nature of living things (Ch. 3-1.4);—and they are also close to Aristotle's view that soul is the first actuality or form of organic bodies. Thus, especially in his concept of Soul, Plotinus bridges the chasm between the eternal and the temporal. And yet, since this bridging requires two quite distinct aspects of Soul, there is the danger that the bridging is only verbal, the word "Soul" being almost equivocal. Indeed, Plotinus sometimes refers to the immanent aspect of Soul as nature, and as such it is almost a distinct emanation from Soul in its transcendent aspect, almost a fourth level of reality.

Body is the third emanation from the One or the fourth if the immanent aspect of Soul, nature, is counted as a separate emanation. Body for Plotinus means bare physical matter, not organic body or living matter since it is organic or living only by virtue of the Soul. With Body the power of the One has become completely expended, just as the light and energy of the sun is completely expended with the darkest, coldest, and most inert thing. Hence nothing at all lies beyond Body save just that, nothing at all. But this nothing at all, this sheer darkness or nonbeing, is for Plotinus the principle of evil which has as such a positive influence on life and the world. In this positive context Plotinus calls it matter, a negative yet quasi-positive asymptote of the One's emanation. Just as the radiation of light from the sun approaches but never reaches absolute darkness, so the emanation of being from the One approaches but never reaches pure matter or absolute nonbeing. Hence it is not matter in our modern sense, and it is not even the pure potentiality which Aristotle called matter; it is more like the nonbeing or void of Democritus and the Epicureans. As such it presents the same problem of the being of nothing, which was attached to Democritus' void and which Plato tried to solve in the *Sophist* (Ch. 3-2.1).

A summary comparison of Plotinus' view of reality with that of Plato may be presented in terms of Plato's divided line:

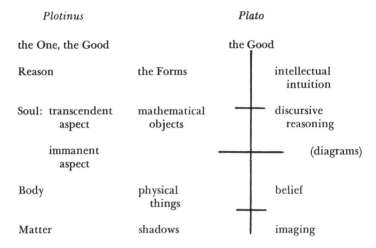

Plotinus		*Plato*
the One, the Good		the Good
Reason	the Forms	intellectual intuition
Soul: transcendent aspect	mathematical objects	discursive reasoning
immanent aspect		(diagrams)
Body	physical things	belief
Matter	shadows	imaging

"Epistrophe" or return is the ethico-religious dimension of the philosophy of Plotinus. Just as for Plato man's true destiny lies in recapturing the union with ultimate reality which he possessed before his earthly fall, so also for Plotinus man's salvation consists in returning to the Godhead from which he was primordially sprung. Since man is born on and of the earth, he must begin there; and his way of salvation consists in a conversion away from preoccupation with the body and physical things and a gradual return first to the life of Reason and finally to a reunion with the One or God. Thus the true life of the Soul, of the Reason, and of the God in man necessarily involves, as it does for Plato in the *Phaedo,* a dying to the pseudo-life of the body. Conversely, the evil life is the life lived in separation from the One, or in union with its opposite extreme, matter, the principle of evil. Just as the One is the Good and the principle of goodness, so its absolute negation, matter, is the principle of evil. It should be noted that for Plotinus the mystical experience of union with God presupposes the realization of rationality in the highest degree; the ideal life is a *super*rational, not an *ir*rational, state of consciousness.

The philosophy of Plotinus, like that of the Stoics, is more notable for its moral than for its logical strength, since it, too, contains some fundamental paradoxes. Two of these, the paradox of freedom and the paradox of evil, are essentially the same as in Stoicism (Ch. 5-4). For Plotinus, as for the Stoics, everything happens by necessity, ultimately by the inward necessity of the One or the Good. The One must, by the necessity of its own nature, emanate Reason; Reason must emanate Soul; and Soul must emanate Body. Thus freedom, for Plotinus, is not choice between different alternative possibilities but rather self-determination to one end; an act is free if and only if it is caused by the agent in question rather than by something outside that agent, even though the agent in question cannot help but cause that act. Yet on the other hand the ethical theory of Plotinus seems to require the freedom to choose between two alternative possibilities: the higher life of the mind and the lower life of the body. This is the paradox of freedom: everything whatever is determined by the One, and yet my ethical acts of choice depend solely upon me. And the second paradox, the paradox of evil, is quite similar. Since, for Plotinus, everything whatsoever emanates out of the Good, how can there possibly be any evil? Because evil is only privation or negation (matter), Plotinus replies, and hence not anything positive, which could have emanated from the Good. But if everything whatever emanates from the Good, how can there be any privation at all? If evil is wholly negative it is nonexistent, and if it is at all existent how can it emanate from the Good? The third paradox in the system of Plotinus is the derivation of plurality from pure unity. Getting multiplicity from the nonmultiplicity of the One sounds very much like getting something from nothing. Here the Neoplatonism of Plotinus seems a regression from the philosophy of the later Plato where Being as power is both one and many.

5-6. *Summary*

Thus ends the Hellenistic-Roman Period of ancient philosophy and with it ancient philosophy as a whole. In the broadest and most general terms the philosophy of the Hellenistic-Roman

Period may be regarded as a restatement of the three-stage
sequence of whole, part, whole-of-parts which was first developed in the Greek era of ancient philosophy. Although Plato
and Aristotle had already expressed the third of these three
stages in their reunion of man as isolated in the Anthropological
Period with the cosmos central to the Cosmological Period, their
thought became a new statement of the first stage of simple union
of man and world when the Skeptics, Epicureans, and Stoics
followed the Sophists, Cyrenaics, and Cynics, respectively, in re-
isolating man and making him the center of their concern to
form a new statement of the second stage. With Neoplatonism's
return to Plato and Aristotle, however, a new statement of the
third stage is effected; and ancient philosophy thus closed with
man once again reunited with his world. Medieval philosophy,
to which we now turn, provides still another, a third, statement
of this natural three-stage sequence, though at a deeper level.

SUGGESTED READINGS

5-1. Zeller, E. *The Stoics, Epicureans, and Skeptics,* trans. O. J.
     Deichel. New York: Russell & Russell, 1962. Chs. 22–23.
5-2. Epicurus. *Letter to Herodotus, Letter to Menoeceus,* and *Princi-*
     pal Doctrines.
     Lucretius. *On the Nature of Things.*
5-3. Epictetus. *Manual.*
     Arrian. *Discourse of Epictetus.*
     Marcus Aurelius. *Meditations.*
5-5. *Plotinus,* trans. A. W. Armstrong. London: Allen & Unwin, 1962.
     Plotinus. *Enneads,* trans. S. MacKenna. London: Faber & Faber,
     1962.

For bibliography, see:
Guthrie, W. K. C. *The Earlier Pre-Socratics and the Pythagoreans,*
     Vol. I of *A History of Greek Philosophy.* Cambridge, Eng.: Cam-
     bridge University Press, 1962. Pp. 493–503.
Owens, J. *A History of Ancient Western Philosophy.* New York:
     Appleton-Century-Crofts, 1959. Pp. 376–77, 393–94, 415–16.

Medieval
Philosophy

While Neoplatonism represents the third, the reunion, stage in relation to its predecessors, it is at the same time in relation to its successors a new and third statement of the first stage of the objective oneness of man and world. Medieval philosophy then presents, first, a new statement of the second stage in its doctrine of the radical contingency or uncertainty of the world and, second, in its doctrine of God as creator of the world a new statement of the third stage, a new reunion of man with objective reality. Like the Neoplatonic one, the medieval synthesis draws heavily on the initial Platonic-Aristotelean reunion. Although medieval philosophy deals with a wealth of philosophical topics, is rich in philosophical insights, and covers a very long period of time—roughly from near the beginning of the Christian era to the middle of the second millennium—it is thus most basically and broadly a continuation of the tradition of ancient philosophy. Moreover, like the Hellenistic-Roman Period of ancient philosophy, medieval philosophy even draws most of its philosophical ideas from the ancients, especially from Plato and Aristotle.

This medieval statement of the three-stage sequence, however, differs from the two statements in ancient philosophy in two main ways. The first and most important difference is, in simplest terms, that ancient philosophy takes the *existence* of the natural world for granted while medieval philosophy does not. This difference is epitomized by and arises from their different conceptions of the nature of God, as we shall shortly see. The second difference is that in medieval philosophy the third stage cannot as easily as in ancient philosophy be identified with a chronologically later period than the second stage, and even Neoplatonism's presentation of the first stage overlaps medieval philosophy chronologically. We might very roughly identify the second stage, the stage in which man questions the reality of the world about him, with Augustine (354–430) and the tradition he founded and the third stage, the reunion of self and world, with Thomas Aquinas (1227–1274) and the tradition he symbolizes. Yet the questioning of the existence of the world, which gives rise to the separated self of the second stage, is in both periods immediately answered by the doctrine of God's creation of the world, a doctrine which reassures man of his place in the world. Hence the difference between the second and third stages in medieval philosophy is more a logical and psychological difference rather than a chronological one, a mood of doubt and separation followed by a mood of affirmation and reunion, though the union of all parts of the world into one systematic whole is certainly more evident in the high scholasticism of the thirteenth century than it is in early medieval philosophy.

The treatment of the idea of God is most fundamentally distinctive of medieval philosophy (It is often said, for example, that in the middle ages philosophy is the handmaid of theology, though this is an oversimplification.); therefore, this treatment is the focal point of the present discussion of medieval philosophy. Since the difference between the second and the third stage in the three-stage sequence is in medieval philosophy more logical and psychological than chronological, this discussion of medieval philosophy is not organized in terms of chronological schools and figures. Furthermore, the main concern of this chapter is with the Christian philosophy of the middle ages, although the distinctive nature of medieval philosophy, as well as many of its peripheral features, is present in medieval Jewish and Muslim philosophy as well as in medieval Christian philosophy. Let us consider first the nature of God as it is distinctively conceived in medieval philosophy and then the question of the existence of God thus conceived.

6-1. *The Nature of God*

The medieval philosophers differed considerably among themselves concerning the nature of God, but through all these differences runs a functional similarity, which, for the sake of synoptic understanding, may be referred to as the medieval conception of God. This conception stands in fundamental, functional contrast to the ancient Greek conception of God. The ancient Greek philosophers, in spite of all their disagreements and differences, conceived of their first principle—God or however it was named—as most fundamentally the cause of motion, change, and order. Anaxagoras' reason functioned to account for the changes and rearrangements of the other seeds and hence also to account for the order of the things in nature. Plato's divine Craftsman accounted for the transition from the indeterminacy of the Receptacle or world stuff to the relative determinacy of the world of nature; he made a cosmos out of chaos. And Aristotle's Unmoved Mover accounted for the change in nature, for the transition from potentiality to actuality. Thus God in ancient Greek philosophy was preeminently the author of change and order. Hence in ancient Greek philosophy the question to which the concept of God is the answer was "Why do things move and change as they do?" "Why should things *exist to* move and change?" seems generally to be an unasked question. Even though the reality *of* change *in* nature was of course an important problem (Ch. 1-3), the very existence of objective nature seems hardly to have been brought into question. ". . . the first principle of all being, as Plato and Aristotle conceived it, integrally explains indeed why the universe is what it is, but does not explain why it exists."[1]

For the medieval philosophers, however, God is Lord of all.

God is therefore the cause of the very *existence* of the universe, the cause of the fact that there *are* things which may, or may not, be changed and ordered. In medieval philosophy the question to which the concept of God is the answer is thus a more fundamental one than that of ancient Greek philosophy, even though it is perhaps a meaningless one by Greek standards. The medieval philosophers like the ancient philosophers, of course, raise and try to answer the question "Why do things move and change as they do?", and their final answer to this question is God as it was with Plato, Aristotle, and others, but the medieval philosophers also raise and try to answer the more fundamental question of why anything should exist in the first place. The medieval philosophers do not, indeed, ask *whether* the world exists as many modern philosophers will be seen to do, but they do ask *why* the world exists. In medieval philosophy, therefore, the question to which the concept of God is the answer is "Why do things exist?" Why do seeds exist to be rearranged, a Receptacle to be ordered, or a primary potentiality to be actualized? Why does anything exist in the first place, granted that once it exists it may be changed and ordered?

This questioning of the very existence of things occurs in two different ways. First, the question may be put objectively, impersonally, logically, metaphysically, or theoretically as has just been done; it may be the head which is questioning. The existence of everything in nature is questionable, so how does anything happen to exist in nature? Put logically, the proposition "X exists," in which X stands for any natural thing or even for the whole of nature, is a contingent rather than a necessary proposition; its denial, "X does not exist," is not self-contradictory even though it happens to be false. In the medieval period this objective form of the question is more characteristic of Thomas Aquinas and the more abstract dimension of medieval philosophy which he represents. Yet the more personalistic Augustine also employs it in a reflection anticipating the extreme doubt stated by Descartes in the seventeenth century when he meditates that everything whatever may be a dream or an illusion (Ch. 8-2), and Descartes's extreme form of the

question will give birth to modern philosophy's extreme separation of the questioning self from his world.

Second, the questioning of existence may occur subjectively,
personally, emotionally, religiously, or practically; the heart
may be doing the questioning. "Oh, why was I ever born?"
"What's the point to life anyway?" "Why did there have to be
such a world?" As Ecclesiastes says, "Vanity of vanities, . . . all
is vanity! . . . What does a man gain from all his toil at which
he toils beneath the sun?" This form of the question is central
to existentialism, whether it is in a religious context or not.
And the answer of the medieval philosophers to the question in
this form is again God. Why does anything exist at all? Because
God brought it into existence.

If God is most fundamentally the cause of the existence of
natural things, then God Himself must be most fundamentally
existence itself. That is to say, existence is the very essence of
God, according to Thomas Aquinas and others. How did these
philosophers arrive at such an idea? They often maintain that
it was revealed to man by God Himself; and in proof of this
contention they frequently cite Exodus 3:14 in which God, in
response to Moses' question, says that He is "I am that I am."
This interpretation of the words transliterated as Jehovah is
questioned by many scholars today, however. Yet the thesis that
God's essence is existence seems to follow logically and immediately from the proposition that God is the cause of the existence
of all other things, for how could He perform this function
unless existence were essential to Him? In any event, God is regarded as essentially "I am"; His essence is existence. God is
now most fundamentally pure existence, and thus He is the
cause of the existence of finite things, rather than mind, Craftsman, Unmoved Mover, self-thinking thought, or even the Good
or the One, as He was for the ancient philosophers.

From this distinctively medieval conception of God's essential
nature as existence or being a number of equally distinctive
properties of God were derived. The first and most important
of these is that God is a necessary being. This follows from
saying that God's essence is existence, for this makes God exist

by the necessity of His own nature independently of any other factor. Many philosophers today, even theological skeptics,[2] are coming to agree that the adequate object of worship in any religion must be a necessary being. But exactly what kind of necessity is this?

One outstanding perennial answer is that the necessity of God is a logical necessity, that to say that God is a necessary being is to say that His nonexistence is self-contradictory or inconceivable. This is the presupposition of and the key to the famous ontological argument (as it has been called since Kant in the eighteenth century) for the existence of God. This argument is given its classical form by Anselm (1033–1109), has been used by many subsequent philosophers, and is still an object of great interest and controversy.[3] Just as the Epicureans inferred from the concept of God as a perfect being that he could not be concerned with the cares of the world, so the ontological argument infers from the idea of God as absolute perfection that He cannot fail to exist. The idea of God, according to Anselm, is the idea of a being than which nothing greater can be conceived; even the atheist has this idea in his mind, for if he did not he could not deny the existence of the being corresponding to this idea. God as thus conceived must also exist outside the mind as well as in the mind, for if He did not, it would be possible to conceive of a still greater or more perfect being, namely one which does also exist outside the mind. But this is absurd, for to conceive of a being greater than God is to conceive of a being greater than the greatest, since God is by definition the greatest or most perfect being conceivable. Hence God must by definition exist outside the mind as well as in the mind.

As one might expect, this ontological argument for the existence of God was strenuously criticized by Anselm's contemporaries and successors. The essential and recurrent core of all these criticisms is that the idea of existence is, after all, still only an idea and hence something mental, that real existence itself is not a predicate, as Kant famously put it in the eighteenth century. God's existence is no exception to this universal rule; the idea of the existence of God is just as much a mental entity as the idea of the existence of a perfect island. So if the idea of

God requires that He exist outside the mind then a perfect island must also, by the same token, exist outside the mind, argues Gaunilo, a contemporary critic of Anselm. If the idea of a perfect island does not imply that island's extra-mental existence, then the idea of God does not imply His extra-mental existence either. Anselm countered Gaunilo's form of the objection by pointing out that the argument applies only to God, though he did not state that the reason for this is that the expression "perfect island" is self-contradictory, if it means absolutely or unqualifiedly perfect, since for a thing to be an island or any other finite thing is for it to lack many perfections, moral perfection, for example. This objection recurred in the middle ages, especially in Thomas Aquinas: while the very essence of God Himself does indeed imply His existence, since His essence is existence, the existence which follows from our idea of God can be only our idea of existence; and from this it does not necessarily follow that God has extra-mental existence. This distinction between different types of existence is tied in with the doctrine of the analogy of being which we noted in Aristotle's philosophy (Ch. 4-5) and which we shall consider again shortly (Ch. 6-4). The most that can be validly concluded from the ontological argument, these critics therefore maintain, is that anyone who thinks of God must think of Him as existing really outside the mind; it does not necessarily follow that He does in fact exist as such a one must think of Him as existing.[4]

On the basis of such criticism Thomas Aquinas and his followers rejected the idea that the necessity of God's being is a logical necessity. The necessity of God is rather an ontological or existential necessity: to say that God is a necessary being is to say that God has *aseity,* that His existence is from Himself *(a se)* and not from another *(ab alio),* rather than to say that it is self-contradictory for humans to deny His existence. The aseity of God is thus simply His *firstness,* the fact that everything else depends upon Him and that He Himself does not depend on anything else. This firstness of God was, of course, also essential to the ancient Greek philosophical concept of God—e.g., Aristotle's God is the first and Unmoved Mover—but in ancient Greek philosophy God is first in the order of change and motion whereas, as we have seen, in medieval philosophy God is, above all, first in the order of existence; the existence of all other things depends upon God. To say that God is a necessary being is thus to say that God is the existence upon which all finite, contingent existents depend for their existence.

Three other important properties follow from the concept of God as existence. First, God is *simple* in the most fundamental sense that in Him there is no distinction between *what* He is and *that* He is, between His essence and His existence, as there is in every being which comes to have existence and then to lose it. Second, God is *one*. There is one and only one God, so Judaism, Christianity, and Islam must be monotheistic religions. If there were, *per contra,* a second God his secondness or otherness from the first God would mean that he is not the ultimate cause of the existence of all things; and this would exactly mean that he is not God, according to the medieval conception of God. And if it were suggested that there could be two ultimate causes of the existence of things, each of whose essence is existence, the reply would follow that then the two "Gods" would be indistinguishable from each other and hence really one. Third, God is the *efficient* as well as the telic or purposive cause of all things since He is the cause of the very existence of purposive things.

Finally, it also follows from the essence of God as existence that He is a creator, in the strictest sense of that term; He makes the matter as well as the form of the world, and He brings it into being out of nothing. This theory was not, indeed, held invariably; and it was often, for example by Aquinas, held to be rationally unprovable and accepted only on faith. Yet it became the position of orthodox Christian philosophy. This view is that God does not make the world out of any antecedent stuff (Plato); He creates any such stuff as well since its existence is contingent. God does not emanate the world out of Himself (Plotinus), for then the world would be God, necessary rather than contingent. Nor, finally, does God merely elicit motion from the world (Aristotle)—although He does this too—since He is responsible for the very existence of the world. Saying that God creates the world out of nothing does not mean that something existed whose name is "nothing" and which was a material on which God worked, for this would make the existence of the nothing-stuff independent of God. Saying that God creates the world *ex nihilo* means rather that while God made the world He didn't make it out of anything, not out of a stuff and not out of Himself. Like the doctrine of God as existence itself, however, the doctrine of God as creator *ex nihilo* is perhaps more based on than found in the Judaeo-Christian revelation, yet it is thus based for only a God Who is existentially responsible for all things would have the power to redeem them.

6-2. *The Existence of God*

Once we have understood the nature of God according to medieval philosophy His existence follows more clearly and certainly than it might otherwise seem to do. Indeed, the core of the arguments for the existence of God is contained most manifestly in the last two properties resulting from the idea of God as existence itself: that He is the creator and efficient cause of all things.

The most famous and influential of these arguments are the five ways of Thomas Aquinas. The first way concludes that God exists as the first cause of change. The second, fourth, and fifth ways conclude, respectively, that God exists as the first efficient cause, the first formal cause, and the first telic cause. But the third way expresses what is fundamental to and implicit in all of the other four ways: the existential necessity of God as required by the existential contingency of the particular things of nature. The starting point of this third argument is that some things about us are actually existent and yet at the same time contingent. Here "contingent" means existentially contingent or dependent in being; existential contingency is the possibility of not existing. And the things about us are certainly existentially contingent, able not to exist, for, as a matter of fact, they come into existence and pass away. From this starting point Thomas concludes that an existentially necessary being is the first cause of the existence which the contingent beings about us happen to have. The argument that contingent existents must indeed have a first cause is essentially the same as that of Aristotle; and, indeed, Thomas's arguments for the existence of God are fundamentally an existentializing of Aristotle's argument, an existentializing brought about by the medieval concept of God as the answer to the question why anything at all exists. For this reason the discussion of Aristotle's argument (Ch. 4-3) should be kept in mind, especially to see why the causal series must have a first member and to see that the first cause is not first in time.

The formulation of the third way or argument from contingency given by Thomas in the *Summa Theologica* is as follows:

> We observe in our environment how things are born and die away; they may or may not exist; to be or not to be—they are open to either alternative. All things cannot be so contingent, for *what is able not to be may be reckoned as once a non-being,* and *were everything like that once there would have been nothing at all.* Now were this true nothing would ever have begun, for what is does not begin to be except because of something which is, and so there would be nothing even now. This is clearly hollow. Therefore all things cannot be might-not-have-beens; among them must be being whose existence is necessary.[5]

This formulation of the argument, which was influenced by the Jewish philosopher Maimonides (1135–1204), contains two non sequiturs. In the first place, from the fact that something *might* not exist it does not necessarily follow that it ever *does* not exist; on the contrary, it could conceivably exist forever as something which might not exist. Actuality does not follow from possibility. In the second place, even if we grant that *each* contingent does fail to exist at some time *or other,* it does not follow that *all* contingent things fail to exist at the *same* time to produce a state of affairs of nothing at all. Like house flies, contingent things could perfectly well be around forever even though none of them lasts very long. However, the formulation of the argument from contingency which Thomas gives in his *Summa Contra Gentiles* is free of these flaws: "Everything that is a possible-to-be has a cause, since its essence as such is equally uncommitted to the alternatives of existing and not existing. If it be credited with existence, then this must be from some cause. Causality, however, is not an infinite process. Therefore a necessary being is the conclusion."[6]

The essence of this argument from contingency is very simple: "contingency" entails "necessity," "dependency" entails "independence," "relativity" entails "absoluteness." A thing cannot be just simply contingent. For a thing to be contingent is for it to be contingent *upon*, for a thing to be contingent upon is for it to be contingent upon *something*, and for a thing to be contingent upon something there must *be* that something upon which it is contingent. The same is true of dependency and relativity. If *everything* were contingent, nothing could be *contingent*, for there would be nothing for anything to be contingent *upon*. For Atlas to hold the world there must be the broad-bosomed sea to support the turtle upon which Atlas stands. Since some things might not be, something else must exist which cannot help but be—a necessary being. "And this," Thomas concludes each of the five arguments, "all men call God."

6-3. *The Relation of Reason and Faith*

This medieval view of the nature of God as essentially existence itself thus throws into question the existence of the objective world of changing nature which was more or less taken for granted by the ancients; this dimension of medieval philosophy epitomizes the second stage, the stage of the questioning self, in the three-stage sequence from whole to human part to reunion of man and his world. Yet the medieval belief in the creative reality of this divine "I am" reaffirms the existence of the changing world of nature and reassures medieval man of his place in it; this dimension of medieval philosophy corresponds to the third stage, the reunion of man and nature. Though nature need not and might not exist, it does indeed happen to exist because God Who is existence itself created it. While the ancients are *assured*, the medievals are thus *re*assured of the reality of nature and of man's bond with her. And they are reassured not by nature herself—obviously not, for it is nature herself which is now called into question—but by something beyond nature, by God.

Furthermore, it must really be God Himself Who effects this reassurance, for otherwise man will not really be reassured. This is the most basic significance of the reason-faith problem which looms so large in medieval philosophy. No merely rationally apprehended God could effect this reassurance, for in so far as He is merely the object of natural reason He is brought within the context of nature; and as such He is Himself brought into question along with the broader context of nature of which He then becomes a part. No, only a *tertium quid,* only a Being lying beyond both objective nature and man's natural mind, is capable of reassuring medieval man of the reality of his bond with nature. On the other hand, however, a completely transcendent God would elude man's natural reason and thus be incapable of reassuring natural man. Man's *rational* reassurance of his place in nature thus requires the God of reason, and man's rational *reassurance* requires the God of faith. Yet this rational reassurance of the reality of nature and of man's bond with her requires that the God of reason and the God of faith be one and the same God. But how can they be? This is the problem of the relation of reason and faith which is so central to medieval philosophy.

Medieval philosophy, in contrast to both ancient and modern philosophy, is distinctively a religious philosophy, whether Christian, Jewish, or Muslim. But is such a union of religion and philosophy, of faith and reason, really possible? This is another way of putting the problem of the relation of faith and reason. Philosophy would seem to involve reason alone; philosophy takes nothing on faith. The great western religions of Judaism, Christianity, and Islam, on the other hand, are grounded on and essentially involve acts of faith in divine revelation. Hence again the problem: How can something be at once philosophical and religious, both rational and based on faith? If a Christian philosophy, for example, is truly Christian it would seem that it cannot be a philosophy, for it involves the acceptance of something beyond reason. And if a Christian philosophy is truly a philosophy it would seem that it cannot accept the Christian revelation on faith, and thus it cannot be Christian in its own inner nature—although it could be Christian in the sense of being held by a Christian or in the sense of being compatible with the Christian faith.

While the idea of a religious philosophy, a rational faith, thus seems to be an impossibility, it is at the same time, for thinkers who are both religious and also philosophers, an apparent necessity. As a modern representative of such thinkers has written, ". . . it is a fact that between ourselves and the Greeks the Christian revelation has intervened, and has profoundly modified the conditions under which reason has to work. Once you are in possession of that revelation how can you possibly philosophize as though you had never heard of it?"[7] As religious men, these thinkers had faith in divine revelation, but as human beings possessed of reason they could not help but rationally philosophize that faith. That transcendent Being Who both questions and reestablishes the reality of nature and man's bond with her must both transcend natural reason yet also be graspable by natural reason. While a religious philosophy may appear impossible, therefore, it is for medieval philosophers inescapably necessary; while the problem of faith and reason may seem insoluble, a solution to it must be found somewhere. But where?

When a problem is caused by the relation between two seemingly unrelatable things, it can be solved or dissolved, it might seem at first glance, either by declaring that the two things are really identical or by declaring that they are so opposite that they cannot possibly have any relation to each other. During the middle ages these two alternatives were represented in almost all the shades of the spectrum spreading from one extreme through a middle position to the other extreme. While conflicting positions were often held at the same time, the broad historical movement may be oversimplified as passing from an initial recognition of the difference between faith and reason to the other extreme of their identification, back then to a middle position of their difference yet intimate union, and ending up finally by a return to the original position of their irreconcilable difference. In order to see the issues more clearly, however, let us consider the three main positions abstractly, the two extremes and the mean between them.

The identification of reason and faith, the first way we shall consider of attempting to solve the problem of a religious philosophy which will reassure man of his bond with nature, has either of two forms: either reason is reduced to faith or faith is reduced to reason. The reduction of reason to faith is required, one may argue, by the very nature of a rational system. Every rational system, and thus every philosophical system, necessarily rests upon first premises or fundamental axioms. "Give me a place to stand and I will lift the world," Archimedes is supposed to have proclaimed, but he did need something on which to stand. These premises are unprovable within the system in which they occur, just because they are the premises of that system. Since they are unprovable and yet accepted as the basis of the whole system, they are simply articles of faith, one may argue. Hence the primary assumptions of any philosophical system are just as much a matter of faith as are the primary beliefs of any religious system, such as Christianity. If the articles of faith which underlie a particular philosophical system happen to be the articles of faith which define a particular religion, such as Christianity, then that philosophy is a Christian philosophy, Christian as well as philosophical. Such a position which grounds reason on faith was approximated by Augustine and especially by Anselm, and its formula is their motto: *credo ut intelligam.* (I believe in order that I may understand.) The foundation of reason is identical with faith, and acceptance of this faith must, therefore, precede the elaboration of a rational system.[8]

The reduction of faith to reason, the other form of their identification, proceeds in the same way except that it emphasizes the rationality of the system rather than the unprovability of the premises. While the premises of any philosophical system are of course unprovable within that system, the fact that a rational system emanates from them makes those premises themselves rational. In fact every premise, as a *premise,* as a statement implying some conclusion rationally, is *ipso facto* rational. On this ground, one may argue, every religion which is articulated into a system having first principles and rationally derived conclusions is also a philosophy, or even a science, since it has the same logical structure as other systems that are universally admitted to be philosophical or scientific. Hence the possibility of a Christian philosophy, for example, requires only the construction of a rational system from premises stating the fundamentals of Christian faith. This position was closely approximated by John Scotus Erigena (about 800–877) who merged reason and faith until they became practically identical; for him true philosophy is identical with, not subservient to, true religion.

Yet, one may argue, these solutions by means of an identification of faith and reason are too facile whether reason is reduced to faith or faith to reason. While philosophical first principles are like articles of faith in being unprovable, and while articles of faith may be like philosophical first principles in rationally implying theorems to form a system, philosophical first principles and articles of faith are still irreducibly different from each other. Furthermore, each type of statement is also different in kind from the fundamental laws of empirical sciences like physics. The first principles of an *empirical science* are, at least in principle and indirectly, verifiable and falsifiable by sensory experience. They are not self-evident; they must sooner or later meet the test of sense experience, and it is always possible that they shall fail to pass that test. *Philosophical* first principles, on the other hand, are self-evidently true or else not true at all; at least this belief has been held almost universally through the history of philosophy.* They are logically necessary propositions, propositions which are true by virtue of the meanings of their terms and which can be seen to be true just by a rational inspection of the meanings of those terms. As Aristotle said, philosophical first principles are definitions. The first principles or articles of faith of a *revealed religion,* like Christianity, however, are neither falsifiable by sensory observations like empirical scientific principles[9] nor logically true by virtue of the meanings of their terms like philosophical first principles. Articles of

---

* This is also true of the first principles of formal sciences, such as mathematics and formal logic. The difference between philosophical first principles and the first principles of systems of logic or mathematics is not in question here, though I should say that the former have existential reference while the latter do not, that philosophical first principles are necessary truths about real existence whereas mathematical and formal-logical premises are necessary truths only about ideas or language. This question is much disputed, but most parties to the dispute would agree that philosophical first principles are logically different from the premises of empirical science.

faith are "the evidence of things *not* seen"; their truth is seen neither by the senses nor by reason but is accepted simply on faith.

To grasp this fundamental difference between empirical science, rational philosophy, and religious faith one need only compare examples of the fundamental statements of each. Compare, for example, the third law of thermodynamics (a principle of an empirical science, physics), the law of noncontradiction (a principle of philosophy, of metaphysics), and the belief in the incarnation of God in Christ (an article of Christian faith). The third law of thermodynamics is verified by experience and could conceivably be falsified by experience, although, of course, it is not at all likely to be. The principle of noncontradiction is verified just by the meanings of its terms and could not conceivably be false; the assertion of its falsity, just in order to avoid being at the same time an assertion of its truth, would necessarily presuppose its truth. But the belief in the incarnation of God in Christ cannot be verified either empirically or rationally. God is not the kind of being Who can be observed by the senses, and His incarnation in Christ is not logically necessary; it can be consistently denied. In spite of the fact that articles of faith are, like philosophical principles, unprovable premises of provable systems, they are, therefore, still irreducibly different from each other. Such a position was held by many medieval philosophers, most notably by both Thomas Aquinas and Duns Scotus (1265–1308) in spite of their other basic differences.

Emphasis upon this fundamental difference leads to the second main way of attempting to solve or dissolve the problem of faith and reason: the assertion of their absolute separation and even incompatibility, even though this separation would seem to destroy natural man's reassurance of the reality of nature as created by God. The classical expression of this position is that of Tertullian (about 160–220): "What has Athens to do with Jerusalem?"[10] Greek reason and philosophy are completely different from and even antithetical to the Judaeo-Christian faith. Articles of faith, say the incarnation or the trinity, completely transcend the grasp of reason. Not only that, articles of faith are even inconsistent or absurd from the point of view of natural reason, one may argue; to say that God (an invisible spirit) is incarnate (a visible body) is to commit the contradiction of saying that God is not God. Although the Christian faith is thus absurd from the point of view of reason, however, this absurdity is itself a reason, in some sense of the word "reason," for accepting the Christian faith. *"Credo quia absurdum est,"* proclaimed Tertullian; I believe because it is absurd.[11] While we might conclude that the rational inconsistency or absurdity of the articles of Christian faith indicates their falsity or meaninglessness, the fideists or "faithists," whom we are now considering, conclude rather that their absurdity demonstrates the limitation of reason and the transcendent truth of revelation. Reason always yields paradoxes and absurdities when it attempts to deal with ultimates, they argue; and in this indirect way reason can be used to demonstrate rationally its own ineptitude, just as Kierkegaard says in the nineteenth century a thief can best be used to catch a thief. From this point of view a Christian *philosophy* is clearly impossible, except in the negative and oblique sense that saying that this is so is rationally philosophizing about Christianity. Faith is faith and reason is reason and never the twain shall meet. Less extreme versions of this separation of reason and faith were held by Bonaventure (1221–1274), Duns Scotus, and William of Ockham (died 1349).

Yet this solution to the problem by means of the absolute separation of faith and reason must be regarded as extreme and inadequate, other thinkers argued, for one fundamental reason: the unity of man. The fideist, the believer, is, as a human being, also necessarily a rationalist, a philosopher (and perhaps the converse is also true), for human beings must always try to make sense out of their beliefs. But ought they to? one might object. This question makes no sense, however, for man has no alternative. He is a rationalizing animal as well as a believing animal, and two aspects of one unified being cannot be essentially or logically opposed. In so far as a belief is irrational and unintelligible to a person, just exactly to that extent is it incredible to him and hence not his belief at all. While the Christian faith, for example, is fundamentally the belief *in* Christ, it is also by that fact a belief *that* certain propositions are true, that Christ is both man and God, for example. For a person really to believe that a certain proposition is true he must be able to make some consistent sense of its meaning, even though he is unable to produce any rational evidence for its truth. Hence while faith and reason are different, they cannot be absolutely opposed and incompatible; Peter Abelard (1079–1142) was a major exponent of this position. If the God of faith is completely foreign to man's natural reason, He cannot reassure natural rational man of the reality of his world.

The conclusion which emerges from this consideration of these alternative attempts to solve the problem of faith and reason, of the possibility of a religious philosophy, in terms of an identification or absolute separation of faith and reason, is that faith and reason are different and yet compatible and even complementary. Each of the two competing theories considered contains a truth, but each exaggerates that truth to the exclusion of the truth of the other theory. The detection and combination of the truths contained in these two theories must be performed by a third, more embracing theory. Such a theory, perhaps the main position during the twelfth and thirteenth centuries, was represented by Abelard, Albert the Great (died in 1280), and Thomas Aquinas; Thomas was influenced in addition by the Muslim philosopher Avicenna (980–1037) and the Jewish philosopher Maimonides (1135–1204).

The theory of the complementarity of faith and reason, of religion and philosophy, maintains that they are irreducibly different but mutually entailing. On the one hand, the pursuit of reason arrives at the point of the rational realization and acceptance of the limitations of reason and hence of the necessity of faith. This is especially evident in medieval Christian philosophy's passage from natural to revealed theology. On the other hand, the act of Christian faith is not a faith in God or in Christ merely; it is a faith in a divinely instituted rational or intelligible order of reality. While these two dimensions of Christian belief—the upward dimension of reason and the downward dimension of faith—are thus complementary and mutually entailing, their relative emphasis varies among the medieval Christian philosophers.

The motto of the downward dimension of revelation is the *Credo ut intelligam* of Augustine and Anselm: I believe in order that I may understand. Faith is seen as prior to reason in the sense of being its foundation. Faith is not merely in God but in the whole God-sprung rational order of reality. "In the beginning was the Word," the *logos* or reason, the fourth gospel begins, and reason was with God and was God, and through it were all things made. Hence faith in God is also faith in reason and the intelligibility of all things made by God through reason. Thus does the Christian faith establish not only the Christian religion but also philosophy and science and all rational endeavors; this is the element of truth in the theory which reduces reason to faith. But this means that the upward path from reason to faith is established too. Therefore *Intelligo ut credam,* I understand in order that I may believe; the pursuit of reason leads inevitably toward its source in a faith in God as the rational author of intelligible nature.

This upward dimension of reason is emphasized more by Abelard and Aquinas than by Augustine and Anselm. The world is intelligible to man's unaided reason, but the full philosophical understanding of this intelligible world necessarily takes man to its source in God. As the source of the world, as its first cause, God can thus be understood by natural reason and expressed in a rational and purely natural theology. But in order to grasp what God is in Himself, distinctly from His extrinsic act of creating the world—for example, that He is a society of three persons—the transition must be made from reason to faith, from natural to revealed theology. "By natural reason we may know those things which pertain to the unity of the divine essence," Thomas writes, "but not those which pertain to the distinction of the divine persons. He who attempts to prove by natural reason the trinity of persons detracts from the rights of faith."[12] Here the word "natural" should be noted. While the doctrine of the trinity transcends natural, merely human, reason, it does not transcend reason *as such,* for God Himself is rational, according to Thomas, so the truths He reveals to man are rational in themselves and to God even though not to natural man. In like manner a grasp of certain things God has ordained for man—like the incarnation in Christ, the sacraments, and the resurrection of the body, for example—requires a transition from natural to revealed theology. With the attainment of this faith in God's supernatural reason, however, the downward passage into man's natural reason is also made possible and even required; at this point, as with Augustine and Anselm, *Credo ut intelligam,* I believe in order that I may understand.

This central mediating position, represented best in the middle ages by Thomas Aquinas, is thus that a religious philosophy is indeed possible, and to a substantial extent even actual, when religion and philosophy, faith and reason, are understood as necessarily involving each other. The religious philosophy of the middle ages is thus to be understood as faith seeking understanding *(fides quaerens intellectum)* and also as understanding seeking and being fulfilled by faith. Man's grasp always surpasses but lures his vision onward; man's dim apprehension always transcends but invites his clear comprehension. The grasp is first of something visible in itself but not to him, to transpose Aristotle's methodological principle (Ch. 4-1.2); and in order to comprehend anything clearly we must first apprehend it dimly. When we do comprehend something clearly, furthermore, this comprehension illuminates and makes intelligible the stages we passed through in order to reach it, just as the released prisoner in Plato's allegory of the cave properly understands his former imprisoned life only from the vantage point he has gained outside the cave. Faith and reason thus form the two mutually entailing and mutually supporting dimensions of one unified spiritual journey. Faith seeks its understanding in reason, and reason seeks its source and meaning in faith. Each is necessary and each requires the other. Reason without faith is empty, and faith without reason is blind.

Such a view of the partnership of reason and faith allows its advocate to reassert a rational belief in the reality of God Who as existence itself bestows existence upon the natural world, which intrinsically lacks it, and it thus reassures the medieval philosopher of the reality of his natural world. Yet this reassuring harmony of reason and faith which reached its peak in the philosophy of Thomas Aquinas soon began to break down into an opposition of reason to faith which began gradually with Duns Scotus and culminated finally in modern philosophy (Ch. 7-1). Some of the reasons for this gradual dissolution of the reassuring union of reason and faith lie in the philosophical problems involved in the medieval conception of God as creative existence.

6-4. *Theological Problems*

Two main problems are involved in this medieval theory of God as both revealed and rationally known as complete and perfect existence or being. One is the problem of the possibility of creation. How could, and why would, a Being Who is already perfect create anything at all, make there be anything in addition to Himself? Of course God as existence itself is *able* to create, and able to create out of nothing, a power which the ancient Greek gods lacked. But the question before us now is what possible reason could a God Who is already complete and perfect existence have for creating anything? This problem has been the source of a lengthy and complicated dialectic, in recent as well as medieval times.[13]

The first answer which occurs on the basis of the medieval conception of God is that the existence which is the essence of God is the *act* of existence *(esse);* and to exist is to act, to act is to cause, and to be a divine cause is to be the cause of a world: to create. To this answer an objection immediately arises, however. If it is God's very essence as active existence to create a world, then God's act of creating is unfree and necessitated like the emanation of the world from Plotinus' One. This charge of divine determinism the Christian philosophers of course deny; God creates freely, for freedom is a high order value and God is perfect goodness. But in that case, the objector continues, there can be no reason for creation at all, for if there were a reason for creation it could only, by hypothesis, be the nature of God Himself, and this has been denied. At this point the medieval Christian philosopher responds that the reason for creation is God's own goodness, that God, like Plato's divine

Craftsman, creates the world because He is good and wants to share His goodness, that He creates the world to glorify Himself. The objector must then reply that if God creates the world to glorify Himself or to share His goodness, then it follows that prior to creation God lacks a perfection, self-glorification or shared goodness, and is therefore not perfectly good at all, which means that He is really not God. Thus the dialectic continues, even into modern times, and we shall meet it again especially in Spinoza, Leibniz, and Kant. We should note, however, that this problem is one which could arise only with the medieval conception of God. The theologies of the ancient Greek philosophers face no such problem because they make no such high claims for God. For them God can reasonably want or need the world because for them God lacks the full perfection which comes only with the medieval identification of God with existence itself.

The other main problem which arises from the medieval identification of God's essence with existence is the problem of the possibility of a relation between God and creatures, between creative and creaturely existence. Conceiving of God as existence itself presents a dilemma between pantheism and agnosticism. If "existence" or "being" is taken univocally, as meaning just one thing, then the existence of creatures must be identical with God. Hence pantheism: all things are God and God is all things. And if "existence" or "being" is taken equivocally, as meaning two entirely different things when applied to God and to creatures, then it follows that the existence of God can have nothing in common with that of creatures. But this means agnosticism; since the finite existence, which alone human beings can know, cannot be predicated of God, He must be completely transcendent and ineffable—a position advocated by the extreme proponents of the separation of reason and faith. Hence either everything is one God-world or else God and world are utterly different. In neither case can there be any relation between God and the world.

This problem of the relation of creatures as beings to God as Being the medieval philosophers could solve more easily than they could the problem of creation, however, perhaps because the ancient philosophers had laid the foundation for the solution. After Parmenides had argued that there can only be one being because (in effect) being has one fixed, univocal meaning, Plato devised a relational concept of being as power, fundamentally active and passive power, which Aristotle developed into his analogical conception of being as both one and many, neither univocal nor equivocal but analogical (Ch. 4-5). This doctrine of the analogy of being *(analogia entis)* Thomas Aquinas and other medieval philosophers inherited and developed as the solution to the problem of the possibility of many beings and therefore also as the foundation for their solution to the problem of the relation between divine and creaturely existence.[14] The relation between divine and creaturely existence is, from a logical point of view, only a special instance of the relation between any one being and another; and theological analogy is thus an application of the general theory of the analogy of being. God exists in a different, but not wholly different, sense than that in which creatures do; God *is* His existence, His essence is existence, while creatures only *have* their existence, they are contingent. In like manner, and more immediately relevant to religious concerns, God loves, fathers, forgives, and so on in a different but not wholly different sense from that in which humans do. Thus both pantheism and agnosticism are avoided by conceiving "being" or "existence" as neither univocal and simply one, nor equivocal and simply many, but rather analogical, both one and many, a bond which prevents all things from falling into nothingness but which also prevents them from collapsing into each other. This medieval solution of the ancient problem of the one and the many will continue into modern times, especially with Continental Rationalism (Chs. 8 and 9), though always with the tendency to lapse either into pantheism or into agnosticism, a tendency corresponding to the tendency either to identify or wholly to separate reason and faith.

6-5. *Summary*

Thus concludes the consideration of the distinctive nature of medieval philosophy: the idea of God as creative existence. The

conception of God as existence throws into question the existence of the natural world, which the ancients took for granted,
but the conception of God as creative reestablishes the existence
of that world. While the God of ancient Greek philosophy was
the answer to the question "Why do natural things *change?*" the
God of medieval philosophy is the answer to the question "Why
do natural things *exist?*" That this medieval question is a new
question is borne out by the fact[15] that the ontological argument for the existence of God is foreign to ancient philosophy.
The ancients might be said to have a tacit ontological argument
for reality or being, but the medievals are the first to have an
ontological argument for the existence of God. Since *something*
must exist, as the ancients (especially Parmenides) rightly believed, the medieval philosophers conclude that this something
can *only* be God because they realize that it is not necessary for
nature or any natural thing to exist. Therefore they find questionable that which the ancient philosophers took for granted,
the existence of the world of nature. Yet the medieval philosophers' question about the existence of nature does not remain
unanswered; though nature need not and might not exist, it
does indeed happen to exist because God created it. While the
ancient philosophers are assured, the medieval philosophers are
thus reassured of the reality of man's natural world. Both are
truly assured of it, however; and this is what will basically distinguish ancient and medieval philosophy from modern philosophy.

   Since this reassurance of the reality of man's natural world is
granted by a God Who transcends nature and natural man, this
reassuring God must be both a God of faith and a God of reason.
Here lies the fundamental significance of the medieval problem
of the relation of reason and faith. Only a God of faith, only a
Being transcending both objective nature and man's natural
reason, is capable of reassuring medieval man of the reality of
his bond with nature. Yet a completely transcendent God would
elude man's natural reason and thus be incapable of reassuring
natural man. While neither can be reduced to the other, faith
and reason must complement each other and the God of faith
must be identical with the God of reason.

With Neoplatonism taken as a new statement of the first stage (with man again not yet separated from the world), medieval philosophy especially in its doctrine of God presents a third statement of the three-stage development from undifferentiated whole to human part to a reunion of man and world. The questioning of the existence of nature involved in the conception of God as existence is a separating of questioning man from nature, a statement of the second stage. But the answering of this question by a transcendent God Who as pure existence Himself bestows existence upon nature then reunites man and nature to form a new statement of the third stage. As transcending nature and man's natural reason this reassuring God must be the God of faith, but knowable as such by man's natural reason, this God must at the same time be the God of reason. As long as man remains bound to a God Who can bring nature and man into being because He is Himself transcendent Being, and as long as natural man can rationally know at least the existence of such a God, he is reassured of his bond with nature and he remains medieval man. If either the God of reason or the God of faith should be lost, however, or if they should become separated from each other, then Western man would also lose his reassurance of the reality of nature and of his bond with nature. This happens in the second part of the story of Western philosophy to which we now turn.

SUGGESTED READINGS

6-1. Gilson, Etienne. *The Spirit of Medieval Philosophy.* New York: Scribner's, 1940. Ch. 3.

Bourke, Vernon J., trans. and ed. *The Essential Augustine.* New York: New American Library of World Literature, 1964. Ch. 3.

Gilby, Thomas, trans. and ed. *St. Thomas Aquinas: Philosophical Texts.* Oxford University Press, 1951. Pp. 69–73, 79–82.

Wolter, A. *Duns Scotus: Philosophical Writings.* New York: Nelson, 1962. Ch. 4.

6-2. Gilson. Ch. 4.

Gilby. Pp. 48–66.

Wolter. Ch. III.

6-3. Gilson. Chs. 1 and 2.
6-4. Gilson. Ch. 5.
    Bourke. Ch. 3.
    Gilby. Pp. 131–36.

For bibliography, see:
Copleston, F. C. *Medieval Philosophy*. New York: Harper, 1961. Pp. 187–88. A brief bibliography with references to more extensive bibliographies.

Part II

MODERN SUBJECTIVISM

Chapter 7

The
Beginnings
of
Modern
Philosophy

7-1. *Transition to Modern Philosophy*

The most basic and general feature of the transition from medieval to modern philosophy is a new, deeper, and more enduring separation of reason from faith. Since philosophy is a rational endeavor, this deeper separation of reason from faith meant for philosophy an increase in the freedom of man's natural reason from the authority of traditional faith and revelation. This new freedom of man's mind from its medieval tie to a revealed, transcendent God Who establishes nature and man's bond with nature will be seen to grow gradually into a new and far stronger statement of the second stage of the three-stage sequence from primordial whole to isolated human part toward a reunion of man and his world. The isolation of the human subject from nature, which develops out of reason's isolation from a transcendent author of nature, will become the most general and fundamental feature of modern philosophy.

The tradition of ancient and medieval philosophy had presented three statements of the second stage, a withdrawal from the objective world of nature to a concentration upon man, but each time this second stage was followed by a statement of the third stage, a reunion of man with the world from which he had become separated. In modern philosophy, however, each attempt to create the third stage of reunion of subjective man with objective world will succeed only in achieving a renewed emphasis upon the second stage, a deepened awareness of the freedom and separation of the knowing and acting subject from his objective world. Thus the separation of the God of reason from the God of faith will lead modern philosophy to a separation of human reason from its original home in nature and to a freedom of the human subject from its original natural ties. Subjectivity, the freedom of the subject from the objective world, therefore will emerge as the defining essence of modern philosophy as a whole.

Secondarily and less fundamentally modern philosophy will be marked by a struggle to achieve the correct definition of this freed human reason in terms of a proper balance between its conceptual and its sensory powers, between sensation and reason in the narrow sense of intellection or conceptualization. Is the new, freed human mind to be defined in terms of its conceptual, logical, theoretical, and deductive activities, on the one hand, or in terms of its perceptual, sensory, observational, and inductive activities, on the other hand? Or is the human mind to be defined in terms of both kinds of activity, and if so, what is the proper balance between them, the appropriate role of each? The various answers to these questions will define the specific movements within the whole of modern philosophy. While each movement will, of course, give some place to both types of mental activity, Continental Rationalism will emphasize deductive, conceptual reason; British Empiricism will emphasize inductive, sensory experience; and the final movement, which is usually called German Idealism and which we will see to be more appropriately called German Voluntarism, will seek a synthesis of rationalism and empiricism in a unified dynamic conception of the mind.

Emphasis upon the subject, the mind, will thus turn out to be the generic feature of modern philosophy, and emphasis upon some particular type of subjective activity will define the specific differences between the various types of modern philosophy. Thus the fundamental motif is the freedom of human reason from its bond with the traditional world of faith, and the subsidiary motif is the definition of human reason in terms of some balance between rational thought and sensory experience. Faith versus reason in the broad sense, and reason in the narrow sense versus sensation; these will be the basic determinants of modern philosophy. Although both of these motifs will become more extreme in modern philosophy than they were in ancient and medieval philosophy, neither is entirely new and they are seldom entirely separate from each other.

In ancient Greek philosophy freedom from the tradition and revelation expressed in the earlier mythology and poetry was essentially won near the beginning of the birth of philosophy in the Milesians, though this freedom kept increasing and reached its peak with Aristotle. In ancient philosophy the main struggle was the attempt to establish the correct relation between reason in the narrow sense and sensation, between rational thought and sensory experience, between conception and perception. Although ancient philosophy was for a time characterized by a vacillation between extreme rationalism, especially in the Eleatics, and extreme sensationism, especially in the Sophists, it culminated in Aristotle's recognition of the distinctness and complementarity of reason and sensation. Reason requires sense experience for the material for its abstraction of universal principles, and sensation requires reason for its discrimination and illumination. In medieval philosophy, however, defined as it was by its reassurance of the existence of nature by means of a transcendent God Whose essence as existence permitted Him to bestow existence upon nature, the main problem was to find the correct relation between faith in this transcendent God and rational knowledge of his transcendent nature and existence. Although medieval philosophy vacillated between the extremes of a complete separation of natural reason and supernatural revelation, for example in Tertullian, and their complete identification, for example in Scotus Erigena, the peak of Aristotelian Scholasticism in the twelfth and thirteenth centuries, represented especially by Thomas Aquinas, saw the development of a middle position maintaining the distinctness yet complementarity of human reason and divine faith. Faith requires reason for its understanding, and reason requires faith as its ground and completion. Both present the same God, that transcendent Being Who is the author of the being of nature. To understand better this interplay of faith and reason and reason and sensation, and also to grasp the mediating position of Thomas Aquinas as a background of the development of modern philosophy, let us use the image of man as created lower than the angels and higher than the brutes. Man is the highest being in the natural order but the lowest being in the supernatural order. Caught in between these two orders of existence, he both shares something with each and also possesses a unique inbetweenness, his own peculiar difference. The supernatural factor in man, that which he shares with the angelic and the divine, is his participation in God's vision by means of divine revelation. The purely animal factor in man, that which he shares with the brutes, is his sense experience, an awareness of the particular and fluctuating features of the things of nature. And his peculiar inbetweenness, his distinctively human characteristic, which marks him off both from the brutes below and the angels above, is his reason, his intellect, his native power of discerning the unchanging and universal characteristics of things through his sense experience. By virtue of his participation in God's vision through divine revelation man can receive a wisdom not achievable by his natural powers. By virtue of his sense experience man gains an awareness which he shares with the lower animals and which contains no distinctively human mark. By virtue of his inbetweenness, however, by means of that native intellect which is his own distinctive and defining property, man can gain a natural and peculiarly human wisdom, an understanding of the universal and fundamental principles of all things acquired by rational abstraction from his natural sensory experience.

Thus did Thomas Aquinas try to hold sensation, reason, and revelation all together in a harmony in which each is necessary and none is reducible to any other. What basically distinguishes late medieval and early modern philosophy is the gradual breaking down of this union and especially the increasing freedom of reason from revelation or faith. The beginnings of this separation of reason from faith may be found already immediately after the death of Thomas in the philosophy of the master dialectician John Duns Scotus. Duns Scotus had a profound distrust of the claims Thomas made for reason, for Scotus held that reason is incapable of ascertaining truth in at least most supernatural matters, that the only certainty here is to be gotten from revelation. While Thomas had of course subordinated reason to revelation, as we have seen, he had held that many theological questions can be settled with certainty by rational philosophy using natural reason without recourse to revelation. Duns Scotus, however, so restricted this area of natural or rational theology as to make it negligible; most of its content was passed to revelation. In addition, the acceptance of this revelation was for Scotus an act of will, which was basically prior to and independent of reason, and here too he disagreed with Thomas Aquinas in making will prior to intellect or reason.

This separation of reason from revelation had two main general consequences which developed concurrently in the years following Duns Scotus' death. On the one hand, the new separation of revelation from reason led metaphysics and theology to become less rationalistic and more mystical. Meister Eckhart (1260–1327) represents most basically a more mystical version of the philosophy of Plotinus. Nicholas of Cusa (1401–1464) presents a mysticism which largely arises from and feeds upon the increasing skepticism about rational or natural theology, and much later Jacob Boehme (1575–1624) presents again a mysticism similar to that of Meister Eckhart.

On the other hand, the new separation of reason from revelation led philosophy itself to become less metaphysical and theological and more naturalistic and empirical; in turning away from faith, reason turned toward sense experience. Roger Bacon (about 1214–1294), a contemporary of Thomas Aquinas, had foreshadowed the spirit of empirical scientific investigation. William of Ockham (who died about 1349) went beyond the restrictions which Duns Scotus had placed on rational theology to the position that natural reason is incapable of demonstrating any theological doctrines at all, that they are only articles of faith. Ockham is perhaps best known in terms of "Ockham's razor," the principle that entities should not be multiplied beyond necessity, though this principle goes back at least to Robert Grosseteste (died 1253). One of Ockham's own formulations of it is "Never should plurality be posited without necessity."[1] The most important logical consequence, or corollary, of "Ockham's razor" was his nominalism, his theory that only individuals really exist, that universals exist only in the mind and in the words and names it employs in classifying individuals. These individuals which alone really exist are known through sense perceptions and the mind's intuitions of them, and all knowledge which transcends sense experience is relegated to faith. Nicholas of Autrecourt (died about 1350) foreshadowed David Hume's eighteenth century critique of causation (Ch. 10-3), reasoning that there is no contradiction in affirming a cause and then denying its supposed effect. He therefore also questioned entities which had been rationally inferred on the basis of the principle of causation: substance as the cause of its qualities, God as the cause of the world, and even the external world as the cause of our ideas of it—a sharp anticipation of what will turn out to be the main feature of modern philosophy.

Thus within the philosophy of this transitional period there is an increased freedom of natural reason from faith and revelation and a turning of natural reason to more empirical and scientific concerns. In addition to this internal philosophical movement, moreover, there were also at the same time parallel social movements. These movements interacted with philosophical thought and profoundly conditioned the rise of modern philosophy. Foremost among them were the Renaissance, the Protestant Reformation, and the development of natural science. As its name implies, the Renaissance was a period of rebirth, a rebirth of natural man freed from the restrictions of the medieval tradition by recapturing the attitudes and culture of ancient Greece and Rome. Renaissance man refused to allow medieval authority and tradition to interfere with his understanding, appreciation, and use of his own natural powers and those of nature generally. Although it started as a revolt against a particular traditional institution, the Protestant Reformation was more basically and generally a revolt against the authority of the whole traditional church. Reformation man refused to allow traditional ecclesiastical authority to stand between him and his God. Thus the Renaissance is analogous to the increased naturalism and empiricism in philosophy represented by such men as William of Ockham, and the Protestant Reformation is analogous to the increased mysticism and individualism in religion represented by such men as Nicholas of Cusa. Both were broader social expressions of the increased freedom from tradition which was characteristic of the philosophy of the time.

The third major force parallel to and interacting with philosophy in this transitional period was the development of natural science. There was, of course, natural science in the middle ages and even in ancient times, but the new freedom from tradition and authority gradually brought about so great a quantitative increase in natural science that it produced something almost qualitatively different. In addition to the general feeling of enlarged physical and spiritual horizons induced by the terrestrial and celestial discoveries of the times, notable advances in this period in the understanding of scientific procedure were to have an important influence upon modern philosophy. The heliocentric theory of Nicolaus Copernicus (1473–1543), though advocated by some ancient thinkers, revised men's notions of their place in the universe and reasserted "Ockham's razor"—the principle of unity and explanatory power in scientific theory. Johannes Kepler (1571–1630) developed Copernicus' heliocentric theory by means of a more refined use of both observation and theory, and Galileo Galilei (1564–1642) explicitly established these as the two equally necessary dimensions of scientific method. Science must proceed free from authority and tradition; "nevertheless, it [the earth] does move," he is said to have murmured after recanting his "heresy." Instead science must be tied to experience and reason, induction and deduction, observation and mathematics. The relative importance of these two dimensions of scientific method will be a matter of disagreement throughout modern philosophy, as has already been indicated and as we shall see in detail later, just as it also was in ancient philosophy in the dialectic between reason and experience.

Thus the spirit of the time, both within philosophy itself and in the broader social movements of the Renaissance, the Reformation, and the development of natural science, was a freeing of man's mind from the authority of tradition. But this freedom was bought at a price, the price of lessened security and solidarity. Like all transitions, this transition from medieval to modern philosophy should be viewed retrospectively as well as prospectively, from the point of view of the old as well as that of the new. From the point of view of medieval philosophy this transitional period was a loss, a loss of security, a loss of the solidarity of man with his God, his church, and his past. Yet from the point of view of nascent modern philosophy it is a gain, a gain in freedom for the individual and his mind from the shackles of tradition and authority. But such gain-in-loss and loss-in-gain is always characteristic of change—in fact this is what change means—and the greater the change the greater the gain and loss. The exact magnitude and nature of this gain in freedom and loss of security and its role in the overall story of Western philosophy may be appreciated better in the Epilogue, however, after we have examined the full development of modern philosophy.

Before turning to the first major movement in the story of modern philosophy, let us now briefly consider the thought of two early modern British philosophers who express both this growing freedom from tradition and also the increased attention to experience and nature. Francis Bacon will emphasize the methodological side of this new, free, naturalistic empiricism, and Thomas Hobbes will present its systematic view of the world. Later we shall see their ideas become fully developed in the philosophy of British Empiricism (Ch. 10).

7-2. *Bacon*

Francis Bacon (1561–1626) compared himself to Aristotle; his *Novum Organum* (New Organon) was intended to replace the old *organon* or methodology of Aristotle. This new organon or methodology is empiricistic rather than rationalistic; Bacon rejected the traditional deductive reason in favor of sensory observation and empirical generalization, and he correctly propounded the basic essentials of the experimental method, although John Stuart Mill in the nineteenth century was to give that method a more detailed and influential form.

Before the new empirical method can be applied, however, the old dogmatic method of reason must be destroyed, and this occurs in Bacon's iconoclasm, his smashing of four types of corrupting idols. The "Idols of the Cave" are the preconceptions and biases peculiar to the individual and distorting his view of nature. The "Idols of the Marketplace" are semantic confusions which mislead us in our attempts to understand nature, confusions arising from ill-defined terms as well as from names for nonexistent things like Fortune and the Prime Mover. The "Idols of the Theatre" are traditional philosophical dogmas, especially the philosophy of Aristotle both as he himself conceived it and as it was modified and accepted in the middle ages. Paramount among these defects of Aristotelianism, according to Bacon, are the scanty attention it pays to experience and its imposition of a preconceived dogmatic method upon the actual, empirical structure of nature. The "Idols of the Tribe," finally, are tendencies innate in the human species to read its own characteristics into nature. Anthropomorphism in all its forms, and especially the belief in inner substances and final causes, leads only to illusion. "The human understanding is no dry light,"[2] Bacon insists.

Bacon seems to think that it is possible to smash these Idols of the Tribe in order that the mind may become a true mirror of nature. But if these are indeed Idols of the Tribe, if they are innate and essential features of the human mind as such, as Bacon also seems to suggest, then apparently they cannot be smashed; they will always remain a distortion in the mirror of the mind, and the human mind must always interpret nature by means of them. This indeed will be the conclusion which Bacon's successors finally will draw. Hume will regard these Idols as the fundamental principle of the mind, the principle of habit or custom (Ch. 10-3.2); and Kant will make them the "a priori forms" which mold human experience (Ch. 11-1.2). Thus even as early as Bacon the structure of the knowing mind begins to intervene between the self and nature; this seed of the freedom and isolation of the subject from his world will gradually grow into the essence of modern philosophy.

Once these idols are smashed the way is open for Bacon's positive method, his new organon. The way to understand nature, and therefore also control it, is to discover what Bacon calls the Forms of things. He insists that these are not Aristotelian forms and certainly not Platonic Forms. They are rather "nature engendering natures," "latent configurations," or "latent processes," "those laws and determinations of absolute actuality, which govern and constitute any simple nature . . . . Thus the Form of heat or the Form of light is the same thing as the Law of heat or the Law of light."[3] In short, Bacon's method is designed to discover the causal laws of phenomena, their determining substructures.

The method consists of three tables of instances of some phenomenon, such as heat, from which an induction is made "to find such a nature as is always present or absent with the given nature, and always increases or decreases with it."[4] The first table, the Table of Essence and Presence, is a listing of *positive* instances of the phenomenon under investigation in order to try to find another feature which is always present with that phenomenon; the assumption is that this accompanying feature is the Form or cause of that phenomenon. Thus in investigating the Form or cause of heat in his Table of Essence and Presence, Bacon gives twenty-seven instances of heat ranging from rays of the sun to aromatic herbs. The use of this table John Stuart Mill later calls the method of agreement. The second table, the Table of Deviation or Absence in Proximity, is a listing of *negative* instances of the phenomenon under investigation, of instances lacking in heat where it might be expected. The use of this table Mill calls the method of difference. The third table, the Table of Degrees or the Table of Comparison, is a listing of degrees of the phenomenon under investigation to see what other feature varies concomitantly, for "no nature can be taken as the true form, unless it always decreases when the nature in question decreases, and in like manner always increases when the nature in question increases."[5] The use of this table Mill calls the method of concomitant variation.* If by the use of these three tables anything can be found which is always present when the phenomenon under investigation is present, always absent when it is absent, and which always varies concomitantly, then that something is the Form or cause of that phenomenon. Thus in the example of heat Bacon uses these three tables to conclude that the Form of heat is *"a motion, expansive, restrained, and acting in its strife upon the smaller particles of the bodies* [which] *while it expands all ways, it has at the same time an inclination upwards."*[6]

Although Bacon's procedure correctly outlines the empirical side of scientific method, it is one-sided in slighting the role of reason. This one-sidedness is manifested in certain serious difficulties in Bacon's method. First, it is probably impossible in practice to obtain a set of instances of a phenomenon which *have only* one other factor in common or a set of instances which *lack only* one other factor. A careful inspection shows that the instances compiled by Bacon in the Table of Essence and Presence have other things besides motion in common, and that the instances listed in the Table of Deviation lack other things in addition to motion. One of these other factors might well be the true Form or cause of heat. Second, it is also probably impossible in practice to produce a set of degrees of a phenomenon which have only one covariant, so once more the Form or true cause might well be one of these other covariants. Bacon does seek to avoid these difficulties by establishing what he calls prerogative instances of various types,[7] pure, typical instances of the phenomenon in question, but this begs the question, for in order to know that an instance is indeed typical one must already know the type which it exemplifies, the true Form of the phenomenon. Finally, Bacon's procedure requires that the Forms be too phenomenal, too empirical, to possess the desired ex-

---

* To these three methods Mill adds two others—the joint method of agreement and difference and the method of residues—though the first of these is hardly more than a combination of the first two methods and the other is really a deductive rather than an inductive procedure. See most any introductory text dealing with inductive logic or scientific method.

planatory causal power. If the induced Form is simply an accompanying observable phenomenon, it is on a par with the phenomenon it is supposed to cause and explain. If, on the other hand, the Form is at a deeper level so that it can indeed cause and explain the observed phenomenon, it would seem to be itself not a sensorily observable phenomenon but rather a rationally inferred, unobservable structure. Bacon's methodology appears to be impaled on the horns of this dilemma.

In order that the Forms may have the desired causal and explanatory power, therefore, we must employ a faculty of rational abstraction similar to Aristotle's, which is quite distinct from sensory observation. In order to rule out all but one of the copresent or coabsent or covariant factors, clearly we must have recourse to some antecedent hypothesis or theory which at least is independent of that particular experience or observation, and this, too, reintroduces the rationalism which Bacon seems to eliminate. For Bacon antecedent hypotheses seem always to be Idols to be smashed, yet his modern followers will conclude that not all of them should or even can be, that prior rational theory is essential to understanding the world. "The men of experiment are like the ant;" Bacon writes, "they only collect and use; the reasoners resemble spiders, who make cobwebs out of their own substance. But the bee takes a middle course, it gathers its materials from the flowers of the garden and of the field, but transforms and digests it by a power of its own."[8] While Bacon apparently regarded himself as a bee, he is in fact more like the ant; he is too afraid of hypothesis and theory. Confined to its sensorily observable aspects, experienced nature as grasped by Bacon's method lacks the illumination which only rational theory can bring.

7-3. Hobbes

Thomas Hobbes (1588–1679), older than Descartes but later in philosophical development, presents in his philosophy a picture of the world which results when reason is reduced basically to sensation; his metaphysics, epistemology, ethics, and politics match and complement the empiricist methodology of Bacon.

The fundamental principle, the metaphysical core, of the philosophy of Hobbes is mechanistic materialism: reality is matter in motion according to deterministic laws, much as Democritus had held earlier and much as Descartes was holding to be true of one half of the world. And the rest of Hobbes' philosophy is a direct manifestation of this metaphysical core. In psychology Hobbes is a behaviorist: man is a machine and his consciousness is a part of the behavior of that machine. In epistemology Hobbes is a materialist and sensory empiricist. Rational thought is literally calculation, a pushing around or rearranging of the pebbles or elements of awareness. (*Calculus* is Latin for pebble.) These pebbles or elements are particular sensations which, when faded and faint, become images and memories. These elementary sensations and the images and thoughts derived from them are simply physical motions in us which are caused by physical motions in some external body. As caused by external bodies, sensations and thoughts are necessarily different from, never identical with, those external bodies or their motions. Sensations and thoughts *re*present but never present those external bodies themselves; thus Hobbes' epistemology is a representationalist one. This theory contains some serious difficulties.

First, the theory presents a difficulty which we noted in the philosophy of Democritus. External bodies and their cognitive effects in us possess only quantitative features and not qualitative ones, only what Locke will later call primary qualities and not secondary qualities. This position is a natural consequence of Galileo's insistence that nature is to be understood mathematically. Yet we experience "secondary qualities" such as colors, sounds, and tastes. Hobbes of course recognized these experienced qualities, but he never explains how it is possible for them to exist in a world of pure quantity. To get qualities from nonqualitive quantities seems like getting something from nothing.

Second, the representationalism of Hobbes' epistemology presents an even more serious problem. Hobbes conceives cognition as a straightforward physical process. An external physical thing, say a tree, emits physical impulses which travel through a medium to a sensory end-organ, e.g., through the air to the eye. They then act on the retina to produce an (electro-chemical) impulse which travels through the optic nerve to (the occipital lobe of) the brain where it produces some sort of physical pattern. Whereupon one is said to see the tree. The first odd thing about this description of vision is that what the person really sees, according to the theory, would seem to be behind his eyes in the back of his brain, instead of out in front of his eyes as he thinks it is. Hobbes handles this difficulty by saying that the brain (or heart) projects the image-event outward back toward the original stimulus object, since every action has an equal and opposite reaction. "The cause of sense is the external body, or object," Hobbes writes, "which presseth the organ proper to each sense . . . which pressure, by the mediation of the nerves, and other strings and membranes of the body, continued inwards to the brain and heart, causeth there a resistance, or counterpressure, or endeavor of the heart to deliver itself, which endeavor, being outward, seemeth to be some matter without."[9]

Even granting this rather dubious external projection of the image, however, the image projected is not and cannot be the same thing as what the person thinks he sees, the original external physical object. The two things must be different at least temporally, since the process takes time; and if change always accompanies time then the two things are also different in character. Thus this theory implies that no one can ever apprehend what he thinks he apprehends. But this may be true, we may object; indeed perhaps we can never apprehend the original things which produce our images. Perhaps so, but if this were really so, we could never know it. If, as Hobbes says, we always know *only* the image-effect and never the thing-cause, then neither Hobbes nor anyone else could possibly know that there *is* any original thing to cause the image-effect. Moreover, since to know that the image which one knows is in fact an *effect* of an original cause implies that one knows that there is an original cause, one could not even know that the image which one knows is an *effect*. That image would have to be the original reality itself, for all one could ever know. Thus in its representationalism Hobbes' theory contradicts itself. If the theory were true it could never be propounded, because then the theorizer could not know that there is any unknown original cause, and if the theory can be propounded, it cannot be true because the propounding of it implies a knowledge of the original cause which the theory denies. This contradiction built into the nature of any representationalist theory will later arise again to plague Hobbes' British Empiricist successors as well as the Continental Rationalists. Its tendency to confine the mind to its own images and ideas already epitomizes and will develop fully into the essence of modern philosophy.

Hobbes' ethical, social, and political philosophy is a simple and consistent application of his basic mechanistic materialism. With Aristotle, Hobbes holds that "good" means "object of desire," or what a thing naturally moves toward, and that "bad" means the opposite. However, Aristotle maintained that what each thing desires or moves toward is its own self-realization, the actualization of its potentiality, but Hobbes holds that it is simply its own self-preservation and self-expression, since (according to his mechanistic materialism) everything is already completely actual and factual and thus has no nature or potentiality to be realized. The natural state of man is thus one in which each man acts for the sake of his own self-preservation and self-expansion. Since one man's acts of self-preservation and self-expansion inevitably impinge upon and imperil those of other men, however, this "state of nature" is also a state of war, a war of all against all, where life is "solitary, poor, nasty, brutish, and short."[10] Thus the human condition is for Hobbes much the same as a situation in mechanics: each body, according to the law of inertia, continues in a uniform state of motion or rest until it is acted upon by another body. Contrary to Aristotle, men do not share any common nature such that the good of one entails the good of all; man is not by nature a political or social animal.

Yet this very individualism is itself something which all men share; individualism is itself a universal nature which founds two fundamental laws of nature. However, they are unlike the "natural law" of Plato and Aristotle in being more descriptive than prescriptive, since Hobbes is a determinist. The first law of nature is "to seek peace and follow it . . . [and] by all means we can to defend ourselves," and the second law of nature is "that a man be willing, when others are so too, as far forth as for peace and defense of himself he shall think it necessary, to lay down this right to all things; and be contented with so much liberty against other men, as he would allow other men against himself."[11] Given the fact that the state of nature is inevitably a state of war destructive of self-preservation, this second law of nature immediately leads to Hobbes' famed social contract in which everyone says to everyone else: "I authorize and give up my right of governing myself to this man, or to this assembly of men, on this condition, that thou give up thy right to him, and authorize all his actions in like manner."[12] Thus is born the Leviathan, that artificial man which is the state. Once more we should note that for Hobbes the state is artificial whereas for Plato and Aristotle it is natural. To put this important point more accurately, for Hobbes the state is a necessary *means* toward the natural end of the self-*preservation* of the *individual* —and in this attenuated sense the state is natural—whereas for Plato and Aristotle the state is a necessary part of the natural *end* of self-*realization* of the human *species*. Notice also how the rugged individualism of Hobbes' natural man follows from the nominalism of his epistemology: since all cognition is sensory and since the senses grasp only the individual or particular and never any universal nature, the good can only be conceived and sought in terms of particular individuals, never in terms of a universal nature of man.

7-4. *Summary*

The primary theme of the transition from medieval to modern philosophy is the separation of reason from faith, the increasing freedom of man and his mind from the authority of tradition, institution, and revelation with its concomitant loss of the solidarity of medieval man with the world of his past. Since natural reason no longer united with the transcendent God of faith Who had reassured medieval man of the reality of nature, the question of the existence of nature as man's natural home begins to be reopened. Can modern man recapture ancient man's assurance of nature from nature herself? This seems to be his initial attempt as is evident in the direct attention paid to nature in the Renaissance, by early modern natural science, and by the early modern philosophers Bacon and Hobbes. Yet Bacon's Idols of the Tribe and Hobbes' representative images seem to come between man and nature to throw into question once more ancient man's natural home. To what can modern man then turn for a new reassurance of his home in nature? Not to nature any longer, nor to God. All that is now left is man himself. Nor can it even be man as a part of nature, as a natural being, for, again, that is exactly what is in question. Modern man's reassurance of his bond with nature can therefore arise only from his own mind, that consciousness which transcends his own natural being and that of nature at large. And thus it is that Descartes will father modern philosophy.

The secondary theme of the rise of modern philosophy is the competition between sensory experience and rational thought as candidates for the nature of man's freed mind. With the revived separation of reason from faith, the freed human mind turns first toward sensory experience for the clue to its nature. The fullest early modern expression of the resulting methodology is to be found in the philosophy of Francis Bacon, and the view of man and his world which corresponds to this empiricistic and naturalistic methodology is presented in the philosophy of Thomas Hobbes. Since both Bacon and Hobbes give only a minor role to the rational, theoretical dimension of human knowledge as established, for example, by Galileo, the next task facing modern philosophy will be that of discovering and utilizing a new concept of reason, one free from revelation and yet also irreducible to sensation and observation. The discovery and utilization of such a concept of reason is the essential feature of the first major movement in modern philosophy and even gives this movement its name, Continental Rationalism. Since the most important characteristics of Continental Rationalism are all contained in the philosophy of its founder, René Descartes, a separate chapter is devoted to him.

SUGGESTED READINGS

7-1. Gilson, Etienne. *The Unity of Philosophical Experience.* New York: Scribner's, 1937. Chs. 3, 4.
Wolter, A. *Duns Scotus: Philosophical Writings.* New York: Nelson, 1962. Ch. 2.

7-2. Bacon. *Novum Organum.* Bk. I, aphorisms xxxviii–lxv; Bk. II, aphorisms x–xv, xx.

7-3. Hobbes, *Leviathan.* Intro.; Pt. I, Chs. 1–2, 5–6, 11, 13–15; Pt. II, Ch. 17.

For bibliographies, see:

7-1. Wolter, A. *Duns Scotus: Philosophical Writings.* New York: Nelson, 1962. Pp. xii–xiii.

7-2, 3. Kennedy, G. *Bacon, Hobbes, and Locke.* New York: Doubleday Doran, 1937. Pp. xli–xlii.

Chapter 8

Continental
Rationalism
in
Descartes

René Descartes (1596–1650), the first of the Continental Rationalists, inherited and attempted to synthesize both medieval philosophy and nascent modern science. His debt to medieval philosophy is manifest in the scholastic terms he employs; and he was especially influenced by, and in turn himself influenced, the mathematical dimension of the spirit of modern science. Although he also wrote on physics and physiology, Descartes's scientific bent was primarily mathematical. His dream of a universal mathematics, which resulted in his development of analytic geometry with its reduction of space to number, prepared the way for his reduction of matter to space or extension, which we will examine, and therefore also the reduction of matter to number. Where Bacon was inclined to be the metaphorical ant by neglecting rational theorizing, Descartes tended to be the spider, under-emphasizing empirical observation and experimentation. Under these influences but inspired by his own special genius, Descartes constructed the system by which he became the father of modern philosophy. All modern philosophy passes through Descartes, not only the Rationalism which he immediately began but also the Empiricism which will react against it and the Voluntarism which will attempt to reconcile their conflict.

8-1. *The Method*

The first matter to be settled is method. Like Bacon, Descartes was convinced that the traditional Aristotelian logic which he had been taught in school was inadequate as a method of demonstration; at best it was good only for pedagogical purposes, for displaying what had already been demonstrated to be true. Unlike Bacon, however, Descartes found the key to his new method in the procedures of mathematics rather than in those of the empirical sciences. In reviewing the history of human thought Descartes became convinced that certainty is to be found only in mathematics, yet he bemoaned the fact that such mathematical certainty had never yet been used as a foundation for a complete system of knowledge. To use the rigor of mathematical reasoning as a foundation for a philosophical edifice was Descartes's dream and the key to his positive method.

This new method as Descartes states it in Part II of his *Discourse on Method* consists of four rules. The first rule is "to accept nothing as true which I did not clearly recognize to be so . . . to accept . . . nothing more than what was presented to my mind so clearly and distinctly that I could have no occasion to doubt it." The second is "to divide up each of the difficulties which I examined into as many parts as possible. . . ." This second rule may be called the principle of division or analysis. The third is "to carry on my reflections in due order, commencing with objects that were the most simple and easy to understand, in order to rise little by little, or by degrees, to knowledge of the most complex, assuming an order, even if a fictitious one, among those which do not follow a natural sequence relatively to one another." This rule we may call the principle of order, in which the order is from simple to complex; note how Descartes here parts company with Bacon in imposing upon the facts a theoretical order, if only as a working hypothesis. The fourth and last rule is "in all cases to make enumerations so complete and reviews so general that I should be certain of having omitted nothing." This we may call the principle of review, a counsel of perfection, as Descartes expresses it, which is something everyone tries to use.

Of these four rules the first we will see to be the most important and influential one. In fact it is the most fundamental element in the story of Continental Rationalism; therefore it should be examined in some detail. As Descartes states the rule, it is from one point of view nothing more than a tautology. "To accept . . . nothing more than what was presented to my mind so clearly and distinctly that I could have no occasion to doubt it" is simply to accept only what one cannot doubt, or to accept only what one must accept. As a tautology, however, this rule is still valuable as a counsel "to avoid precipitation and prejudice in judgments."

More important in the rule is the expression "clearly and distinctly," by virtue of which this first rule has rightly been named the principle of clarity and distinctness. What does Descartes mean by *clarity* and *distinctness?* In Principle XLV of his *Principles of Philosophy* Descartes defines his terms: "I term that clear which is present and apparent to an attentive mind. . . . But the distinct is that which is so precise and *different from*[1] all other objects that it contains within itself nothing but what is clear." The most important idea, as we shall see increasingly, is that of distinctness, the idea that a thing is so sharply marked off from all other things that it contains nothing of them within itself. If we add this definition of distinctness to Descartes's first rule, we can see that he vows to accept nothing as true unless it is so sharply marked off from all other things that it contains nothing of them within itself. The true and therefore the real consist of things which are sharply cut off from each other. It is not too early to begin to ask whether this is indeed true. Are all true ideas and true realities sharply marked off from all other things? What about time, for example? Can a moment of time be adequately thought of as sharply cut off from all other moments of time? Or what about causation? Is an effect absolutely distinct from its cause? Or finally, what about being or reality itself? What is there from which the whole of being can be sharply cut off? Nothing at all, but then there is nothing from which being is distinct, so being is not distinct from anything. You may recall that this was one of the reasons for Anaximander's notion of being as the *apeiron,* as indeterminate, indefinite, or indistinct (Ch. 1-1). Before long we will begin to see the consequences of Descartes's adoption of this rule of distinctness in the content of his philosophy and the philosophies of his followers.

The general method established by these four rules is that of analysis, intuition, and deduction. When faced with a problem—above all, of course, the problem of the nature of the reality man inhabits—we must first divide that problem into distinct parts and arrange them in an order beginning with what is logically primitive or axiomatic (with what is "most simple and easy to understand") and ending with what is logically derivative or in need of demonstration, with what is complex. Like the mathematician, we begin with axioms and deduce theorems; however, unlike the mathematician of today, we must first use a process of skeptical analysis to make absolutely sure that our axioms are self-evidently and indubitably true rather than just arbitrarily postulated. At each point in the deduction the proof of the theorem must be intuited as being just as self-evident as the original axiom. If *A* is self-evidently true, and if the implication of *B* by *A* is self-evidently true, then *B* is self-evidently true. This is, in part, Descartes's dream of a universal mathematics, and it is what most obviously makes him the founder of the movement of Continental Rationalism.

8-2. *Application of the Method*

The application of Descartes's method falls into two stages, a negative and a positive one, because of the method itself. Since the first rule is to accept nothing except what is so clear and distinct that it cannot be doubted, we must first consider all beliefs to see which must be skeptically rejected as dubitable. Furthermore, the second and third rules say that a problem must be broken up into parts and the parts arranged in a deductive order beginning with what is axiomatically true, so of course one must first reject all beliefs which are not axiomatically true but which need proof. So Descartes begins the application of his method, in the first *Meditation* and in Part III of the *Discourse on Method,* with a skepticism which starts mildly with doubt about things which do frequently deceive us and culminates in the hypothesis of an evil genius or devil who employs his whole energy in rendering false every last belief. It is very important here not to conclude that Descartes ever actually thought that all these beliefs are false—that there is no good God, that Descartes has no body, etc.—for then we might charge Descartes with inconsistency when he later incorporates these beliefs into his philosophy. In this skeptical, negative stage Descartes is *not* saying that all these beliefs are false; he is saying rather that they are all *dubitable,* and hence unfit to be his axiomatic starting point. He is saying that while they may well in fact be true, they must be *proven* true since they are not, by themselves, so clear and distinct that he cannot doubt them. Thus Descartes's skepticism is a methodological rather than a doctrinal one; it is skepticism as a tool for the establishment of a nonskeptical philosophy.

8-2.1. *The Self*

The positive stage of the application of the method, the stage of the construction of a system of philosophy, begins when Descartes discovers one belief which is self-evidently or indubitably true, which is so clear and distinct that he cannot doubt it. This discovery is the famous *"Cogito, ergo sum," "Je pense, donc je suis,"* "I think, therefore I am." If an evil genius deceives Descartes in every one of his beliefs, then it necessarily follows that he must exist just in order to be deceived, he says in his second *Meditation.* Or, as he puts it in Part IV of his *Discourse:* "Whilst I thus wished to think all things false, it was absolutely essential that the 'I' who thought this should be somewhat." If you should object that it is possible to doubt even that you exist, Descartes would reply that you must exist just in order to exercise that doubt since that doubt is itself a certainty. And if you should rejoin that you can even doubt that you doubt that you exist, and doubt that you doubt that you doubt that you exist, Descartes would reply that, since at each point you are affirming that you are doubting, that bit of doubting must be a certainty, and hence also you must be a certainty to perform that bit of doubting. The doubting process clearly need not terminate once and for all at some one particular doubt. Rather an endless series of doubts posits the doubt and the doubter *at each and every stage* in the series. For this reason the *"cogito"* might better be a *"dubito,"* "I doubt, therefore I am." The point is that an affirmation of complete skepticism is self-refuting because the affirmation of anything, even of complete skepticism, is after all necessarily an *affirmation of something,* even if it is only of complete skepticism. "I am, I exist, is necessarily true *each time that I pronounce it."*[2]

This *"Cogito, ergo sum "* is not an inference or argument in spite of the suggestion of the word "therefore." If it were an inference, the "I am" would be the conclusion and the "I think" would be a premise, and the validity of the inference would require another, tacit, premise such as "All thinking things exist." But this premise is even more dubitable than the conclusion that "I exist" since it generalizes to *all* thinking things. If this premise were established as the conclusion of an inference, some *other* premise would have to be established, and so on. Every inference must have an unprovable starting point or premise, and if the conclusion of the inference is to be true as well as valid, that premise must be true even though unprovable. Precisely such an unprovable yet self-evidently true starting point is what Descartes has been seeking in his skepticism and which he thinks he has found in his *cogito.* The same was true of Plato in his dialectic (Ch. 3.1-2) and of Aristotle in his ontology or first philosophy (Ch. 4-5), though their indubitable first principle was not the self.

The *cogito* is thus an axiom or necessary proposition rather than an inference. It is not a *logically* necessary proposition, however, since the definition or meaning of "thinking" does not entail the concept of existence, as the meaning of "square" does entail that of rectangle. In fact, as we saw in the discussion of the ontological argument for the existence of God (Ch. 6-1), it is very questionable that *real, extra-judgmental* existence is entailed in the meaning of any concept at all. In any case we can see that *thinking* does not entail existence, that the proposition, "Thinking does not exist," is not logically self-contradictory, no matter how egregious it may be practically. No, the necessity of the *cogito* is rather a *practical* or *existential* necessity, and Descartes seems to agree with this point when he says, "I exist is necessarily true *each time that I pronounce it . . . or mentally conceive it.*"[3] The proposition, "I do not exist," contains no internal, logical contradiction; there is rather a practical or existential contradiction between the proposition and the fact of its assertion and asserter. The proposition does not contradict itself; the proposition contradicts, speaks against, the *proposer* of the proposition. While it could possibly be true with logical consistency that you do not think or that you do not exist, you cannot possibly *assert* or *believe* that it is true with practical or existential consistency. If you really did not exist and think, then you certainly could not assert that you do not exist and think, nor assert anything at all. If, therefore, you assert or believe anything at all, you must assert or believe that you exist and think in order to make the assertion or have the belief. This is the true meaning and force of Descartes's *cogito*.

Descartes's way of putting this account of the meaning and force of the *cogito* is to say that it is "clear and distinct," and in so doing he reaffirms and generalizes his first rule:

> I am certain that I am a thing which thinks; but do I not then likewise know what is requisite to render me certain of a truth? Certainly in this first knowledge there is nothing that assures me of its truth, excepting the clear and distinct perception of that which I state, which would not indeed suffice to assure me that what I say is true, if it could ever happen that a thing which I conceived so clearly and distinctly could be false; and accordingly it seems to me that already I can establish as a general rule that all things which I perceive very clearly and very distinctly are true.[4]

Descartes has already told us what he means by "clear and distinct" (p. 179), but he does not say what he means by "very." In the light of the discussion of the *cogito*, however, we can see that *"very* clear and distinct" means necessary or inescapable, at least practically or existentially if not logically or semantically. And since Descartes has generalized this rule of clarity and distinctness, we may formulate the following general rule: *Accept all and only those propositions whose contradictories contradict either themselves or yourself.* This rule provides a clear indication of the logical and rationalistic motif of Descartes's thought. It clearly presupposes the truth of the principle of noncontradiction—or perhaps it is rather Descartes's psychological and decisional way of putting the principle of noncontradiction, for he does not establish that principle as an explicit and formal part of his procedure. Such a rule also reinforces our earlier prediction that the items in Descartes's world will be absolutely distinct from and independent of each other, for the truth of a necessary proposition—one which is true simply because of the meanings of its own terms—is absolutely distinct from and independent of every other consideration. That this prediction does come true will be evident later.

I think, therefore I exist. But what am I? What is the nature of the self whose existence has been established? I am a thinking thing, Descartes replies, since it is my thinking that is indubitable. This is thinking in the broad sense of consciousness, however, not just cerebration. "What is a thing which thinks? It is a thing which doubts, understands, affirms, denies, wills, refuses, which also imagines and feels."[5] Consciousness is the only property which I can now know I possess since it is the only property the assertion of which is practically or existentially necessary or indubitable.

> I am, I exist, that is certain. But how often? Just when I think; for it might possibly be the case if I ceased entirely to think, that I should likewise cease altogether to exist. I do not now admit anything which is not necessarily true: to speak accurately I am not more than a thing which thinks. . . .[6]

One can imagine, as John Locke did, Descartes's drowsy ego nodding frantically to keep itself in existence. But if Descartes's ego has at this point no other property than consciousness, it is at least also a *thing* or *substance* which has that property. Some commentators have objected that the thinking does not necessarily involve any underlying substance or thing to do the thinking, that there might perfectly well be a thinking without a thinker, an action without an agent. Indeed, some commentators have gone even further to suggest that developments in modern science show that this is actually the case, that the fundamental realities are actions or events and that substances or things are simply derivative constellations of these actions. For Descartes, however, this is inconceivable; for him the idea that thinking requires a thinker, a thing or substance which thinks, is so self-evident that he never even discusses the issue. It was no more possible for him to have a predicate without a subject in Latin or in French than it is for us to do so in English. This fact expresses Descartes's pervasive rationalism, his belief that the structure of thought reflects the structure of reality.

8-2.2. *God*

The second step in Descartes's construction of a philosophical system by means of his method is the discovery of God. God's existence is concluded from three different arguments.

The first argument, which he presents in the middle of *Meditation* III and in Part IV of the *Discourse,* consists in inferring the existence of God as the necessary cause of Descartes's idea of Him. The first premise of the argument is the principle of sufficient reason or law of causation.

> Now it is manifest by the natural light that there must be at least as much reality in the efficient and total cause as in its effect. For, pray, whence can the effect derive its reality, if not from its cause? . . . And from this it follows, not only that something cannot proceed from nothing, but likewise that what is more perfect—that is to say, which has more reality within itself—cannot proceed from the less perfect.[7]

"The natural light," "the light of nature," or "the light of reason" is one of the concepts which Descartes inherited from medieval philosophy; it means man's natural power of reason for gaining certain knowledge of necessarily true first principles. This "natural light" and the principle of sufficient reason which it reveals are not officially and formally established by Descartes, so from this point of view they appear to be unwarranted, ad hoc assumptions. Yet so to regard them would be a mistake, for "the natural light" is at least functionally identical with the power of grasping something so clearly and distinctly that it cannot be doubted, a principle which Descartes formally and officially established in his first rule and which he has explicitly manifested in his *cogito*. Indeed, we can demonstrate that this principle of sufficient reason is as clear and distinct and as necessarily true as the *cogito*, for its contradictory is self-contradictory, even logically or semantically self-contradictory, since the meaning of "effect" entails the concept of cause.

This *ex nihilo nihil fit* principle "is not only evidently true of those effects which possess actual or formal reality, but also of the ideas in which we consider merely what is termed objective reality."[8] Here again Descartes uses medieval terms. By "actual or formal" he means what "objective" means today, that is real, extra-mental reality; and by "objective" he means what "subjective," means today, what is thrown *(iacere)* before *(ob)* the mind. Even though the pink elephants which the drunk sees do not exist apart from his mind, they do have a mental or "objective" reality as objects before his mind. Any characteristic which has "objective" reality as an object before the mind may also have "actual" reality in the extra-mental world, and this "actual" reality may be either "formal" or literal or else "eminent" or subsumed at a higher level. For example, the characteristic of being a vegetable exists objectively in the idea of it, actually and formally in vegetables, and actually and eminently in human beings who, while they are not formally or literally vegetables, do possess vegetable characteristics subsumed in a higher form.

> If the objective reality of any one of my ideas is of such a nature as clearly to make me recognize that it is not in me either formally or eminently, and that consequently I cannot myself be the cause of it, it follows of necessity that I am not alone in the world, but that there is another being which exists, or which is the cause of this idea.[9]

One such idea does exist, the idea of God, and the recognition of the existence of this idea as one whose reality is such that Descartes could not have caused it is the second premise in the first argument for the existence of God. The reason that I could not be the cause of my idea of God is that it is of an infinite and perfect being while I am finite and imperfect. Since the idea of God contains infinity and perfection objectively or by representation, the cause of that idea must also contain infinity and perfection, for otherwise more would be coming from less and hence something from nothing. A cause which contains infinity and perfection is by that fact an infinite and perfect being, and this is just exactly God. Hence the idea of God can only have been caused by God. So the conclusion follows that God exists.

One way of criticizing this argument is to insist that I myself can indeed be the cause of the idea of God, even though I am finite and imperfect, since as finite I can cause the idea of a finite being and as negative I can negate that idea to produce the idea of an infinite being (nonfinite), and since as imperfect I can cause the idea of an imperfect being and as negative I can negate that idea to produce the idea of a perfect being (not imperfect).

Descartes counters this criticism by insisting, in agreement with Plato, that a recognition of something as finite and imperfect presupposes an idea of infinity and perfection. "For how should it be possible that I should know . . . that I am not quite perfect, unless I had within me some idea of a Being more perfect than myself, in comparison with which I should recognize the deficiencies of my nature?"[10] If the critic now goes a step further to state that he himself has no idea of an infinite and perfect being, then what can his statement itself be about? If the critic really has no notion whatsoever of an infinite and perfect being, then what is he talking about when he claims that the idea of God is not present in his mind and when he urges that Descartes has not proven the existence of God? And if the critic, now more cautious, refuses to make any such claim and contents himself with the assertion that the word "God" brings nothing whatever to his mind, then Descartes can reply that he has the idea of God in *his* mind and that one instance of the effect is sufficient to require the cause. Whether or not anyone else has an idea of God, therefore, God must exist to be the cause of Descartes's idea of Him. Finally, if the critic were to object that not even Descartes has an idea of God as an infinite and perfect being, the critic would have to be ignored since his existence has not yet been recognized in Descartes's philosophy.

A more telling objection is that the validity of Descartes's argument logically requires that Descartes's idea of God be God Himself. One of the premises in the argument is that the idea of God contains the properties of infinity and perfection, but this premise can only mean that the idea of God is itself an infinite and perfect being and is therefore itself God. If the idea of God is not itself an infinite and perfect being, then its cause need not be infinite and perfect, in which case the conclusion of God's existence does not follow. If on the other hand the conclusion of the existence of an infinite and perfect cause does logically follow, then its effect must be an infinite and perfect being; the idea of God must be God. So Descartes's first argument proves either too little or too much.

The second argument for the existence of God, which Descartes presents in the latter part of the third *Meditation* and in a very condensed form in Part IV of the *Discourse,* has two stages. The first stage of the argument claims that God must exist as the ultimate cause of the *origin* of myself (Descartes). If I had originated myself I would have made myself perfect, and since I am certainly not perfect I cannot be the author of my own existence. Moreover, Descartes seems rather unclearly to suggest, if any one of my ancestors had originated himself he too would have made himself perfect. Hence no human being (if there are any human beings other than Descartes) can have originated himself, so we must look for the origin of our existence in God. Descartes seems not to put much stock in this first stage of his argument, and rightly so, since at most it implies only the existence of some being more powerful than man, not an infinitely powerful and perfect being.

The second stage in the argument concludes that God must exist as the cause of the continuation of myself over time, granting that I have once been brought into existence in the first place, on the ground that no antecedent moment of my life is a sufficient cause for the next. Descartes writes:

> For all the course of my life may be divided into an infinite number of parts, none of which is in any way dependent on the other, and thus from the fact that I was in existence a short time ago it does not follow that I must be in existence now, unless some cause at this instant, so to speak, produces me anew, that is to say, conserves me.[11]

When confronted with the objection that this cause of the continuation of my existence could be some being other than God, say my parents, Descartes reverts to his first argument by replying that any such other cause would have to be a thinking being (since I, the effect, am a thinking being) and would thus have to have the idea of God, or in any event that at least Descartes himself has the idea of God, and this idea of God must have been caused, according to the first argument, by God Himself. Hence this second ar-ument, in both its stages, necessarily involves the first argument.

What is especially important and interesting in this second stage of the second argument is the atomizing of time, change, and causation which Descartes effects in his premise. One's life, and presumably any other enduring thing that happens to be, may be divided into an infinite number of parts, we saw him say; and no one of these parts is in any way dependent upon or necessarily connected with any other.

> It is as a matter of fact perfectly clear and evident to all those who consider with attention the nature of time that, in order to be conserved in each moment in which it endures, a substance has need of the same power and action as would be necessary to produce and create it anew, supposing it did not yet exist; so that the light of nature shows us that the distinction between creation and conservation is solely a distinction of the reason [merely mental].[12]

Here we are reminded of ancient Zeno's paradoxes and their conclusion that one can never get from one point of a continuum, temporal or spatial, to another point because another point, an infinity of points, is always in between. This similarity is not superficial, for Descartes agrees with Zeno that whatever is mentally distinguishable is really distinct. Any continuum, for example, any moment of time no matter how short, is mentally divisible into shorter moments, so any moment, no matter how short, must be really divided into shorter moments, according to Zeno and Descartes. Thus there can be no least moments of time; the least must be the infinitesimal. This concept reflects Descartes's rationalism, his belief that the real corresponds to the rational.

This atomizing of time provides us with the first confirmation of our prediction that atomism would follow from Descartes's rule of clarity and distinctness. Since his rule says that he will accept as true only what is clear and distinct, and since to be distinct means to be sharply distinct from and cut off from all other things, then it follows that in order for a part of time, or of any other continuum, to be accepted as true it must be clearly distinct from and thus in no way dependent on any other part of that continuum. Therefore, "All the course of my life may be divided into an infinite number of parts, none of which is *in any way* dependent on the other."[13] Each part must contain within itself only what is clear, only what belongs to itself. "Everything is just itself and not another thing," to quote the motto of Bishop Samuel Butler. From one point of view this motto is tautologically true, yet if it means that no event can have any dependency upon or connection with any other event, then God is not only the ultimate cause but the only cause. Descartes rejects this conclusion, but it will be drawn by the Occasionalists who followed him as implicit in and demanded by his principles (Ch. 9-2).

The third and last argument for the existence of God, which Descartes presents in the early part of the fifth *Meditation* and in Part IV of the *Discourse*, is the ontological argument which was discussed in connection with Anselm. Descartes writes:

> On reverting to the examination of the idea which I had of a Perfect Being, I found that in this case existence was implied in it in the same manner in which the equality of its three angles to two right angles is implied in the idea of a triangle. . . . Consequently it is at least as certain that God, who is a Being so perfect, is, or exists, as any demonstration of geometry can possibly be.[14]

In short, God, a Perfect Being, who lacked real existence, would just not be a Perfect Being, would just not be God. This third, ontological argument must not be confused with Descartes's first, causal argument. While both of these arguments, unlike the second argument, proceed from the idea of God, the first one concludes that the existence of God is the cause of that idea while the third one affirms that the existence of God is semantically contained and logically implied in that idea. Descartes also presents a revised version of Anselm's reply to Gaunilo's charge that the validity of this ontological argument would imply that a perfect island must exist. "Although I cannot really conceive of . . . a mountain without a valley, . . . it does not follow that there is such a mountain in the world. . . . [But] from the fact that I cannot conceive God without existence, it follows that existence is inseparable from Him, and hence that He really exists."[15] Thus the idea of God is the only idea which entails actual existence.

The essential and recurrent core of the many criticisms of the ontological argument was presented in connection with Anselm's argument. Even if the idea of existence is contained in the very idea of God, it is still the *idea* of existence rather than real, extramental existence. If one's concept of God semantically contains the note of His real existence, why then of course one cannot conceive of God as really nonexistent. As Descartes puts it, "it is not within my power to think of God without existence (that is of a supremely perfect Being devoid of a supreme perfection). . . ."[16] But, the critic insists, it does not necessarily follow that anything outside our minds corresponds to this concept, for, as Descartes himself goes on to say, "thought does not impose any necessity upon things."

Thus the second step is completed in Descartes's reconstruction of the world; I am now certain that there is a God as well as myself. Before continuing with the third and last stage in this reconstruction, however, we must digress to consider briefly the notorious so-called circle in Descartes's argument. This apparent circle is neatly stated by a contemporary of Descartes, Antoine Arnauld, in his *Objections* to (and published with) Descartes's *Meditations:*

> . . . I have . . . an uncertainty as to how a circular reasoning is to be avoided in saying: the only secure reason we have for believing that what we clearly and distinctly perceive is true, is the fact that God exists. But we can be sure that God exists, only because we clearly and evidently perceive that; therefore prior to being certain that God exists, we should be certain that whatever we clearly and evidently perceive is true.[17]

This is indeed a genuine problem because Descartes does many times assert (here at the close of the fifth *Meditation*) that

"before I knew Him [God], I could not have a perfect knowledge of any other thing," and yet he claimed that he cannot
know God until after he has known several other things, especially his four rules and the *cogito*. But Descartes's reply to
Arnauld's objection removes this apparent circle in a very
simple way:

> I distinguished those matters that in actual truth we clearly perceive
> from those we remember to have formerly perceived. For first, we
> are sure that God exists because we have attended to the proofs
> that establish this fact; but afterwards it is enough for us to remem-
> ber that we have perceived something clearly, in order to be sure
> that it is true; but this would not suffice, unless we knew that God
> existed and that he did not deceive us.[18]

In other words, God comes first only as the guarantor of the
veracity of our *memory* of previous demonstrations; in the
logical order of demonstration He still comes last so far as the
point we have now reached is concerned, and thus there is no
logical circle.

At a deeper level, however, God guarantees not only the
reliability of our memory but also that the validity of Descartes's
method will correspond to the truth of extra-mental reality. Descartes's reiteration that God guarantees our memory of clear and
distinct perceptions means that God guarantees that what we
must *believe* to be true must actually *be* true of *extra-mental*
reality. The acceptance and rigorous application of the four
rules does guarantee that all the conclusions reached thereby
will be logically valid and even psychologically indubitable. But
this guarantee still leaves the gnawing worry that reality itself
may fail to comply with the way in which we must indubitably
understand it. This worry may be removed, however, if we can
assure ourselves that our method must necessarily reflect the
way reality itself is constructed. Such an assurance can obviously
not come from within the method itself nor from extra-mental
reality itself, for the extra-mental veracity of that method is
exactly what needs support. Hence the guarantor of the method
must be something which is independent both of the method
and the independent world; and what could be more indepen-

dent and real than God Himself, the ultimate reality and cause of all things? Since God is both the cause of all things and perfectly good, it necessarily follows that He would not have made our minds in such a way that they must accept something as indubitably true unless it is in fact really true. This point will come out more explicitly in the third and last stage of Descartes's reconstruction of reality, the demonstration of the existence of the physical world. Thus to say that before I knew God I could not have a perfect knowledge of anything also means that before we know that an omnipotent and perfectly good God exists, we cannot be certain that our subjectively necessary way of understanding things corresponds with the structure of independent reality. God guarantees the correspondence of reason and reality that is essential to rationalism. In so doing He reassures Descartes of the reality of the external world in a way which is analogous to and historically derived from the reassurance of the reality of nature granted to the medieval philosophers by their God.

8-2.3. *Matter*

"Nothing further now remains but to inquire whether material things exist"; thus Descartes begins his sixth and last *Meditation*. His argument that they do indeed exist is the same in structure as his first argument for the existence of God.

> If the objective reality of any one of my ideas is of such a nature as clearly to make me recognize that it is not in me either formally or eminently, and that consequently I cannot myself be the cause of it, it follows of necessity . . . that there is another being . . . which is the cause of this idea.[19]

Just as the idea which was the starting point of his first argument for the existence of God was the idea of God, so also now the idea whose presence in Descartes's mind requires the existence of the physical world is precisely the idea of the physical world. Just as God must exist to be the cause of Descartes's idea of Him because Descartes himself, as a finite and imperfect being, does not contain the infinity and perfection inherent in the idea of God, so also there must now really exist a material world to be the cause of Descartes's idea of it because Descartes himself, as a thinking being, does not contain the reality presented in the idea of the material world.

This point is established in the latter part of the second *Meditation* in Descartes's analysis of the piece of bee's wax. The very essence of matter must be that in it which abides through all change. But what in the piece of wax remains constant throughout the loss of its honey sweetness, flowery odor, color, shape, size, temperature, and so on? Only its extendedness, only the fact that it is an extended or spatial thing, so the idea of matter is essentially the idea of extension. Thus Descartes follows Democritus, Galileo, and Hobbes in holding that material things can be known to possess only the primary or quantitative qualities; the secondary or sensible qualities are in the mind. Furthermore, since extension or space is identical with matter, Descartes agrees with Empedocles and Anaxagoras that there cannot be any empty space, so the motion of one thing requires the motion of all other things, much as the entry of a person through the front door of a packed bus requires the simultaneous exit of somebody else through the back door. Since matter is extension, since I (Descartes) am only a thinking being, and since thought does not contain extension either formally (literally) or eminently (subsumed in a higher form), it follows that I cannot be the cause of my idea of the material world. The same conclusion also follows, Descartes points out, from the fact that the idea of the material world often comes to me against my will. Having been brought up on Freud, you may at this point object that the idea of the material world could very well be caused by one's own mind involuntarily and even unconsciously. Although this may be true of you, however, it cannot be true of Descartes, of the mind he established in the *cogito,* for that mind is only a consciousness. Since the only established volition is a conscious one and since the idea of the material world sometimes enters the mind contrary to that conscious volition, it follows that the mind itself is not the cause of its idea of the material world.

Hence the cause of the idea of the physical world must be something outside the mind. But why couldn't this something be "God Himself, or some creature more noble than [the] body in which the same is contained eminently"?[20] Because, Descartes argues,

Since God is no deceiver, it is very manifest that He does not communicate to me these ideas immediately and by Himself, nor yet by the intervention of some creature in which their reality is not formally, but only eminently, contained. For since He has given me no faculty to recognize that this is the case, but, on the other hand, a very great inclination to believe that they are conveyed to me by corporeal objects, I do not see how He could be defended from the accusation of deceit if these ideas were produced by causes other than corporeal objects. Hence we must allow that corporeal things exist.[21]

Note that the starting point of the argument has shifted from the *idea of* material objects, as something merely present in and contemplated by the mind, to the *belief in* the real, extra-mental existence of material objects. While God as an infinite being could perfectly well produce in my mind the idea of material things without there really being any, as a perfect and, therefore, undeceiving being He could not make me have to believe in the real, extra-mental existence of material things unless they existed, for if He were to do this, He would be compelling me to believe a falsehood and thus deceiving me. Is it indeed the case that one cannot help but believe that material things really exist? To this question Descartes answers, "Yes," but we shall later see Berkeley answer the same question, "No" (Ch. 10-2.2). Even supposing that one cannot help but believe that material things—in so far as they are extended—really exist outside the mind, does it follow that they do in fact exist merely because we have to believe that they do? Yes, Descartes replies, because God guarantees that the structure of reality must correspond to the structure of the mind.

8-3. *The Resulting World Picture*

The world Descartes has reconstructed consists of his self or mind as a thinking thing and two things outside his mind: God as infinite being and matter as finite extended being. Yet the latter two realities, God and matter, sometimes seem to be more in the mind than outside it. We have already seen that the validity of Descartes's first argument for existence of God requires that God be identified with Descartes's mental idea of Him, and the same thing seems to be true of matter. The matter whose existence Descartes establishes is pure extension, the object of geometry; and this seems to exist only in the mind. From this point of view, therefore, Descartes really establishes only the existence of a certain abstract concept or idea rather than the existence of something quite independent of the mind. This suspicion is supported by the fact that the analytic geometry which Descartes discovered consists essentially in the reduction of extension to number, for, unless we are Pythagoreans, we moderns are even less inclined to think that numbers have independent, extra-mental existence than that extension does. This tendency to merge the objective and extra-mental with the subjective and mental, which lies at the heart of Descartes's rationalism, is the opposite and introverted side of the extroverted holism and hylozoism of the ancient Cosmological philosophers. It is also the beginning of subjectivism, the statement of the second stage in the three-stage sequence, which will become the essence of modern philosophy.

Descartes's view of the world also includes human minds other than his own, but he never attempts to demonstrate their existence. This deficiency may result from the fact that his usual method of demonstration (that something exists as the cause of the idea of it) would not work with other human minds since the reality contained in Descartes's ideas of them is sufficiently finite and imperfect that Descartes's own mind could be the cause of those ideas, unless, as in his clincher in the argument for the existence of matter, Descartes holds that God created him so that he cannot help but believe that other human minds really exist outside his own mind and that God would be deceiving him unless this belief were true. This problem of the existence of other finite minds is one which will concern the British Empiricists and many of their twentieth century followers. The material world likewise seems to consist of only one substance, extension; at least Descartes gives no official reason for believing that there is more than one material substance, and his identification of matter with extension and his denial of empty space also seemingly make all bodies merge into one. Thus only three individual beings seem logically to exist in Descartes's official world—God, self, and matter—and all of them seem logically to be of the nature of the self or mind. Indeed, these three beings seem at times to merge into only one being, as we shall see shortly.

The theory of truth and error presented in the fourth *Meditation,* a digression from Descartes's systematic reconstruction of the world, makes everything that comes from God good and true because God is not a deceiver. Hence we have truth and goodness in so far as we participate in God or being, and we err and sin only in so far as we do not participate in God or being, only in so far as we participate in nonbeing. Error—the form of evil with which Descartes is primarily concerned in the construction of his philosophy—is caused by the will's act of judgment overshooting the understanding's clear and distinct ideas. The understanding is weak and limited in the extent of its clear and distinct ideas, Descartes maintains, while the will is unlimited and infinite, and as pure will it is identical with the infinite will of God. Thus somewhat paradoxically the infinite and divine in us is the source of error, but only because it is conjoined in us with a principle of limitation and negativity, the understanding. Error can be avoided only by restraining the will to assent only to those ideas which are clear and distinct. But what in us can thus restrain the will, another and higher will? Clear and distinct ideas restrain the will in the sense of forcing the will to assent to them; this is one of the meanings of Descartes's first rule, to accept only "what was presented to my mind so clearly and distinctly that I could have no occasion to doubt it,"[22] which means that the will *must* accept ideas which are clear and distinct. But what is to restrain the will from assenting also to ideas which are not clear and distinct? Such restraint would seem to require another and higher will, but Descartes does not explicitly discuss or avoid this problem.

From its sharp division of all nondivine reality into thought and extension, Descartes's philosophy originates the mind-body problem, a problem of the nature of the relation between the mind and the body, which will plague subsequent Continental Rationalism. For Descartes the mind is a substance whose nature is thought, and the body is another substance whose nature is extension. Each is conceived so clearly and distinctly from the other that they can have no real connection. Each is conceived separately and can exist separately. Yet experience tells us that mind and body interact with each other, for when I will my finger to wiggle it wiggles, and when I receive a blow, I feel pain. But how can two absolutely separate substances possibly interact? Descartes's answer to this logical question is a physiological theory. The pineal gland in the center of the brain is the seat of the mind through which flow all the neural impulses from and to all the various parts of the body. Descartes conceives of these impulses as small bodies and calls them animal spirits. As these animal spirits pass through the pineal gland they sometimes affect the mind, as in the experience of bodily pain, although at other times, as in dreamless sleep, they do not; and likewise the mind sometimes affects them, as in conscious volition, although in unconscious and autonomic bodily activity it does not. When this theory was criticized on the ground that it violates the law of the conservation of energy, since energy would be passing out of and into the physical system, Descartes replied that the mind does not inject additional energy into the physical system but only redirects the energy already there in the animal spirits—an unsatisfying reply since such redirection would surely itself require energy.

Not the inaccuracy of Descartes's physiology but the invalidity of his logic should be the subject of our criticism, however. How can that which is unextended, the mind, occupy a place, whether that place is in the pineal gland or elsewhere? If it occupies only an extensionless, geometrical point, on the other hand, how can it make contact with an extended body to influence it? And how can an extended body ever make any impression upon an unextended thought? Two things which are so absolutely different that they have nothing to do with each other can, of course, have nothing to do with each other. "East is east and west is west, and never the twain shall meet." Descartes's problem is not the lack of adequate empirical facts. His problem is that he has defined "mind" and "body" in such opposition to each other that it is logically impossible for them to interact. The reason that he has so defined them is in order to have an apodictic demonstration of the existence of each. The *cogito* establishes one's own existence only by restricting it to consciousness; the doubting of everything makes clear and distinct only that an unextended thought exists. The proof that it must be a real material world rather than one's own mind which is the cause of one's idea of the material world requires that matter be something in no way characteristic of mind, for if it were, the mind could construct its idea of the material world without there having to be any material world at all. So matter is unthinking extension whereas mind is unextended thought. Hence Descartes's mind-body problem follows logically from the application of his method. In this method the first rule and especially the principle of distinctness are the determining factors. Only what is distinct is true and real, and the distinct is that which is distinct *from* all other things, that which contains within itself nothing of anything else. Hence if mind and body are to be true and real, each must be clearly and distinctly separated from the other and hence contain nothing of the other in itself. But if this be true, they can have no possible relation to each other.

The impossibility of mind-body interaction produces an even more serious problem, however: the logical impossibility of knowing that any bodies or material things even exist at all. We know that material things exist, according to Descartes, only because they act upon our minds to produce ideas of them in us. But if bodies cannot possibly act upon minds, then minds cannot possibly have any ideas of bodies or even know that there are such things as bodies, whether or not they act upon our minds. Either this conclusion is valid or else Descartes's argument for the existence of the material world is invalid. Thus Descartes's mind-body problem (and indirectly the principle of distinctness which lies behind it) is the source of the epistemological subjectivism or solipsism—only *(solus)* the self *(ipse)* exists—which will become the central feature of modern philosophy. If ideas are to be conceived as distinct, absolute entities, they cannot be produced by bodies and cannot inform us that bodies even exist.

8-4. Summary Analysis

Descartes's principle of distinctness has led to atomism. For anything to be true and real it must be absolutely distinct from all other things, both in its conception and in its existence, as we have seen. Yet from another and less obvious point of view Descartes's principle of distinctness leads paradoxically to monism. It does this indirectly, first, by means of the consequences of his atomism. Since Descartes draws from his principle of distinctness the atomistic conclusion that every spatial and temporal event "may be divided into an infinite number of parts, none of which is in any way dependent on the other,"[23] it follows that no finite thing can have any causal efficacy whatever, for causal efficacy necessarily involves just such dependency. It therefore follows that in Descartes's philosophy only one being possesses any power, activity, or efficacy, namely God. Thus Descartes's second argument for the existence of God proves too much—if it proves anything—for it proves not only that God is the cause of Descartes's existence but even that God is the only cause of anything, that there are no secondary causes. In the second place, Descartes's principle of distinctness leads to monism directly, just by virtue of what is involved in its very meaning. Since distinctness is a relation, for a thing to be distinct from something else is for it to be related to and dependent upon that something else as the term of its relation of distinctness. If each thing is "distinct-from-everything-else," then each thing contains "everything-else" within itself in one monistic whole. This paradoxical fact will culminate in the dialectic of Hegel (Ch. 12-3.2). Thus everything necessarily involves everything else, a form of monism: reality is a relational network of terms.

Both of these paths from the principle of distinctness to

monism are present when Descartes admits a monism of substance in Principle LI of his *Principles of Philosophy:* "And when we conceive of substance, we merely conceive an existent thing which requires nothing but itself in order to exist. To speak truth, nothing but God answers to this description . . . ." While Descartes's philosophy is explicitly and officially a dualism of mind and matter, it is thus also, because of his principle of distinctness, implicitly and at a deeper level a tension and vacillation between atomism and monism. Its monistic pole will be developed by the Occasionalists and professed by Spinoza to continue the story of Continental Rationalism, and while still paradoxically connected with the monistic pole, its atomistic pole will become the most obvious feature of the philosophy of Leibniz who will conclude the story of Continental Rationalism.

SUGGESTED READINGS

8-1. *Discourse on Method*. Pts. I–III.

8-2.1. *Meditations* I and II.

8-2.2. Ibid., III–V.

8-2.3. Ibid., VI.

8-3. "Objections and Replies to the Meditations," *Meditations.* 1st ed.
   Principles of Philosophy. Pt. I., Prins. LI–LIII; Pt. II, Prins. X–XI,
   XVI–XVIII, XXIII.
   Passions of the Soul. Pt. I., Art. XXXI and XXXIV.

For bibliographies, see:
Anscombe, E., and P. T. Geach, *Descartes: Philosophical Writings*.
   New York: Nelson, 1954. Pp. xlix–liv.
Smith, N. K. *New Studies in the Philosophy of Descartes*. London:
   Macmillan, 1952. Pp. vii–ix.

Chapter 9

Continental
Rationalism
After
Descartes

The immediate followers of Descartes, noting the centrality of his method and its special influence upon his metaphysics, tended to take exception either to Descartes's method or to his metaphysics; Pascal is the main example of the former alternative, and the so-called Occasionalists of the latter.

9-1. *Pascal*

Blaise Pascal (1623–1662) fits into the story of Continental Rationalism primarily as a reaction against it. Gifted in science and a genius in mathematics (he was one of the founders of probability theory and laid the foundation for calculus), Pascal had an unusually forceful religious experience which made him regard science and mathematics, whose core he saw in Descartes's method, as having only a very limited applicability and a very diminished importance. Pascal interprets the difficulties which we have seen in Descartes's metaphysics as conclusive proof of the inapplicability of the rationalistic method to the problems of metaphysics. The moral of Cartesian rationalism is for Pascal that reason inevitably becomes bogged down in paradoxes when it attempts to grasp ultimate reality—paradoxes like the absolute separation yet intimate interaction of mind and body and the radical atomism yet absolute monism of reality. Descartes's rationalistic method, which Pascal calls *l'esprit géometrique,* Pascal accepts as valid in, but restricted to, specific scientific disciplines, especially insofar as they are mathematical. Rationalism cannot validly be extended to the problems of metaphysics, to questions as to the nature of ultimate reality, both because it cannot establish its own premises and because it requires that its objects be finite, definite, and limited—that they be "clear and distinct"; whereas ultimate realities, God for example, are infinite and unlimited and by no means clear and distinct. Pascal also accepted as valid in a restricted domain the less rigorous method of the empirical sciences which he sometimes refers to as the reason of effects. This is the method of statistical probability rather than mathematical deduction, and by adding this method he reintroduces the inductive method of Bacon which was slighted by Descartes while retaining the deductive method stressed by Descartes and slighted by Bacon. In this sense Pascal is more nearly a bee than the antish Bacon and the spiderish Descartes.

Over and above the deductive and inductive methods of the head, however, Pascal places a method of the heart which he sometimes calls *l'esprit de finesse;* this last method alone is capable of dealing with ultimates, especially in theology, religion, and ethics. "The heart has its reasons, which reason does not know";[1] the demands of our hearts are just as real and worthy as the demands of our heads, and therefore the felt need for a belief may be a reason or justification for its truth. This method of the heart predominates in the famous "religious wager," which Pascal presents in *Thoughts,* No. 223, although the other two methods are also at work there. Since the head can neither prove nor disprove the existence of God, and since we have everything to gain by believing in Him and a great deal to lose by not doing so in case that belief is true, the heart's desire for such a gain is a legitimate reason for believing in God, a theory which anticipates the famed "will to believe" or "right to believe" of the nineteenth-twentieth century American psychologist-philosopher William James.

Therefore, what Pascal essentially represents is a protest against rationalism as a philosophical method, especially in the area of metaphysics and theology, and the substitution of the reason of the heart. Pascal's protest is a voice crying in the wilderness, however, for Descartes's rationalism had gained too much impetus to be stopped so quickly.

9-2. *The Occasionalists*

The philosophers called the Occasionalists accept Descartes's method, but they modify his metaphysics by explicating and endorsing certain implications of that method; thus they write the second chapter in the story of Continental Rationalism. This explication of the consequences implicit in Descartes's method by the Occasionalists has two main steps.

Arnold Geulincx (1624–1669) took the first of these two steps. Reflecting upon the mind-body problem in Descartes's philosophy, Geulincx concludes that, contrary to Descartes, there cannot be any interaction between mind and body, since neither contains the characteristic of the other, either formally or eminently. The mind contains no extension by which it could produce any bodily event, and body contains no thought by which it could produce any mental event. Furthermore, bodily events cannot be produced by other bodily events either, because, following Descartes, each bodily event is absolutely distinct from and in no way dependent upon any other bodily event. God, however, does contain the reality of material things eminently or in a pure, sublimated form (although of course not formally or literally); thus God is the cause of each and every bodily event. When the mind wills the finger to move, it is not the mind but God Who causes the finger to move, although God causes the finger to move upon the occasion of the mind's so willing it. This is the reason for the name "Occasionalism." Geulincx stops short of having God be the cause of *mental* events, however, and retains intra-mental causation; in so doing he does not go as far as Descartes seems to go in his second argument for the existence of God (Ch. 8-2.2).

Nicole Malebranche (1638–1715) took the second of the two

steps in drawing and accepting the consequences of Descartes's method. Malebranche agrees with Geulincx in denying all material causation, but he also denies all intra-mental causation as well. God is the cause of all mental events, of all ideas, as well as the cause of all physical events because, following the line Descartes laid down in his second argument for the existence of God, every mental event is just like every physical event in being absolutely distinct from and in no way dependent upon any other mental event. Thus there are no natural, finite causes at all; God is not only the first cause but the sole cause of all things, a conclusion we noted as latent in Descartes's philosophy. Our mental decisions and our bodily actions are never causes but only occasions for God's causation of other mental or bodily events. Since no bodily event can cause any mental event, moreover, no physical object can be the cause of anyone's mental idea of *it*—another conclusion which we saw as latent in Descartes's mind-body problem. Therefore your idea is not really an idea *of* a physical object, as you take it to be; rather your idea "of a physical object" is really your idea of *God's* idea of that physical object, since God is the cause of your idea. This point will be expanded by Berkeley in his development of British Empiricism (Ch. 10-2.2). Thus for Malebranche all knowledge is "vision in God." More than that, Malebranche therefore also maintains that all finite minds dwell in God's mind, that God is "the place of minds" just as space is the place of bodies; bodies still remain separate from God but only as impotent effects. This concept is almost the mental half of Spinoza's identification of nature with God, for Spinoza has only to locate bodies as well as minds within God and to make both merely expressions or modifications of God's being.

9-3. *Spinoza*

Baruch (Benedict) Spinoza (1632–1677) writes the third chapter of the story of Continental Rationalism and thus forms the link between Descartes and the Occasionalists, on the one hand, and Leibniz on the other. We will consider Spinoza's metaphysics, epistemology, and ethics or ethico-religion in that order.

9-3.1. *Metaphysics*

Spinoza's theory of reality is the core of his philosophical system; and it essentially consists of three basic concepts: substance, attribute, and mode.*

"Substance" is defined at the beginning of Part I of the *Ethics* as "that which is in itself and is conceived through itself; in other words, that the conception of which does not need the conception of another thing." This definition permits the existence of only one substance, a point which Descartes with his similar definition of substance grudgingly conceded (Ch. 8-4). Only one thing can exist which is not in anything else; a second thing which is not in anything else would at least have to be in reality or in the universe, in which case it would be in something else. And there can be only one thing which does not need anything else for its conception and being; a second thing which did not need anything else would need the first thing just for its secondness. This proof that there is only one substance is quite similar to Parmenides' proof that there is only one being and the medieval philosophers' proof that there is only one God—a point which hints at a conclusion to be drawn shortly, that substance is God. According to the definition of "Substance," it must be infinite, since it is not limited by or dependent upon anything else; and its infinity means both that it must have an infinity of attributes, since it is not limited in quality, and also that it must be eternal, since it is not limited by time.

Substance must, therefore, also be the first cause of all things and not caused by anything save itself. Spinoza says that Substance is the cause of itself *(causa sui)*, though this seems to involve the contradiction that it exists (as cause) before it exists (as effect). Substance is not an efficient or final cause, however, but a formal or logical cause of all things, their immanent generating formula. From Substance, Spinoza writes, "infinite things in infinite ways, that is to say, all things, have necessarily flowed, or continually flow by the same necessity, in the same way as it follows from the nature of a triangle, from eternity and to eternity, that its three angles are equal to two right angles."[2]

---

* These are presented mostly in the *Ethics* Pt. I.

The generation of all things from Substance is therefore like a mathematical system in which all the theorems are generated from only one primitive concept. Just as the theorems in a mathematical system must be implicit in the axioms and primitive concepts in order to be implied by them—a situation sometimes referred to as "the paradox of implication"—so also all things must already be implicitly contained in Substance in order to be formally caused by it. Here we should note the tension between complete pluralism and absolute monism which we saw in Descartes's system (Ch. 8-4): everything is implicitly one but explicitly many. The center of a circle is, on the one hand, a simple extensionless point and yet, on the other hand, the infinity of other points which the center as center implies and necessarily generates—the infinity of points on each of the infinity of radii leading to the infinity of points on the circumference. So also for Spinoza reality is both simply one as the substantial center of existence (*natura naturans,* nature naturing) and yet also the infinitely many things which it necessarily implies or formally causes (*natura naturata,* nature natured).

As has already been hinted, Substance is God, a term so central to and so often expressed in Spinoza's philosophy that Spinoza has been called the God-intoxicated philosopher. Just like the One of Plotinus, Spinoza's God emanates the world out of Himself without any freedom of choice. For the existence of this God Spinoza presents three arguments, or possibly four, depending upon how they are divided. One is the familiar ontological argument discussed in connection with Anselm and Descartes. A second is that God must exist because His nonexistence would have to have a cause and because nothing other than God is great enough to cause His nonexistence. A third argument is that the existence of any finite thing entails by the meaning of "finite" an infinite being or God. All of these arguments are logically circular; take the third one, for example, "If . . . there is nothing which necessarily exists excepting things finite, it follows that things finite are more powerful than *the absolutely infinite Being* [if any], and this (as is self-evident) is absurd. . . ."[3] Here Spinoza is clearly presupposing the conclusion to be proven, that "the absolutely infinite Being" for finite things to outpower does indeed exist. Of course, the *concept* of "the absolutely infinite Being" exists, but that a reality corresponding to this concept exists is just exactly what needs to be proven and what Spinoza here assumes. In this assumption that what is true of thought must be true of reality is the rationalism which Spinoza inherits from Descartes and the Occasionalists and carries to a further stage.

Attribute is the second basic concept of Spinoza's metaphysics. "By attribute, I understand that which the intellect perceives of Substance, as if constituting its essence."[4] This statement makes an attribute seem to be something in the mind of the perceiver rather than in the nature of Substance itself. In Proposition 19 of Part I, however, the attributes seem to be really present in Substance. Whether the attributes are independently real or only mental representations is a much debated and very important point because, as we shall see in a moment, on this point hinges the reality of the finite world. Substance must have an infinite number of attributes because Substance is infinite or unlimited in all respects, but of these we human beings know only two: thought and extension, the same two as Descartes's but now made the attributes of a single Substance rather than of two different ones, mind and body.

In considering the relation between the two attributes of thought and extension we are also dealing with the mind-body problem, although at a cosmic level. On this problem Spinoza holds two different but related views. First, he holds an *ontological double-aspect theory:* thought and extension are in their being or reality but two aspects or attributes of one and the same Substance. In this way he solves Descartes's mind-body problem at the deepest level. Mind and body have no interaction—a conclusion implied but rejected by Descartes's philosophy—but this is no flaw because two beings or substances do not exist to interact; there is only a single Substance which expresses itself in mental and bodily behavior. ". . . the mind and the body, are one and the same individual, which at one time is considered under the attribute of thought, and at another under that of extension. . . ."[5] Second, Spinoza holds a *methodological parallelism:* " . . . when things are considered as modes of thought, we must explain the order of the whole of nature or the connection of causes by the attribute of thought alone, and when things are considered as modes of extension, the order of the whole of nature must be explained through the attribute of extension alone. . . ."⁶ The world may be considered either physically or spiritually, but when we start explaining things in one way, say by science, we must stick to that way and not jump to the other way, say by religion.

Mode is the third and last of the basic concepts of Spinoza's metaphysics. "By mode I understand the modifications of Substance, or that which is in another thing through which also it is conceived."⁷ The infinite modes of Substance are intellect and will (through the attribute of thought) and motion and rest (through the attribute of extension), and the finite modes are all the particular things and events in the world when regarded as modifications of the one Substance or God. Are these finite, individual things which make up the world we experience real? Are we really distinct from God? The answer to this moot question depends partly on whether the attributes are real in God or only our mental perspectives and partly on whether the modes are really distinct expressions of the attributes or only our limited ways of seeing them. For those who view Spinoza's philosophy from the point of view of Substance, from the point of view of the axiom or primitive concept of Spinoza's system, finite things are no more than the illusions or opinions which Parmenides contrasted with the single true Being. But for those who view Spinoza's philosophy from the point of view of the attributes and modes, from the point of view of the consequences or theorems constituting the system, finite things are real and Substance is only their unifying ground. This question can probably never be settled conclusively, but an examination of Spinoza's third kind of knowledge indicates the most likely answer.

9-3.2. *Epistemology*

Spinoza's theory of knowledge is mostly contained in Parts II–IV of the *Ethics,* and it is a consistent companion to his metaphysics. The most general point to note about Spinoza's epistemology is that while the purpose of knowledge is mainly if not entirely the salvation or beatification of the knower, faith and revelation play no part whatever. We know in order to be saved, but we are saved only through our rationally acquired knowledge and not through any special revelation. Thus Spinoza's position is much like that of the ancient philosophers, especially Plato and Aristotle, except, as we would expect, the way of wisdom to salvation is conceived in accordance with the principles of rationalism. Spinoza believes we can be happy only when we fully love, but we can fully love only what we rationally understand.

Spinoza's way of wisdom to full knowledge and happiness has four stages, although he combines the first two into a single one. The first stage is "knowledge from vague experience," "from individual things, represented by the senses . . . in a mutilated and confused manner";[8] this stage is immediate sense experience and much the same as the imaging at the lowest level of Plato's divided line. The second stage is knowledge from signs or vicarious experience, an imaginative awareness; and this is analogous to Plato's second stage of belief. These first two stages Spinoza combines into "knowledge of the first kind" which he calls opinion or imagination, much as Plato makes "opinion" the combination of his imaging and belief. The third stage is reason or "knowledge of the second kind"; its essential feature is the use of abstract universal concepts arranged in a system, and it is therefore much the same as the discursive reasoning at the third level of Plato's divided line. The fourth and final stage of knowledge Spinoza calls "intuitive science" and "knowledge of the third kind"; it consists in seeing things "under the aspect of eternity," in seeing things as modes of God. Where discursive reason sees all things as distinct yet interconnected in one coherent system of theorems implied by axioms formed from primitive notions, intuitive reason sees all things as fused in a single primitive notion—just as we see each theorem of Euclid's geometry as quite separate from every other theorem and from the axioms by which they are implied while God would see the whole system together as latent in a single small set of basic ideas. Thus Spinoza's highest stage of knowledge is like Plato's intuition of the Good and Plotinus' mystical union with the One:

Plato	*Plotinus*	*Spinoza*
intuition of the Good	union with the One	4. intuitive science, seeing all things as God (third kind)
knowledge of the Forms	Reason	
discursive reasoning	Soul, transcendent aspect	3. reason, logical system (second kind)
diagrams	Soul, immanent aspect	
belief	Body	2. signs
imaging	Matter	1. vague experience

(2. signs and 1. vague experience bracketed as) (first kind)

Spinoza's theory of the nature of truth and error fits consistently into this ladder of knowledge, this way of wisdom. Descartes had maintained a correspondence theory of truth, that truth consists in the correspondence of our ideas with independent reality. This theory was a consequence of his sharp division of material substance from mental substance and of his belief that our clear and distinct ideas are caused by external things. After the Occasionalists had shown on the basis of Descartes's own principle of distinctness and its consequent mind-body dualism that material things could not cause mental ideas and therefore could not be the objects and verifiers of ideas, that all ideas must be ideas of ideas and especially of God's ideas, Spinoza then consistently took the final step of making ideas and minds, on the one hand, and bodies, on the other, into two aspects of a single Substance, God. Thought and extension thus have an indirect connection through God, even though they are not directly connected with each other.

The consequence of this for Spinoza is a coherence rather than a correspondence theory of truth. Ideas are not to be measured according to whether they are caused by and correspond to material things because no direct connection exists between ideas and material things.[9] On the contrary, ideas are to be measured according to their own reality wholly within the attribute of thought with no direct reference to matter at all. Furthermore, *every* idea is true insofar as it really is an idea, insofar as it is a mode of God through his attribute of thought. "All ideas are in God," Spinoza writes, "and insofar as they are related to God are true . . . and . . . adequate."[10] Even the ideas of nonexistent things are to some extent true, for they "are comprehended in the infinite idea of God, in the same way that the . . . modes are contained in the attributes of God."[11] While all ideas are true just because they are really modes of God, not all ideas are equally true, however, for they do not all manifest Substance or God with equal adequacy. "Knowledge of the first kind alone is the cause of falsity; knowledge of the second and third orders is necessarily true,"[12] Spinoza writes. Furthermore, knowledge of the third kind, intuitive reason, is at least higher if not truer than knowledge of the second kind, systematic reason; and truth and error seem in general to be matters of degree. Truth is a matter of the degree to which an idea expresses the whole of reality as it is fused together in God. Correlatively, error is a matter of the degree to which an idea is constricted to some individual part of reality, to some particular mode of God. In short, the bigger an idea the truer it is, and the smaller it is the falser it is. Thus the very truest idea—the most adequate, clear, distinct, comprehensive, and eternal idea—is the idea of God, where "of" means both about and by: God's idea of Himself, for God is reality itself. The very falsest idea—the most inadequate, confused, indistinct, and ephemeral idea—would be the most restricted and fleeting feeling.

These degrees of truth or adequacy correspond to Spinoza's four-rung ladder of knowledge; the mounting of the ladder to the highest kind of knowledge is a growth in the comprehensiveness of awareness of what is involved in any particular thing, passing through the stage of seeing all things as involving everything else (the second kind of knowledge), and culminating in the vision of God as the unity of all things (the third kind of knowledge). Your initial contact with another person, for example, is a fleeting sense impression of some very limited aspect of his being—his eyes or his hair. But his eyes or his hair cannot be adequately understood all alone because they are his, after all, because they are merely limited aspects of a total person. Through the addition of other experiences, both direct and vicarious, you gradually gain a more adequate conception of that person, one which embraces more and more different features as expressions of one single being. But then you begin to see that you cannot adequately understand this person without reference to his friends, family, and society, for these are as much a part of his being as his hair or eyes; "no man is an island." Finally you begin to see that this person's associates and society require for their adequate understanding, and therefore also for his, an understanding of the whole world which contains and conditions them and to which they are essentially related. Thus it is that the completely adequate, comprehensive, or true understanding of anything, no matter how small or insignificant, requires finally an understanding of everything else whatsoever. Hence the completest or truest possible understanding is the understanding of reality itself, which Spinoza calls God, as manifesting itself in all the many limited perspectives to which your gaze was initially restricted. Each and everything is like the "flower in the crannied wall":[13] to know it all in all is to know what God and man are.

The same point may be made conceptually and abstractly by recalling our earlier reflections upon the implications of Descartes's principle of distinctness (Ch. 8-4). Spinoza agrees with Descartes that the true is the distinct.[14] But he sees what Descartes seemed not to see, that for a thing to be distinct from all other things is for it necessarily to involve all other things as a part of its very meaning and being. Thus Spinoza expands one of the implications of Descartes's principle of distinctness into a theory of being and truth as a single unity of interlocked multiplicity.

9-3.3 *Ethics*

The moral philosophy of Spinoza, which is at the same time a secular, philosophical religion, is the final and consummating part of his *Ethics;* and this ethico-religion is a consistent expression and application of his metaphysics and theory of knowledge. The theory begins, much like Aristotle's and Hobbes's, by defining "good" as object of desire; and it is also like Aristotle's in conceiving the object of desire as the fullest possible realization of each person. However, this similarity stops as soon as we understand the nature of this self-realization in Spinoza's ethics: a mental realization of what is already in fact an actuality, namely that I am already perfect, complete, and fully real in my identity with God. The task of life is not, as it was with Aristotle, to make real that which is now only potential. In Spinoza's ethics the task of life is rather to realize or to comprehend the fact that each person is already realized as a mode of Substance or God. Indeed, according to Spinoza there are no unrealized potentialities at all.

Freedom is usually thought to be a prerequisite for morality; Kant, for example, will make it a "moral postulate" on the ground that "I ought" implies "I can" (Ch. 11-2.2). Spinoza affirms a *metaphysical* freedom only for God and not for man, however, except insofar as man is identical with God, although, as we shall see, man may, or perhaps even must, possess a human *moral* freedom. For Spinoza there is no freedom in the sense of indeterminacy, in the sense of man's being confronted with two or more unactualized possibilities whose realization or nonrealization depends upon his act of will. Such supposed freedom of choice from alternatives is for Spinoza simply ignorance of the causes necessarily determining the future.[15] In fact, no real possibilities exist at all; everything is either necessarily existent or logically impossible. "Whatever we conceive to be in God's power necessarily exists,"[16] and whatever is not in God's power cannot possibly exist since God is the cause of all things. Indeed, Spinoza argues,[17] to say that either God or man might have made or might make things different is to commit the contradiction of placing a limitation on a Being Who is by definition infinite, for the alleged alternative possibility would either have to be better than the one realized, in which case God in His perfect goodness would necessarily produce it, or else worse, in which case it is impossible for it to be produced by a good God. In any case no alternatives are possible and hence no freedom of choice from among them is possible. For Spinoza there is freedom in the sense of self-determination, however, in the sense of being free *from* all outside forces. Of course this freedom belongs strictly speaking only to God, but it also belongs to man in so far as he is a mode of God.

In addition to this metaphysical freedom of self-determination, however, Spinoza's ethics also contains another kind of freedom which is relevant to moral man. But this human, moral freedom is a goal rather than a precondition of moral action. It is the freedom which consists in *seeing that* everything is necessarily determined and that man is self-determined insofar as he is identical with God; it is a consciousness of necessity which comes with the second and third kinds of knowledge. Yet having freedom (or anything else, for that matter) as an ethical goal seems to imply that we are antecedently free to realize or not to realize that goal, that we have a freedom of choice from two alternative possibilities. But Spinoza, of course, has ruled out such freedom. If everything whatever is determined, then is not our seeing or not seeing all things under the aspect of eternity *itself* determined? If it is, is it not pointless for Spinoza to exhort us to seek the first alternative and avoid the second? But if it is not, then real alternatives are possible and free human choice from among them is possible.

Out of this divine determinism emerges an optimistic fatalism, which is quite similar to that of the Stoics. Spinoza's ethics teaches us

> how we ought to behave with regard to the things of fortune, or those which are not in our power . . . ; for it teaches us with equal mind to wait for and bear each form of fortune, because we know that all things follow from the eternal decree of God, according to that same necessity by which it follows from the essence of a triangle that its three angles are equal to two right angles.[18]

While we must be fatalists in the sense of realizing that everything is determined, we also become optimists as soon as we see that everything is determined for the best since the determiner, God, is perfectly good. Things seem bad only when we have an inadequate understanding of them, only when we have torn them from the total context. When we see them necessarily involved in the total network of things and thus gain an adequate understanding of them, we see that they are and must be good.

Immortality is granted in Spinoza's ethics in two senses, although neither of them is a personal immortality of the individual human. First, every person, and indeed everything whatever, is immortal as a mode of the eternal Substance or God; this immortality is given from the start and is not a prize to be won. In the second place, however, a more specific kind of immortality can be won by ethical striving; this is the *consciousness* of oneself as immortal which comes in the second and third kinds of knowledge. Insofar as one enlarges oneself to include all reality, one sees all things under the aspect of eternity; and here time and therefore mortality disappear. Seeing things as temporal and therefore mortal is seeing them with the senses and the imagination, with the first kind of knowledge; here life is enslaved by the passions, as the Stoics also said. However, seeing things with the second and third kinds of knowledge is seeing them with one's reason and therefore seeing them and oneself as timeless or immortal; this is reason's mastery over the passions.

Correspondingly, two levels of happiness are offered by Spinoza's ethics. The genuine philosophical sage and religious saint who has achieved the third kind of knowledge has the beatitude of a mystical yet rational identification with God. Such a state is both knowledge and love, the one requiring the other, and both the man's knowledge and love of God and God's knowledge and love of the man. Spinoza calls it the intellectual love of God in which God loves Himself through one of His human modes. For the person who falls short of the third kind of knowledge, and perhaps even possesses little of the second kind, Spinoza's ethics offers liberation and consolation without the experience of union with God. Recognition that everything is eternally preserved in God brings consolation by removing the tragedy of time; God will wipe away all tears. Recognition that everything in the world is necessarily determined also brings consolation, for then whatever happens is seen, as it was by the Stoics, to be a necessary part of the life of God. Recognition that the world is as perfect as possible—that it is not only the best of all possible worlds (as Leibniz will say) but even the only possible world—also brings consolation and peace. As with the Stoics so also with Spinoza, God's in His earth and all's right with the world.

9-3.4. *Summary*

On the basis of the Rationalist principle that what is true of thought is true also of reality, Descartes's principle of distinctness paradoxically entails both metaphysical atomism and metaphysical monism. It entails metaphysical atomism because to conceive a thing as clearly distinct from everything else is to conceive it without reference to anything else, and the identity of thought and reality means that the thing thus conceived must likewise have no relation to anything else. It also entails metaphysical monism, however, because to conceive something as distinct from everything else is to conceive it as just that, as something-distinct-from-everything-else, as something necessarily involving everything else in its very nature as distinct from them; and the identity of thought and reality means again that the thing thus conceived must likewise involve everything else within itself in the very distinctness which it has from them. This paradoxical union of atomism and monism also arises from the deductivism of the Rationalists, for a deductive system is one which is squeezed into one in the axiom set and also split into many in the multiplicity of theorems.

In Descartes's philosophy this metaphysical atomism and monism exist in unreconciled tension with the atomism explicitly predominating. In Spinoza's philosophy they are brought together and reconciled as equally necessary properties of distinctness, deduction, and the world; yet the monistic pole predominates since the Occasionalists helped Spinoza to the conclusion that reality itself must be identified with the single

Substance or one God. In the philosophy of Leibniz, the last chapter in the story of Continental Rationalism, to which we now turn, the attempt will be made to combine the positions of Descartes and Spinoza to give full due to both atomism and monism.

9-4. *Leibniz*

Although Gottfried Wilhelm Leibniz (1646–1716) was fourteen years younger than John Locke, the founder of British Empiricism, Locke begins a new story while Leibniz ends an old one. Leibniz's philosophy is most basically, within the context of this story of Continental Rationalism, the attempt to combine Descartes's dominant atomism with Spinoza's dominant monism. The result is an historical analogy: Pythagoras : Parmenides : Anaxagoras : : Descartes : Spinoza : Leibniz. Where Pythagoras maintained a dualism of Limited and Unlimited manifested in a pluralism of numbers, and where Parmenides reduced this dualism and pluralism to a strict monism, Anaxagoras maintained a pluralism of seeds each of which possesses the properties of Parmenides' single Being (Ch. 1-2 to 1-4). Analogously, where Descartes maintained a dualism of thought and extension which reduced to a radical atomism and where Spinoza combined this dualism and atomism into the monism of a single Substance, Leibniz will present a pluralism of "monads" each of which possesses the properties of Spinoza's single Substance. Leibniz will atomize Spinoza's Substance just as Anaxagoras pluralized Parmenides' Being, even though from another point of view the philosophy of Leibniz will remain as monistic as that of Spinoza.

9-4.1. *Metaphysics*

Leibniz's theory of reality is first and most fundamentally concerned with all possible worlds, not merely with this actual one we inhabit; and the determinant of possibilities and possible worlds is the principle of noncontradiction: a thing cannot both have and not have a given property at the same time and in the same respect. In order to understand what Leibniz means by *a possible world,* we must first distinguish between the possible and the actual and the necessary. The possible and the necessary are, for Leibniz, based solely on the law of noncontradiction: a thing is possible if and only if it is not self-contradictory, and a thing is necessary if and only if its contradictory is self-contradictory. By the same token something is impossible if it is self-contradictory. Thus an isosceles triangle is possible, a three-sided triangle necessary, and a four-sided triangle impossible. Whatever is necessary is of course also actual, and whatever is impossible is also nonactual, but only some possible things are also actual. That which renders some possibilities actual is God, as we should expect and as we will see in detail in the next section. Now *a possible world* or compossibility is simply a possibility which consists of possibilities, a complex possibility, a self-consistent set of self-consistent essences. Such complex possibilities or possible worlds are Leibniz's first concern, for it is from these possible worlds that the actual world was selected.

Propositions true in all possible worlds, and therefore also true in the actual world, are for Leibniz "truths of reason" or necessarily true metaphysical propositions. In contrast to these necessary truths of reason Leibniz places "truths of fact" which are true only contingently upon the truth of something else; this contrast between two kinds of truths we shall later see reflected in Hume's contrast between "relations of ideas" and "matters of fact" (Ch. 10-3.1). Let us now turn to the most important of Leibniz's truths of reason or metaphysical principles about all possible worlds, since they depict the most fundamental features of reality as Leibniz sees it. The first five of these principles constitute Leibniz's unique vision of the world, and the last three save as appearances what the first five principles render unreal.

First, all possible worlds must consist of indivisible, individual substances which Leibniz calls monads (from the Greek word for unit). Each of these monads is absolutely self-contained and unrelated to anything else; in Leibniz's picturesque language, monads have no "windows." This isolation of the monads follows perfectly from Descartes's principle of distinctness;

each monad is so completely distinct from all other monads that each contains within itself nothing of any other and not even any real relation to any other. All relations are thus internal to the monad; monads have no external relations. Therefore, the whole history of each monad is contained entirely within and developed solely out of its own nature. Nothing happens to monads from the outside; they only spin out their own internally determined characteristics. We can already see how similar each monad is to Spinoza's Substance, except, of course, that there are many monads. From the monads' lack of external relations it follows that each monad is indestructible and unconstructible. Just as nothing can change the nature of triangularity which remains eternally just what it is, so also nothing can change the nature of a monad. Also like triangularity, however, the actuality or nonactuality of each monad does depend upon something outside it, namely God.

Second, the essence of each monad is force or activity rather than matter or extension, according to Leibniz; thus dynamics replaces the geometrics of Descartes. Moreover, Leibniz goes even further to declare that matter or extension is unreal. His main argument for this crucial preposition is that real extension consists of external relations, of relations of a monad (or of a part of a monad) to something outside itself, and that, as we have seen, there cannot be any external relations, that monads have no windows. From this Leibniz draws the conclusion that the quantitative characteristics which Democritus, Epicurus, Hobbes, and Descartes had declared to be the only objectively real properties of things are in fact just as subjective as the qualitative characteristics—that primary qualities are just as subjective as secondary ones. The quantitative characteristics of extension, size, shape, etc., are for Leibniz only "well-founded phenomena"; and in this position against Descartes and Locke he will soon be joined by Berkeley and Kant.

Third, Leibniz therefore also maintains that every monad is mental or spiritual in nature. While the essence of each monad is force or activity rather than extension, this force or activity is immaterial and spiritual just because it is unextended. This is the first genuine metaphysical idealism in the history of Western philosophy, the first clear example of a philosophy which maintains that reality is ultimately of the nature of mind. This position seems to follow from Descartes's mind-body dualism and therefore also from his principle of distinctness. As we have already suggested (Ch. 8-3), if matter is conceived so distinctly that it cannot act upon or have any relation to mind, then matter cannot produce ideas of itself in the mind, and the mind cannot know that matter even exists. Although each of the Rationalists before Leibniz asserted the real existence of matter (even though for Spinoza it is only an attribute of Substance or God), the Occasionalists and Spinoza embraced the position implicit in Descartes that the mind is in contact only with minds and ideas. From this Leibniz has only to take one step to the logical conclusion that we cannot know or say that there really is any such thing as matter. A quite similar sequence will be observed from Locke to Berkeley (Ch. 10-2.2).

Fourth, in his famous principle of the identity of indiscernibles Leibniz maintains that identity in nature is identity in number, that the difference between two individuals must always be qualitative as well as numerical. Some of the court ladies and gentlemen reputedly tried to refute this principle by searching the palace gardens for two identical blades of grass, but needless to say any two blades of grass they produced could always be found to differ at least slightly in their properties. This principle of the identity of indiscernibles may have been one of the things Lewis Carroll had in mind in his creation of Tweedledum and Tweedledee. While these two boys are allegedly identical in their qualities or "tweedleness," they still remain two, Dum and Dee. Yet Leibniz would surely have pointed out that they have at least some qualitative differences. Thus each of Leibniz's monads is the only possible instance of its type or species.

Fifth, Leibniz's principle of continuity says that the world is a continuum of monads in which each monad differs from the next only infinitesimally. Nature avoids leaps and vacuums, Leibniz believes. No matter how similar two monads are, there is always some other monad between them which is more similar to each than they are to each other. While the principle of the identity of indiscernibles says that no place is filled twice in the continuum of monads (since two things cannot be identical in nature), the principle of continuity says that every possible place in the continuum of monads is filled. Together these two principles thus declare that there is exactly one instance of every possible kind of thing.

This continuum of monads is a vertical rather than a horizontal one, moreover; it is a hierarchy of being, and Leibniz divides it into three main segments (even though this scale contains no real discontinuities). The lowest segment of this vertical continuum consists of "swooning" or "stunned" monads or *"petites perceptions"*; these monads are the unconscious mental life which is definitive of inorganic and vegetative existence. The next higher segment is that of souls, the conscious sensory life characteristic of animals. And the highest segment consists of spirits or minds, which possess the rationality and self-consciousness peculiar to human beings. Whether God constitutes a fourth and even higher level in the continuum of monads is a question which will be considered later.

The last three of Leibniz's principles we shall consider are designed to reinstate as mere appearance items in our experience which have been barred from the status of reality by the first five principles; they are designed to save the appearances. The first of these is a principle of virtual space or extension. Although space or extension has been declared unreal on the ground that it involves external relations, although reality has been declared to consist only of units of spiritual force which act entirely out of themselves, still, according to Leibniz, the monads' self-representation is necessarily projected on a spatial or material plane. While space or extension is thus not objectively real, it is a well-founded phenomenon because each monad must experience itself and its world as if they were spatial. This view will lead to Kant's famous theory of space as the form of outer sensation (Ch. 11-1.3).

Secondly, a principle of virtual aggregation accounts for our experience of the congealing of matter into individual substances like trees and tigers. Monads appear clustered together into colonies under the rule of a dominant monad, even though no such clustering can really take place because it would involve the external relations which are incompatible with the "windowlessness" of monads. The dominant monad in each virtual aggregation of monads gives each composite things its own special nature. Thus you as a human being are a colony of monads of all three types—swooning, souls, and spirits—but you are the particular person you are because this colony is dominated by one particular monad, and you are a human being because this dominant monad is a mind or spirit.

Last and perhaps most famous is the principle of preestablished harmony. This principle saves the phenomenon of the interaction among the things which make up the world when such interaction has been barred from reality by Leibniz's rejection of external relations. Although the monads cannot really have any interaction with each other, since each is absolutely self-contained or windowless, according to Leibniz, the appearance of such interaction results from the fact that God preestablished at the beginning of creation that the activities of each monad would be synchronized with those of every other. Leibniz explains this principle by means of an analogy to a number of clocks which tick on independently of each other while keeping the same time because they have been synchronized at the start and constructed in such a way as to retain this synchrony. An apter analogy today might be to liken each monad to a television set playing off its own copy of the same taped program with no interaction with any other set, where the tapes and the sets were synchronized with each other at the start of their playing. To this analogy we should add, however, that these television sets form a vertical continuum ranging from one of infinitesimal size and clarity through all possible degrees of size and clarity to one of infinite size and clarity. While the program presented in each set is the same as that presented in every other, each set projects the program out of itself in its own unique way without any influence from anything outside itself save that of the television synchronizer. Thus God is the only external agent for Leibniz, the only being with any external relations—a new expression of the principle of Occasionalism (Ch. 9-2)—though, as we shall later see, this seems incompatible with one of Leibniz's conceptions of God, namely as a monad, since no monad is supposed to have any windows.

This principle of preestablished harmony is also Leibniz's ultimate solution to the mind-body problem initiated by Descartes, although Leibniz actually handles this problem at three different levels. In the first place, Descartes's gap between mind and body is bridged by Leibniz's concept of force. The essential nature of each thing is force, and mind and body or thought and extension are simply two different aspects of this single reality. At this level Leibniz's solution is quite similar to that of Spinoza who made thought and extension (mind and body) two attributes of one Substance. In the second place and at a somewhat deeper level, however, the mind-body problem is also solved by denying one half of the dualism, since force is for Leibniz unextended and mental. Here there is no mind-body problem because there is really no body, although certain monads, the swooning ones, represent the body. However, this solution simply transfers the problem to a deeper level. While there is now, metaphysically, no mind-body problem, in its place at the deepest level of analysis there is a mind-*mind* problem, or rather a monad-monad problem, for mind monads are conceived so distinctly from body monads that they can have no relation whatever. At this final level Leibniz solves the problem, as we have seen, with the principle of preestablished harmony: while mind and "body" monads have no windows through which they could interact, the insulated actions of each mirror those of the other since God has foreordained that every monad shall act out its history in synchrony with every other. Leibniz's solution to the mind-body problem is thus in the last analysis the same as the Occasionalists', although the occasions for God's synchronizing actions are now only mental units rather than both mental and physical ones.

The principle of preestablished harmony means also that every monad is metaphysically free, within the limits of the existence which it receives from God and its preestablished harmony with all other things, for every monad determines by itself what it will do since it has no external relations to anything else, and this is Leibniz's conception of freedom. With Spinoza

Leibniz holds that genuine freedom is self-determination, a freedom from external determination in which one is the cause of one's own actions. No real freedom of indeterminism or choice from alternative possibilities exists; such supposed freedom of choice is really ignorance of the "alternative" which one's nature is determined to enact. Rather strangely, however, Leibniz does grant freedom of choice to God, here disagreeing with Spinoza, though we must now consider reasons for thinking that Leibniz cannot consistently do this.

9-4.2. *Theology*

The most basic function of God in the philosophy of Leibniz is to account for the fact that our world has been chosen for actualization from among all the possible worlds. Here Leibniz invokes the principle of sufficient reason: nothing can be actual or fail to be actual without a sufficient or adequate reason. This principle was also important in Descartes's arguments for the existence of God and matter; *ex nihilo nihil fit,* and the more perfect cannot come from the less perfect (Ch. 8-2.2).

What in fact is the sufficient reason for the existence of this actual world we inhabit? God, of course. God is the agency by which possibilities become actualities, by which essences come into existence; and this is the first of Leibniz's several arguments for the existence of God. This first argument, that God 'must exist as the sufficient reason for the world, is essentially the same as the causal arguments proposed all through philosophical history and perhaps most famously by Thomas Aquinas (Ch. 6-2). A second argument Leibniz uses is similar to one which had been put forth by Augustine: Eternal truths ("truths of reason") require the existence of an eternal mind as their habitat, since a truth must be known by some mind. A third argument is Leibniz's special version of the ontological argument. God must necessarily exist if He is possible since, by the definition of "God," nothing is beyond Him to prevent the actualization of this possibility. And God is of course possible since His conception involves no contradiction. A fourth argument is one which is unique to Leibniz, that the existence of God is implied by the principle of preestablished harmony, that God must exist to account for the apparent interaction among monads whose windowlessness prevents any real interaction. The important question here of course is whether any such preestablished harmony does indeed exist. Perhaps on the contrary the apparent harmonious interaction of things is mere illusion, or perhaps, and more hopefully, the things in the world really do have windows through which they are externally related to and really interact with other things rather than God's Occasionalistically making them think that they interact when they really do not.

What is God's reason for creating our world rather than some other? Leibniz claims that God creates for a moral reason, not for a logical or metaphysical one. Unlike the God of Plotinus and Spinoza Who is bound by His nature to bring forth actualities, the God of Leibniz, like the divine Craftsman of Plato and the God of the medieval Christians, created the world by an act of free will, so Leibniz claims, which therefore means that He is also free not to create it. But why then did He create it? Again Leibniz's answer is much the same as that of Plato and the medieval philosophers: God freely chose to create this actual world because He is good and because He saw that it is better to create this world than not to do so. More than that, this actual world in which we live must be "the best of all possible worlds," according to Leibniz, for if another possible world were better than this one then the goodness and omnipotence of God would require Him to create it. While this position may sound optimistic, Voltaire in his *Candide* made it look pessimistic: If this vale of tears is indeed the best of all possible worlds, how terrible the others must be!

This guarantee that the goodness and omnipotence of God will produce the best of all possible worlds raises the question whether any other world than this one is really possible after all, a problem similar to those we saw confronting medieval Christian theology (Ch. 6-4). If God is both omnipotent and perfectly good, He seemingly cannot help but actualize that world which is best of all the possible ones. And from this it seems inevitably to follow that these other worlds are not really possible at all, since the goodness of God makes their realization impossible. But this brings us back to Spinoza: everything possible actually and necessarily exists; there can be no unactualized possibilities. Thus it appears that Leibniz would have been more consistent had he withheld freedom of choice from God as he did from men.

The theology of Leibniz is also complicated by the fact that it contains at least two and probably even three different and conflicting doctrines of the nature of God. First, Leibniz espouses the traditional Judaeo-Christian conception of God as creator and as radically different from the world by virtue of the fact that He is infinite while it is finite. Second, Leibniz presents a doctrine of God as the Supreme Monad at the top of the vertical continuum of monads, and thus God differs only infinitesimally, rather than infinitely, from the next lower monad on the continuum. Third, he sometimes speaks of God as though He were the emanator of the world rather than its creator; here God fulgurates or sparks off the world from His own being. The second of these conceptions, that of God as the Supreme Monad continuous with the other monads, seems most consistent with his general theory but hardest to reconcile with Christianity. This ambivalence concerning the nature of God epitomizes the basic ambivalence in Leibniz's philosophy and its relation to the philosophies of his predecessors.

9-5. *The Story of Continental Rationalism*

Continental Rationalism is essentially based on two principles: Whatever is truly thought must be distinct, and whatever is true of thought is true of reality. From these two fundamental premises follows the conclusion that whatever is truly real must be distinct in just the way that we conceive it. But this distinctness of the real necessarily involves it in a tension between atomism and monism. Reality must be atomistic because, as Descartes saw, a thing which is clearly distinct from everything else must have no dependency on or relation to anything else. Yet reality must also be monistic because a thing which is distinct from everything else in just the way we conceive it must also be just that really: a thing-distinct-from-everything-else and hence necessarily involving everything else in its very concept and essence.

This paradoxical union of atomism and monism also results from the deductivism of the Rationalists, for a deductive system is one in which the many theorems are united into and with the one set of axioms.

In the philosophy of Descartes atomism and monism exist in unreconciled tension with atomism explicitly predominating. In the philosophy of Spinoza they are reconciled as equally necessary properties of thought and the world, but monism predominates since the causal impotence of finite atomic things yields the conclusion, by way of the Occasionalists, that only the one God is truly real. In the philosophy of Leibniz, finally, atomism and monism are reconciled in the plurality of monads each of which is a monistic Spinozistic Substance, but this reconciliation becomes specious in view of the ambivalent nature and role of Leibniz's God. If God is a monad, the result is an atomism more extreme than Descartes's, for then God, like other monads, has no windows through which to preestablish a monistic harmony of all things. If God is an omnipotent and perfectly good creator, on the other hand, He is apparently bound by His nature to emanate or fulgurate out of Himself the monads constituting the actual world; but then no other world is really possible, and all things are contained in and necessarily flow from God—a monism hardly distinguishable from that of Spinoza.

The reconciliation of monism and atomism is rendered even impossible, furthermore, and the Cartesian tension between them is even made necessary, by Leibniz's very statement of his metaphysical system. Since Leibniz's own mind must be a windowless monad according to his system, it follows that Leibniz cannot know that there is any other monad than himself. This is solipsism, the doctrine that only the self can be known; and it will continue to grow into the fundamental feature of modern philosophy. And the Leibnizian self which alone can be known is just as monistic as the monolithic reality of Spinoza, although instead of Leibniz and his world being one with God the world and God are one with Leibniz. Yet neither Leibniz nor anyone else can really believe this solipsism, so existence must be granted to other monads outside Leibniz's own. Since none of these monads has any windows, however, the result is again a radical atomism.

This unreconciled tension between monism and atomism is thus contained in Leibniz's very statement of his philosophy, even though at first glance that tension would seem to be removed by a synthesis of monism and atomism in the concept of monads. Hegel will claim that this fundamental tension or dialectic is the mark of truth, and in so doing he will frame a new and characteristically modern conception of reality which forms the conclusion of the story of modern philosophy. Before this conclusion comes about, however, Continental Rationalism first gives rise to its apparent opposite, British Empiricism.

SUGGESTED READINGS

9-1. Pascal. *Thoughts*. Especially Nos. 72, 77, 79, 144, 229, 230, 233, 234, 252, 277, 278, 282, 283, 346–48, 358, 384, 393–95, 412.
9-2. Malebranche. *Dialogues on Metaphysics*, trans. M. Ginsburg. Pp. 21–29, 51–61.
9-3. Spinoza. *Ethics*. Pt. I except for Appendix; Pt. II from beginning to Prop. 13 (exclude the notes) , Props. 21, 32–36, and 40 from note 2 to end of Pt. II; Pt. III, Props. 6–9; Pt. IV, Props. 19–25, 28, 31, 35–37, 64; Pt. 5, Prop. 14 to the end.
9-4. Leibniz. *Monadaology*.
_____ *Discourse on Metaphysics*. Especially Secs. VIII, IX, XII, XIV, XV, XXVI, XXVIII, XXX, XXXIII.

For bibliographies, see:
9-1. Turnell, M., trans. and ed. *Pascal: Pensées*. London: Harvill, 1962. Pp. 423–24.
9-2. Rome, B. *The Philosophy of Malebranche*. Chicago: Regnery, 1963. Pp. 331–51.
9-3. Hallett, H. F. *Benedict de Spinoza*. University of London: Athlone Press, 1957. Pp. xv–xvi.
9-4. Loemker, L. E., trans. and ed. *Gottfried Wilhelm Leibniz: Philosophical Papers and Letters*. Vol. I. University of Chicago Press, 1956. Pp. 102–113.

Chapter 10

British
Empiricism

Empiricism in Britain goes back at least to Bacon and Hobbes—indeed, even to Ockham—and the first of the three great Empiricists we shall consider (Locke) was a contemporary of Spinoza and older than Leibniz; however, the full development of British Empiricism came after, and partly as a reaction against, Continental Rationalism. The story of Continental Rationalism seems to tell us that logical reason, when carried to an extreme, shuts us up within ourselves away from objective reality. Since this subjective isolation is intolerable to the sound common sense of all men, however, even to that of the Rationalists, each of the Continental Rationalists escapes from his self-created isolationist impasse by fiat or a tour de force: Descartes through interactionism, Malebranche through occasionalism, Spinoza through his identity with infinite Substance, and Leibniz through preestablished harmony. This Rationalist series of impasses and tours de force seems to indicate that we should reject the Rationalists' reason and return to common sense and the sensory experience on which it is based.

The Empiricists' choice of sense experience as their avenue to reality inevitably produces a corresponding sensory picture of the world, just as the Rationalists' choice of reason necessarily resulted in a corresponding rationalist picture of the world. The objects of reason and its rational concepts are stable, timeless, universal, and necessary forms; this we saw first with Plato (Ch. 3-1.1) and again with the Continental Rationalists. We can only expect, therefore, that a world depicted solely by such rational concepts will have these same characteristics. It will be necessary and deterministic through and through, emphasis will be on universals and unity with a consequent leaning toward monism, and it will include the inevitable tendency to regard the finite, temporal world as unreal or inadequate with time, causation, change, and plurality tending to become factitious. The objects of sensory experience and its sense images, on the other hand, are changing, temporal, particular, and contingent; this we have already seen especially in connection with Plato, and we shall now be seeing it again in British Empiricism. The world as depicted exclusively by sensory experience will therefore inevitably possess these same features. An Empiricist world will be contingent through and through with no necessary reason for anything; it will be radically particularized and plurified with universal forms either wholly absent or greatly attenuated; and time, causation, change, and plurality will be seen as inexplicable ultimates. In order to see this prediction verified, however, we must go on to the story of British Empiricism. Locke will formulate the position and expose some of its implications; Berkeley will adopt some of these implications, rejecting others, and thus modify the original position; and Hume will accept these implications and, in general, draw Empiricism to its logical conclusion.

10-1. *Locke*

10-1.1. *Epistemology*

John Locke (1632–1704) devotes Book I of his *Essay Concerning Human Understanding* to an attempt to refute the theory of innate ideas, for he regards this theory as the root of rationalistic dogmatism and authoritarianism and as the basic opposite of the empiricism which he himself espouses. Locke's criticisms of the theory of innate ideas thus form the negative stage preliminary to the positive stage of the construction of empiricism, and Book I therefore has essentially the same function as Bacon's iconoclasm and Descartes's methodological skepticism. Locke conceives of the innate ideas which he wants to refute as ones which are consciously present at birth, and the recurrent core of his argument is simply that such ideas are not actually to be found. Leibniz and others who believed in innate ideas objected that Locke's target was a straw man, since the defenders of the theory of innate ideas had never maintained that they are to be found consciously present in newborn infants. The theory was rather that certain ideas and principles are *unconsciously* or *latently* present at birth; and their reason for holding this, as we saw in connection with Plato (Ch. 3-1.3), was that these abstract ideas and universal principles cannot be obtained from sensory experience of concrete particular things. At this point the real issue is joined, for Locke maintains that all knowledge whatsoever is acquired by external things affecting the mind in sense experience, though the story of British Empiricism may vindicate his opponents' claim that this will not yield universal principles. Thus the real issue in Locke's debate over innate ideas is the issue between rationalism and empiricism, and Locke's attempted refutation of the theory of innate ideas amounts to his choice of empiricism.

In thus choosing empiricism Locke lays down his fundamental thesis, a thesis Bacon and Hobbes had also accepted, although in a less explicit and emphatic way. The mind is at birth a *tabula rasa,* a blank tablet or clean slate, and everything we learn is written on this tablet of the mind by sensory experience. Locke's most central concept is that of an idea, and it is very important to note that Locke means by "idea" any object of consciousness rather than an act of consciousness. *"Idea is the object of thinking,"* is the opening statement of Book II of the *Essay.* Ideas are thus what we are aware of, not the awareness itself.

Ideas as objects of consciousness come from two sources or types of experience: sensation of external bodies and reflection upon internal mental operations aroused by those sensations.

While ideas are the objects of thought, qualities are the causes of ideas; and of these qualities two kinds in material things are especially important: the primary and secondary qualities to which we have referred so often. By the primary qualities Locke means the quantitative features of things, their size, weight, shape, etc.; and by the secondary qualities he means the qualitative features of things, their colors, sounds, odors, etc. Slightly contrary to present-day ordinary usage, however, secondary qualities are declared by Locke to be extra-mentally present in material objects, but only as potential and not as actual. More exactly, the secondary qualities of things are for Locke only the powers of the primary or quantitative qualities to produce in our minds the corresponding qualitative sensations. While that tree is actually tall, heavy, and broad in its objective existence, its green and brown colors are only capacities possessed by its quantitative structure to make us see green and brown. Moreover, "had we senses acute enough to discern the minute particles of bodies," "*the now secondary qualities of bodies would disappear* . . . and instead we should see an admirable texture of parts of a certain size and figure."[1] Such a reduction of the actuality of the objective world to quantitative and mathematically treatable properties is essentially the same as Descartes's thesis that the essence of material things is extension, and both are expressions of the general modern tendency to see the objective world through the eyes of the physical scientist and to wastebasket all qualities in the subjectivity of the mind.

Locke's treatment of one idea, the idea of substance, is particularly important because it shows already the influence of the sensory approach to reality. The idea of substance, according to Locke, is a particular collection of ideas or perceived qualities plus an inability to conceive how or why they hang together. Since we sense only the qualities of a substance, say the size, color, shape, etc., of a horse, we do not and cannot sense any substance which stands under them and holds them together.

> . . . because we cannot conceive how they should subsist alone, nor one in another, we suppose them existing in, and supported by, some common subject; which support we denote by the name substance, though it be certain that we have no clear or distinct idea of that thing we suppose a support.[2]

Indeed, a person speaking of substance has no idea of it at all "but only a supposition of he knows not what . . . ."[3] This also holds true of mental substances or minds as well as of material substances or bodies, though as we shall shortly see Locke regards the existence of his self as absolutely certain.

"The simple ideas we receive from sensation and reflection are the boundaries of our thoughts; beyond which, the mind . . . is not able to advance one jot; nor can it make any discoveries, when it would pry into the nature and hidden causes of those ideas."[4] Here in these fundamentals of Locke's philosophy we can already glimpse the skepticism which we will now see emerge in his theory of knowledge.

The objects of knowledge, as we have just seen, are ideas. The definition of the act of knowing and its knowledge product follows immediately: *"Knowledge is the perception of the agreement or disagreement of . . . ideas . . . .* In this alone it consists."[5] Locke identifies three types or "degrees" of such knowledge (or four if probable knowledge is counted as a separate type). The first type is *intuitive* knowledge, the perception of the agreement or disagreement of ideas immediately, without the intermediation of any other ideas, as for example that squares are rectangular. The second type is *demonstrative* knowledge, a mediated perception of the relation of two ideas by means of the relation of each to a third. The syllogism is perhaps the clearest example of demonstrative knowledge: we perceive the agreement of the idea of *Socrates* with the idea of *mortal*, for example, by means of the agreement of each with the idea of *man,* the middle term. Each of the constituent comparisons in demonstrative knowledge must be a matter of intuitive knowledge; for example, we must know intuitively the agreement of the concepts *man* and *mortal*. These two types of knowledge yield certainty, according to Locke; and when taken together they are much like Descartes's method of intuition and deduction. To these two kinds of knowledge Locke adds, however, a *sensitive* knowledge of "the existence of particular external objects by that perception and consciousness we have of the actual entrance of ideas from them."[6] When we notice that the objects of intuitive and demonstrative knowledge are *ideas* while the objects of sensitive knowledge are *external physical things,* and when we recall that all ideas derive from particular sensations, we arrive at the two most fundamental problems in Locke's philosophy and in British Empiricism as a whole.

10-1.2. *Nominalism and Solipsism*

Locke's fundamental thesis is a sensory empiricism, the view that all kowledge derives from sensory experience. In making the transition from Rationalism to Empiricism we noted the peculiar characteristics of the objects of sensation in contrast to those of the objects of reason. While the objects of reason are stable, universal, necessary forms, the objects of sensation are the unstable, fluctuating, particular, contingent features of physical things. Locke's first two types of knowledge, intuitive and demonstrative, he declares to be theoretically certain; the propositions exemplifying these two kinds of knowledge are universally and necessarily true; for example, "Man is mortal."

The first of the two fundamental problems in British Empiricism is the problem of how, or whether, such universal, necessary, and certain truths can possibly be derived from objects or experiences which are utterly particular, contingent, and uncertain. Plato and the Continental Rationalists claimed that this is not possible, that universal and necessary truths must be delivered by reason independently of sense experience. Locke, by virtue of his empiricist thesis, has of course repudiated any such nonempirical, rational truths. Aristotle agreed with Locke's position that all knowledge derives from sense experience, and Aristotle also agreed on the existence of universal and necessary truths, intuitive and demonstrative knowledge. Aristotle was able to do this consistently, however, only because he also recognized a faculty of reason distinct from that of sensation and, correlatively, the presence of unchanging, necessary forms in the changing, contingent objects of sense experience. If Locke also were to do this, or something like it, then this first problem in his epistemology would evaporate. But Locke seems not to do this, although his position is not entirely clear. While there are *"nominal* essences," he says, abstract complex ideas to which we have annexed distinct general names, *"real* essences" must forever remain unknown to us, and Locke thus seems to have only the faculty of sensation and correlatively only changing and contingent objects of cognition. That this is in all likelihood Locke's position emerges from the fact that his Empiricist successors will espouse it themselves as an explicit nominalism (universals are only names; only particulars are real) required by Empiricism. And the consequence of this espousal which will be drawn by Hume is that a consistent Empiricist must attenuate his claims to universal and necessary truths, to intuitive and demonstrative knowledge, even further than Locke did in his earlier noted renunciation of such knowledge of substance. The first fundamental problem in Locke's epistemology is thus the apparent incompatibility between his sensory empiricism with its particular and contingent objects and his intuitive and demonstrative knowledge of universal and necessary truths.

The other fundamental problem in Locke's epistemology is that he has defined knowledge and its object in such a way as to land him, strangely enough, in the impasse of his Rationalist opponents, the impasse of solipsism. The first premise leading to this impasse is the proposition that we can know only ideas. "Since the mind, in all its thoughts and reasonings, hath no other immediate object but its own ideas, which it alone does or can contemplate," Locke asserts at the beginning of Book IV, "it is evident that our knowledge is only conversant about them." The second premise leading to solipsism is that these ideas, which are all that we can know, are in our minds. "There is nothing more certain than that the idea we receive from an external object is in our minds: this is intuitive knowledge."[7] From these two premises there follows necessarily the conclusion that we can know only what is in our own minds, that we can have no knowledge of external, extra-mental things. This is the impasse of solipsism. Since solipsism is unacceptable to Locke's sovereign common sense, however, this impasse must be escaped. It cannot be escaped logically, for it follows deductively from Locke's fundamental premises, so it must be escaped by a tour de force, by forcing in a logically forbidden knowledge of the external world. This tour de force is the concept of "sensitive knowledge," a knowledge of external things.

Locke is of course aware of this problem, and he struggles courageously but unsuccessfully to avoid it:

There can be nothing more certain than that the idea we receive from an external object is in our minds: this is intuitive knowledge. But whether there can be anything more than barely that idea in our minds, whether we can thence certainly infer the existence of anything without us which corresponds to that idea, is that whereof some men think there may be a question made; because men have such ideas in their minds when no such thing exists. . . . But yet here, I think, we are provided with an evidence that puts us past doubting; for I ask anyone whether he be not invincibly conscious to himself of a different perception when he looks on the sun by day, and thinks on it by night. . . . If anyone say, "A dream may do the same thing, and all these ideas may be produced in us without any external objects;" he may be pleased to dream that I make him this answer: (i) That it is no great matter whether I remove his scruple or no; where all is but dream, reasoning and arguments are of no use, truth and knowledge nothing. (ii) That I believe he will allow a very manifest difference between dreaming of being in the fire, and being actually in it. But yet if he be resolved to appear so sceptical as to maintain that what I call 'being actually in the fire' is nothing but a dream, and that we cannot thereby certainly know that any such thing as fire actually exists without us; I answer that we certainly find that pleasure or pain follows upon the application of certain objects to us, whose existence we perceive, or dream that we perceive, by our senses; this certainty is as great as our happiness or misery, beyond which we have no concernment to know or to be.[8]

The theoretical problem Locke thus simply dismisses on the ground that its insolubility leaves unaffected man's sovereign common sense and its concern with practical life—a subordination of theory to practice which we shall see strengthened in British Empiricism and in the philosophy of Kant. Yet the theoretical problem still remains: if I can know only what is *in* my mind, I cannot also know what is *outside* my mind. Locke tries to hedge this conclusion by changing the object of "sensitive knowledge" from an external thing to something which is *both* inside and outside the mind, namely the *entrance* of an idea into the mind from outside. "Sensitive knowledge" then becomes the "perception . . . of the actual entrance of ideas from [external things]."[9] Yet this answer is clearly unacceptable. If I can apprehend only what is inside my mind, then I can apprehend the allegedly entering idea only while it is inside my mind, and this means that I cannot apprehend its very entrance itself. To observe something entering something is to observe it first outside and then inside that something, and the observation of things outside the mind is what Locke has prohibited.

At this point one may well wonder why Locke sticks to his statement that the mind can know only its own ideas. Instead of tinkering with our sensitive knowledge of the outside world to try to make it conform to the proposition that the object of knowledge is always an idea, why does he not cling robustly to the objectivity of knowledge and simply reject the assumption that we can know only our own ideas? Because he cannot; and the reason he cannot is that his sensory empiricism forces him, as it also forced Hobbes, to describe cognition as if it were a purely physical process analogous to writing with chalk on a clean slate, even though Locke regards cognition metaphysically as immaterial and unextended.

Hobbes's physical theory of cognition forced him to conclude that we can never know the original thing which we think we know, that we know only a later effect of it, although for Hobbes this idea-effect is entirely material in consistency with his materialistic metaphysics, and although Hobbes claimed that the idea-effect which alone we can know is external to us since it is projected out of us by an "outward endeavor." The situation in Locke is essentially the same, except that Locke regards the idea-effects as mental entities and keeps them within the mind rather than projecting them outward. As the image of the *tabula rasa* suggests, Locke seems to regard cognition, while immaterial or unextended, as a quasi-physical process in which a primary quality of a physical substance acts, through mediaries, upon a quasi-physical but metaphysically immaterial mind to produce an idea which is the terminus and object of knowledge. Since this idea is in the mind, all that we can know is the contents of our own minds. This must mean that we cannot legitimately know the external cause of the idea, or even that it has any external cause, and therefore that we cannot legitimately know even that the idea is an effect (since *effect* requires *cause*). Locke should also have been bothered by one factor in this situation which bothered Descartes's followers and critics, namely how an extended material body can act upon an unextended immaterial mind.

Locke does go so far as to grant that the presence of an idea does not assure us that any corresponding external object exists except at the moment of the sensation, but he claims that such assurance is indeed present at that moment.

> . . . this knowledge extends as far as the present testimony of our senses, employed about particular objects that do then affect them, and no farther. For if I saw such a collection of simple ideas as is wont to be called man existing together one minute since, . . . I cannot be certain that the same man exists now, since there is no necessary connection of his existence a minute since with his existence now. . . .[10]

(Compare the last clause with Descartes's second argument for the existence of God, Ch. 8-2.2.) What Locke overlooks, however, is that a present idea must be later than its supposed cause, since the causal process takes time; and one can, therefore, never be sure that any idea has a corresponding external object. While one might be able to be sure of the existence of a copresent cause, the external cause of an idea is never copresent with it but is always temporally antecedent to it.

Locke thus faces a problem peculiar to his Empiricism in trying to derive certainty from sense experience, but he also lands in essentially the same solipsistic impasse as his Rationalist opponents. Although Locke tries to escape from this impasse by means of his concept of sensitive knowledge, the impasse will remain with British Empiricism, as will be increasingly evident; and Berkeley and Hume will retain the impasse and reject Locke's sensitive knowledge.

10-1.3. *Metaphysics*

Although Locke's philosophy is more epistemological than metaphysical, he presents a picture of the world which is much closer to that of Descartes than we might expect from his Empiricist opposition to Descartes's Rationalism.

In the first place, the world includes myself, and of my own existence I have intuitive knowledge; to show this Locke even uses Descartes's *dubito ergo sum.* Locke seems not to realize that the objects of knowledge in general and of intuitive knowledge in particular have been restricted to ideas, for the self which perceives ideas is certainly not an idea itself. Later Berkeley and Hume will realize this fact, however, and will conclude therefrom that either our knowledge of ourselves is of a very peculiar kind or else quite nonexistent. Second, the world includes God; of this we have demonstrative knowledge and thus "more certainly know that there is a God, than that there is anything else without us."[11] Once more Locke seems to neglect the fact that the objects of knowledge in general and demonstrative knowledge in particular have been restricted to ideas. If this restriction is consistently applied it must mean that we cannot have any knowledge of God as a real being outside our minds, that the only "God" we can know, demonstratively or otherwise, is our idea of God, as seemed to be the case with Descartes. Third, the world includes physical bodies; of this we have "sensitive knowledge" as we have seen—although once again such external physical bodies cannot consistently be objects of knowledge if the objects of our knowledge are confined to ideas. Fourth and finally, the world also contains other finite minds, minds other than my own and God's. Here at last Locke, however, frankly accepts the consequence which he had dodged in connection with self, God, and bodies, namely, that we cannot have any knowledge of other finite minds since our knowledge is restricted to our own ideas. The existence of other finite minds Locke accepts only on faith in divine revelation, though in adding that their existence is "highly probable" he apparently forgets that probability can have no meaning in the absence of all evidence. We should recall that the Continental Rationalists also experienced difficulty in establishing the existence of other minds; Descartes was mostly silent on the point, and the Leibnizian monad has no windows. The existence of other finite minds will also become a severe problem for the remaining British Empiricists.

Locke thus presents a world of minds and bodies. My mind

and God's, Locke says, I know with certainty—yet according to his principles neither is really known at all because as known each must be merely an idea. Bodies I know with the practical certainty of "sensitive knowledge," Locke claims—yet according to his principles it can again be only my ideas and not bodies themselves which I know. Other finite minds, here quite in accordance with his principles, are unknowable but accepted on faith. Thus the implications of Locke's philosophy outrun and conflict with his explicit claims. While the philosophy implies, and even states, that he can know only his own ideas, Locke claims that he can know a number of things which are not ideas.

10-1.4. *Political Philosophy*

Locke's social and political philosophy, presented especially in the second of his *Two Treatises of Government,* is the social manifestation of his epistemology and metaphysics, and it therefore contains the same conflict between logical implication and explicit claim. Locke's social and political philosophy may be most basically characterized as a moral individualism, and these two words indicate the two main historical influences on Locke's doctrine. From Richard Hooker (1553–1600) Locke inherits the tradition of natural law ethical and social theory expressed especially in Plato, Aristotle, and Aquinas. One central idea of this natural law tradition is that of the natural moral community: man is by nature both moral and social. From Thomas Hobbes and from the Empiricist epistemology held by both Hobbes and Locke, Locke inherits the concept of a natural nonmoral individualism: society and morality are human conventions. These two sources Locke combines into his own theory of moral individualism: society and the state are human conventions as with Hobbes, but the natural individual is moral as with Hooker. While man is not by his essential nature a political animal, he is as a natural, presocial, individual a moral being who has received moral rights from God.

In Locke's "state of nature" prior to the social contract individual human rights exist, but common power to enforce them does not; so this common power is created by the social contract. These natural rights are, for Locke, life, liberty, and estate; and all of these together he calls property, for they are what are naturally proper to every man, what belong to his own nature prior to contracts and conventions. Locke's justification for his assertion that man has these natural rights is that they are self-evident, that they are seen to be true by reason or "the light of nature." Such a justification is easier to understand within the context of a Rationalism like that of Descartes, however, than within the context of Locke's Empiricism, for how can a light of nature or reason exist to apprehend such self-evident, stable, universal, necessary truths as the natural rights of man if the only access to reality and truth is a sense experience of uncertain, unstable, particular, contingent things?

The fundamental theoretical problems (apart from the practical ones) in Locke's political philosophy are entirely analogous to and derivative from the fundamental problems of his epistemology. In his epistemology the fundamental problems are, first, how to obtain stable, universal, necessary, rational truths when one is in cognitive contact only with fluctuating, particular, contingent, sensory things and, second, how to arrive at a knowledge of extra-mentally real existents when the objects of knowledge are always our own mental ideas. Analogously and derivatively, the fundamental theoretical problems in Locke's political philosophy are, first, how to justify a Cartesian "natural light" with its rational grasp of universal and certain truths about the natural rights of all men on the basis of merely sensory experience of particular and contingent things and, second, how to justify the objective truth of this theory on the basis of Locke's cognitive restriction to his own subjective ideas. Once more, in political philosophy as in epistemology—and in the former because in the latter—the logical implications of Locke's principles and general statements outstrip and prohibit his particular explicit claims. This point will become more manifest in the work of Locke's Empiricist successors, Berkeley and Hume, but a clear picture of it as it stands in Locke's works can be seen in the excellent summary statement of Locke's political theory in George Sabine's *History of Political Theory*, pages 524–26.

10-2. *Berkeley*

George Berkeley (1684–1754), Irishman and Anglican Bishop of Cloyne, is the second great British Empiricist. The logical core of Locke's philosophy maintains, as we have seen, that one can know only particular and contingent sensory ideas within one's own mind. Yet Locke also claims that he can know with certainty (practical or theoretical) three causes of these ideas: bodies, his own mind, and God. Berkeley's basic contribution is that he proceeds one step further in carrying out the implications of the logical core of Locke's philosophy, and thus he writes the second chapter in the story of British Empiricism. Berkeley does this by overtly espousing the nominalism implied in making sensation the only mode of cognition and by denying any material cause of ideas. Let us first consider Berkeley's nominalism, his denial of universals, and then his mentalism, his denial of matter.

10-2.1. *Nominalism*

Berkeley's nominalism is quite explicit in the Introduction to his *Principles of Human Knowledge*. In it he denies the existence of abstract ideas, which he regards as having "occasioned innumerable errors and difficulties in almost all parts of knowledge,"[12] on the ground that it is impossible to "conceive separately, those qualities which it is impossible should exist so separated."[13] Berkeley says he does not deny the existence of general ideas, however; "an idea which considered in itself is particular, becomes general by being made to represent or stand for all other particular ideas *of the same sort.*"[14] Yet this seems to imply that the sort of which they are the same is itself an abstract idea. However that may be, Berkeley is less concerned with developing a nominalistic theory for its own sake and for its other implications than he is with using nominalism as a basis for his proof of the nonexistence of matter, partly because he is convinced that materialism is conducive to atheism and skepticism. Berkeley claims that we cannot possibly have an abstract idea of the existence of a thing apart from its properties. Since he thinks he can show that the properties of so-called material things are mental, he concludes that their existence is mental too. Again, Berkeley claims that we cannot possibly have an abstract or separate idea of the primary qualities apart from the secondary ones. Since he agrees with Locke and will also claim to prove that the secondary qualities are actually mental, it will follow that the primary qualities, and therefore all the properties of so-called material things, are also mental. Other logical implications of Berkeley's nominalism, of his rejection of abstract ideas, will be drawn by Hume, especially in criticizing the notion of causal connection. But let us turn to Berkeley's own use of his nominalism to establish his mentalism.

10-2.2. *Mentalism*

Berkeley's disproof of the existence of matter may be divided into two arguments, the first of which is simply a clear statement and acceptance of the implications of Locke's position: The objects of knowledge are ideas, and ideas are mental. The *esse* or existence of ideas is their *percipi*, their being perceived.[15] While these two propositions seem to imply the conclusion that we cannot know anything outside our own minds at all (Ch. 10-1.2.), Berkeley draws only the less-sweeping conclusion that we cannot meaningfully talk about anything nonmental or not of the nature of mind. Thus matter cannot exist, or more accurately, to say that matter exists is nonsense.

The second argument against the existence of matter is based on the destruction of the existential distinction between primary and secondary qualities, and here Berkeley agrees with Leibniz. As we have just seen, Berkeley argues that we cannot possibly separate the primary qualities of things from their secondary qualities. We cannot sense or imagine any quantitative structure without certain qualities; every seen shape must have some color, every heard vibration some sound. Now everybody from Democritus to Locke admits that secondary qualities are mind-dependent, subjective, and mental, Berkeley argues; and if any further proof of this fact were required we need only be reminded that insofar as they are known, secondary qualities are ideas and that ideas are of course mental. From these two premises it follows that primary qualities are also mental; and since all the qualities of so-called material things are either primary or secondary ones, it follows finally that all the properties which we call material are really mental.

At this point in the argument, however, the determined materialist may claim that even if he grants that all the *properties* of material things are mental, at least a nonmental, material *substance* or substratum still remains underlying these properties. But Berkeley will not permit this escape from his conclusion, for such an alleged underlying material substance, he agrees with Locke, is an unintelligible "I know not what." When the materialist speaks of a "material substance," Berkeley argues quite in line with the nominalism of his sensory empiricism, "no other meaning [is] annexed to those sounds but the idea of *Being in general,* [an idea that is] . . . the most abstract and incomprehensible of all other."[16] Our senses acquaint us only with the concrete properties of things and not with any supposed metaphysical substratum—what does pure substance look like, or sound like, or taste like?—so a sensory empiricism must reject such a word as nonsensical. And when the badgered materialist claims finally and desperately that material substances exist at least as the causes of mental ideas, Berkeley closes his case by reiterating that since we know only ideas we cannot know that any extra-mental causes of them even exist.

> Again, I ask whether those supposed originals or external things, of which our ideas are the pictures or representations, be themselves perceivable or no? If they are, then they are ideas and we have gained our point; but if . . . they are not, I appeal to anyone whether it be sense to assert a color is like something which is invisible; hard or soft, like something which is intangible; and so of the rest . . . an idea can be like nothing but an idea . . . .[17]

From these arguments Berkeley concludes a metaphysical idealism or mentalism, a theory like Leibniz's in maintaining that reality is of the nature of mind:

> . . . all the choir of heaven and furniture of the earth, in a word all those bodies which compose the mighty frame of the world, have not any subsistence without a mind, . . . their *being* is to be perceived or known; . . . consequently so long as they are not actually perceived by me, or do not exist in my mind or that of any other created

spirit, they must either have no existence at all, or else subsist in the mind of some Eternal Spirit; it being perfectly unintelligible, and involving all the absurdity of abstraction, to attribute to any single part of them an existence independent of spirit. To be convinced of which, the reader need only reflect and try to separate in his thoughts the *being* of a sensible thing from its *being perceived*.[18]

In short, if there were external bodies, it is impossible we should ever come to know it; and if there were not, we might have the very same reasons to think that there were that we now have.[19]

This refutation of the reality of matter would seem to make Berkeley a solipsist, however, since all that he knows are his own ideas. But Berkeley, like Descartes, avoids this conclusion by arguing that reality contains another mind beyond his own, namely that of God. Since our ideas are passive and yet come and go, they must have a cause; and this cause must of course be a mind since only minds and their ideas exist. Berkeley argues in concert with Descartes that this causal mind is not his own since many of these ideas come to him against his will, since the world of nature keeps dinning into him however hard he tries to shut it out. Notice that this premise presupposes Descartes's theory that the mind is wholly conscious and self-controlled. From this Berkeley concludes that the cause of these ideas must be some mind or spirit more powerful than himself. When he notes the wondrous order in the world composed of these ideas he concludes finally that this spirit is God, a being infinite in power as well as in goodness—even though all that follows from the argument (if it be valid) is a mind that is great, but not necessarily infinite, in power and goodness. Equipped with God as an eternal and all-powerful mind, Berkeley is now in a position to answer the objection that if physical things are only collections of ideas they must evaporate when no one is perceiving them, that the fire must be annihilated when we leave the room and be created *ex nihilo* when we return:

> There was a young man who said, "God
> Must think it exceedingly odd
>   If he finds that this tree
>   Continues to be
> When there's no one about in the Quad."[20]

However, physical things are not annihilated when humans forget them because, Berkeley argues, they are always perceived by the unblinking omniscience of God:

> Dear sir:
> Your astonishment's odd:
> *I* am always about in the Quad.
> And that's why the tree
> Will continue to be,
> Since observed by
> *Yours faithfully,*
> God.[21]

Thus Berkeley's refutation of materialism is at the same time, he believes, a demonstration of theism, so sound philosophy produces an enlightened piety.

While God's omniperception thus saves physical things from annihilation, however, Descartes might have objected that it would appear to do so only at the cost of making God a deceiver, for in Berkeley's view God rather than the physical world implants the ideas of physical things in our minds. Indeed, we should note that Berkeley's argument for the existence of God is essentially the same as Descartes's argument for the existence of matter. However, Berkeley meets this objection by denying Descartes's claim that we cannot help but believe in the existence of matter (Ch. 8-2.3). While Berkeley agrees with Descartes that we cannot help having ideas of physical things since they are dinned into us against our will, he holds that we can indeed avoid believing in the reality of physical things. We can avoid believing that any real material world exists corresponding to and causing these ideas of physical things; and we should do so, he thinks, for the reasons he has given. While God does implant in us the ideas which constitute the world of nature, He does not make us believe that this world of nature is metaphysically material. We do that ourselves through insufficient reflection and inadequate attention to the philosophy of Berkeley.

The world as pictured in the results of Berkeley's arguments contains only ideas and the three types of minds or spirits which perceive them: God, oneself, and other finite (presumably human) minds. While we know our own minds directly, according to Berkeley, we know God and other human minds only indirectly, God being known as the cause of certain of our ideas. We know other human minds only by analogy to our own. Berkeley writes, "A human spirit or person is not perceived by sense, as not being an idea. . . . Hence it is plain we do not see a man . . . but only such a certain collection of ideas as directs us to think there is a distinct principle of thought and motion, like to ourselves, accompanying and represented by it."[22] Since we directly know our own minds and our own bodily behavior, and since we experience other bodily behavior similar to our own, we infer by analogy that this other bodily behavior must be connected with a mind like our own. Hume will expose the weakness of such arguments from analogy, pointing out that their modicum of validity can obtain only when we have had past experience of other instances of the inferred term, and of course Berkeley grants that we have never experienced an instance of another human mind. Furthermore, we should carefully note that the Divine Mind or God could perfectly well be the cause of those experienced patterns of bodily behavior which we infer to be caused by another human mind—just as He is the cause of the bodily behavior of inanimate things. "There is not any one mark that denotes a man, or effect produced by him," Berkeley himself remarks, "which does not more strongly evince the being of that Spirit who is the Author of Nature."[23] Thus the hypothesis of God explains the phenomena without recourse to the additional hypothesis of other human minds, for anything that man can do God can do and better. Descartes's recognition of this fact may well be the reason that other finite minds are so conspicuously absent from his official world view. Hence Berkeley would have kept closer to his principles if he, like Locke, had held that the existence of other finite minds is accepted only on faith in divine revelation; on this particular point and contrary to the general situation, Locke is more advanced than Berkeley in accepting the implications of sensory empiricism.

While reality thus consists of ideas and minds, we can never have an idea of minds or spirits because they are themselves the perceiv*ers* of ideas rather than the ideas perceiv*ed*. The *esse* or being of ideas is *percipi* or being perceived, but the *esse* or being of minds is *percipere* or perceiving. However, we can and do have "notions" of minds, according to Berkeley, because "what I know, that I have some notion of."[24] But Berkeley never gives any clear notion of what he means by a "notion," though he does say, however, that "we comprehend our own existence by inward feeling or reflection, and that of other spirits by reason"[25]—both of which would seem to involve ideas. Moreover, his general position that the objects of knowledge are ideas seems to indicate that we can in fact have no knowledge of any mind or spirit. To draw this conclusion, however, would be to evacuate Berkeley's universe completely, since matter has already been removed and since ideas depend upon minds. To have the world that he wants Berkeley must qualify his sensory empiricism, and his explicit claims, especially of a knowledge of minds as well as of ideas, therefore lag behind and conflict with the logical implications of his principles. In rejecting the notion of external material things Berkeley goes further than Locke did in accepting the implications of their common doctrine, but in retaining the existence of minds outside ideas he still does not follow sensory empiricism to its final conclusion.

10-2.3. *The Problem of Unperceivable Causes*

A distillation of the preceding discussion reveals that Berkeley's fundamental problem is the presence in his alleged empiricism of unperceivable causes. Berkeley's division of the world into minds and their ideas is basically the distinction between causes and effects, in which only the effects, the ideas, can actually be perceived. Berkeley has indeed removed Descartes's and Locke's dualism between ideas and *material* causal objects, a dualism which made it impossible to know material objects themselves, or even that they exist. Berkeley clearly sees the difficulty caused by this idea–material cause dualism. ". . . we have been led into very dangerous errors," he writes, "by supposing a twofold existence of the objects of sense—the one *intelligible* or in the mind, the other *real* and without the mind . . . for how can it be known that the things which are perceived are conformable to those which are not perceived . . . ?"[26] Moreover, he continues, "So long as we attribute a real existence to unthinking things, dis-

tinct from their being perceived, it is not only impossible for us
to know with evidence the nature of any real unthinking being,
but even that it exists."[27]

While avoiding this idea–material cause dualism by making
physical things consist of God's perceptions, however, Berkeley
still retains another dualism: the dualism of ideas and their
Divine cause. So long as Berkeley agrees with Descartes and
Locke in having a correspondence theory of truth, a theory
which makes truth consist of a correspondence between ideas
and extra-mental realities, he must have this dualism of idea and
Divine cause in order to account for the possibility of truth and
error. With a correspondence theory of truth and lacking material things, error and truth would be indistinguishable without
God as the objective, extra-mentally real cause of true ideas.
Since Berkeley still retains the essentials of the idea–external
cause dualism of Descartes and Locke, though without their
material causes, it follows that he is driven to the same impasse
as they: the impasse of being confined to one's own subjective
ideas, of being unable to get to real, external things (now God
and other finite minds). This impasse is quite apparently present
in Berkeley's own statements if we make only two omissions
from and one addition to the last passage quoted: "So long as
we attribute a real existence to . . . things, distinct from their
being perceived [by us], it is not only impossible for us to know
with evidence the nature of any real . . . being, but even that it
exists." Berkeley does escape from this solipsistic impasse, but,
like Descartes and Locke, only with the tour de force of unperceivable causes: God and other finite minds. Can unperceivable causes be allowed in a consistent empiricism? Hume
will say, "No," and will thus conclude the story of British
Empiricism.

10-3. *Hume*

David Hume (1711–1776) of Scotland is the last in the trilogy of
the great British Empiricists. Hume's conclusion of the story of
British Empiricism consists essentially in drawing the ultimate
logical conclusions from Locke's and Berkeley's premises—or at
least as nearly so as probably any philosopher has ever done.

Whereas Berkeley eliminated matter from Locke's Cartesian world of mind, matter, and God on the ground that matter is unperceivable, Hume eliminates mind and God as well, insofar as they are unperceivable, thus leaving only ideas. Since God, one's own mind, and other finite minds are not ideas but unperceivable substances which are the alleged causes of ideas, their existence is just as empirically unacceptable as the existence of the material substance which Berkeley had banished. "We have no perfect idea of anything but of a perception," Hume writes in Section Four of his *Treatise on Human Nature.* "A substance is entirely different from a perception. We have, therefore, no idea of a substance." Thus substances and all other unperceivable entities must be banished from a consistent empiricism. To observe this elimination of all unperceivable substances we will examine first Hume's epistemology and then the use he makes of it in metaphysics and theology.

10-3.1. *Epistemological Framework*

Hume's basic theory of knowledge is essentially the same as that of Locke and Berkeley: a radical sensory empiricism. The elements of knowledge which Locke and Berkeley called ideas Hume calls perceptions, and all perceptions are either impressions or ideas. "By the term *impression* . . . I mean all our more lively perceptions, when we hear, or see, or feel, or hate, or desire, or will. . . . ideas . . . are the less lively perceptions, of which we are conscious, when we reflect on any of those sensations or movements just mentioned."[28] Thus impressions are immediate sensations, and ideas are the imaginative and memory images which are copies of them. All perceptions, impressions and their idea-copies, have their source in sensation; and sensation, according to Hume, is either external or internal. The act of knowing anything is then the compounding or transposing or augmenting or diminishing of these impressions or ideas.

The product of these cognitive operations upon sensory materials is knowledge, and Hume divides all knowledge or all knowable propositions into two types: "relations of ideas" and "matters of fact." Relations-of-ideas are propositions which are universally and necessarily true, and following Locke, Hume subdivides this type of knowledge into intuitive and demonstrative knowledge. The truth of relations-of-ideas is based solely on the law of noncontradiction; such propositions, like Leibniz's truths of reason, are ones whose contradictories involve contradictions, either in themselves (like, "Marsupials lack pouches.")—in which case they are instances of intuitive knowledge—or by means of other propositions (like, "Wallabies lack pouches.")— in which case they are instances of demonstrative knowledge. Here we must raise the same question which was raised in connection with Locke (Ch. 10-1.2): How is it possible to get the stable, universal forms or concepts whose analysis constitutes such universal and necessary certainties from the utterly particular and contingent uncertainties of sensory impressions? How can we possibly know that *all* marsupials *must* have pouches, for example, if we have access to no universal forms and possess only sense impressions of this particular marsupial or that, no two of which are exactly the same? This problem is akin to those of induction and causation which will be considered later, and it is a question which will be of special interest to Kant.

Matter-of-fact knowledge, which Hume also calls moral reasoning, is concerned with real existence like Locke's sensitive knowledge. Like Leibniz's truths of fact, moreover, matter-of-fact propositions are those which lack certainty because their contradictions are perfectly consistent. To see clearly Hume's contrast between relations-of-ideas and matters-of-fact, compare the following two propositions: "All black berries are black," and "All blackberries are black."[29] While the first proposition is certainly true because it is self-contradictory to assert that some berries which are black are not black, the second is not necessarily true (and in fact is actually false) since it is not at all self-contradictory to assert that some examples of the species known as "blackberry" are some color other than black. In fact, as the farm-boys say, "Blackberries are red when they're green." Thus the first proposition is an example of relation-of-ideas knowledge and the second a case of matter-of-fact knowledge.

10-3.2. *Application to Causation*

Having developed this epistemological framework, Hume proceeds to apply it to the major problems of metaphysics and especially to the metaphysical entities of Locke and Berkeley. Every entity, in order to be admitted as legitimate, must conform to the criterion of Empiricism: "Show me the impression!" "When we entertain . . . any suspicion that a philosophical term is employed without any meaning or idea (as is but too frequent)," Hume writes, "we need but inquire, *from what impression is that supposed idea derived?*"[30] The first term to which Hume applied this criterion is *causal connection,* since (as was evident in examining Berkeley's problem) causal connection is the foundation for all belief in real existence or matters of fact, the foundation for all our inductive generalizations.

In analyzing this concept of causal connection three characteristics soon come to light: contiguity or the spatial touching of the cause and effect (as the bat strikes the ball, for example), the temporal succession of cause and effect, the effect following the cause in time, and some kind of power which seems to flow mysteriously from the cause into the effect to produce a necessary connection between them. The first two characteristics present no problem for they easily meet the criterion of "Show me the impression"; we immediately sense the spatial and temporal juxtaposition of a cause with its effect. In the case of remote causes this juxtaposition occurs only by means of intermediate causes, but still it is there. The third characteristic, the supposed necessary connection between cause and effect arising from a mysterious power flowing from one into the other, presents a problem, however; and Hume's solution to this problem by means of his Empiricist analysis of the term "necessary connection" constitutes probably his most famous contribution.

Such an alleged necessary connection between cause and effect is, in the first place, certainly not knowable on purely logical grounds, as a relation-of-ideas truth, according to Hume, because there is no contradiction in affirming the existence of the cause while denying that of its effect.

> The mind can never possibly find the effect in the supposed cause, by the most accurate scrutiny and examination. For the effect is totally different from the cause, and consequently can never be discovered in it. Motion in the second billiard ball is a quite distinct

event from motion in the first; nor is there anything in the one to suggest the smallest hint of the other.[31]

In the second place, the alleged necessary connection is not seen in empirical or matter-of-fact knowledge because, try as we may, we can find no sensory impression of this alleged connection.

> When we look about us toward external objects . . . we are never able . . . to discover any power or necessary connection; any quality, which binds the effect to the cause, and renders the one an infallible consequence of the other. The impulse of one billiard ball is attended with motion in the second. This is the whole that appears to the *outward* senses. The mind feels no sentiment or *inward* impression from this succession of objects: consequently [nothing] . . . can suggest the idea of power or necessary connection.[32]

This is, of course, just the conclusion we should expect to be drawn in an exclusively sensory empiricism for the objects of the senses are only the particular, unique, and contingent aspects of things. Since this supposed necessary connection between cause and effect is thus neither logically nor empirically discoverable, Hume concludes that it cannot be what we are referring to when we link cause and effect together.

To what then does the expression "necessary connection" refer? What is the empirically real connection between cause and effect? Hume finds the key to the answer to this question in the fact that we do not link two things together as cause and effect until after we have experienced them together a number of times.

> . . . this idea of a necessary connection among events arises from a number of similar instances which occur of the constant conjunction of these events. But there is nothing in a number of instances, different from every single instance. . . . except only, that after a repetition of similar instances, the mind is carried by habit, upon the appearance of one event, to expect its usual attendant, and to believe that it will exist. This connection, therefore, which we *feel* in the mind, this customary transition of the imagination from one object to its usual attendant, is the sentiment or impression from which we form the idea of power or necessary connection. Nothing farther is the case.[33]

Thus cause and effect are not linked together objectively by any necessary connection or metaphysical bond between them in themselves, for there is not and cannot be any sensory experience of such a bond. Rather the perception of a cause and the perception of its effect are linked together subjectively by our minds when we get into the habit of expecting the one to accompany the other after they have always or usually done so in the past. Since we have often seen and heard an explosion follow the lighting of the fuse of a fire-cracker, for example, we are unable to avoid flinching in expectation of an explosion after the lighting of the fuse of a fire-cracker—even though we know perfectly well that it may turn out to be a dud. Inductive generalizations are thus "customary conjunctions."

Causal connection is therefore really only customary or habitual conjunction, and Hume defines it accordingly: A cause is *"an object followed by another, and whose appearance always conveys the thought to that other."*[34] The necessary connection is thus a subjective or psychological or mental one, but this important fact should be carefully noted. While Hume finds no objective, physical, or metaphysical necessary connection, his theory and definition of causation do require a subjective, mental or psychological, necessary connection or power, a connection expressed in the fact that thought is always and necessarily conveyed from the idea of the cause to that of the effect. This point more than any other of Hume's Kant will regard as "awakening" him from his "dogmatic slumber."

What, then, is the conclusion of the whole matter? A simple one; though, it must be confessed, pretty remote from the common theories of philosophy. All belief of matter of fact or real existence is derived merely from some object, present to the memory or senses, and a customary conjunction between that and some other object . . . having found, in many instances, that any two kinds of objects— flame and heat, snow and cold—have always been conjoined together; if flame or snow be presented anew to the senses, the mind is carried by custom to expect heat or cold, and to *believe* that such a quality does exist, and will discover itself upon a nearer approach. This belief is the necessary result of placing the mind in such circumstances. It is an operation of the soul, when we are so situated,

as unavoidable as to feel the passion of love, when we receive bene-
fits; or hatred, when we meet with injuries. All these operations are
a species of natural instincts, which no reasoning or process of the
thought and understanding is able either to produce or prevent.
At this point, it would be very allowable for us to stop our philosophical researches. In most questions we can never make a single
step farther; and in all questions we must terminate here, after our
most restless and curious inquiries.[35]

10-3.3. *Application to Unperceivable Causes*

Hume does not in fact stop here, but his continuation is
almost anticlimactic. Since belief in all real beings, beings other
than perceptions, rests upon the causal relation, and since the
causal relation is only a subjective connection in our minds
without any corresponding objective validity, belief in anything
beyond our own perceptions, while subjectively or psychologically necessary and inescapable, is entirely lacking in objective
validity. Thus he destroys one pillar of Continental Rationalism, that whatever is true of thought is true of reality (Ch. 9-5).
In its stead is the principle of habit or custom, which was for
Bacon an Idol of the Tribe, and an attendant supremacy of
practice over rational theory. On this basis any claim to war-
ranted belief in such metaphysical entities as material substance,
the soul, free will, and God must, in accordance with the dictum
with which Hume closes his *Enquiry Concerning Human Understanding,* be committed to the flames, "for it can contain
nothing but sophistry and illusion." Let us see in detail how this
is accomplished.

Since volition is a type of causation, the will is subject to necessity and determination just as much, but also just as little, as
are physical events. Experience shows that our voluntary acts
follow from our characters and that the latter are conditioned
by environmental influences; however, we must remember that
there is, according to Hume, no objectively necessary connection
between any two events, and therefore none exists between our
voluntary acts and our characters or environments. Thus, according to Hume, there is no free will if "free will" means that
voluntary acts are uniquely different from mechanical ones in

having no relevant antecedents, no causes, but free will does exist in the sense that voluntary acts are not objectively necessitated by their antecedents; they are not under compulsion. Thus all actions are equally free and equally unfree.

Material substances Hume rejects on the Berkeleyan ground that they are not perceivable.

> By what argument can it be proved, that the perceptions of the mind must be caused by external objects, entirely different from them, though resembling them (if that be possible) and could not arise either from the energy of the mind itself, or from the suggestion of some invisible and unknown spirit, or from some other cause still more unknown to us? By experience surely. . . . But here experience is, and must be, entirely silent. The mind has never anything present to it but the perceptions, and cannot possibly reach any experience of their connection with objects. The supposition of such a connection is therefore without any foundation in reasoning.³⁶

The mind or self falls on the same ground, and in this Hume goes beyond Berkeley and Locke to explicate a point which is only implicit in their theories. "Philosophers begin to be reconcil'd to the principle, *that we have no idea of external substance distinct from the ideas of particular qualities,*" Hume writes in the Appendix to his *Treatise.* "This must pave the way for a like principle with regard to the mind, *that we have no notion of it, distinct from the particular perceptions.*"

> It must be some one impression, that gives rise to every real idea. But self or person is not any one impression, but that to which our several impressions and ideas are supposed to have a reference. If any impression gives rise to the idea of self, that impression must continue invariably the same, thro' the whole course of our lives; since self is supposed to exist after that manner. But there is no impression constant and invariable. . . . All . . . are different and distinguishable, and separable from each other, and may be separately consider'd and may exist separately, and have no need of anything to support their existence. . . . For my part, when I enter most intimately into what I call *myself,* I always stumble on some particular perception or other, of heat or cold, light or shade, love or hatred, pain or pleasure. I never can catch *myself* at any time

without a perception, and never can observe any thing but the perception . . . I may venture to affirm of . . . mankind, that they are nothing but a bundle or collection of different perceptions, which succeed each other with an inconceivable rapidity, and are in a perpetual flux. . . . The mind is a kind of theatre, where several perceptions successively make their appearance; pass, repass, glide away, and mingle in an infinite variety of postures and situations. . . . The comparison of the theatre must not mislead us. They are the successive perceptions only, that constitute the mind; nor have we the most distant notion of the place, where these scenes are represented, or of the materials, of which it is compos'd.[37]

Thus does Hume clearly and unfalteringly affirm the implication of Locke's and Berkeley's principle that the mind can know only ideas.

10-3.4. *Application to God*

Finally, God too is subject to the same fate, for Hume's position on theology is a consistent application of his general philosophical position: there can be no valid proof of God, but from force of habit or instinct we cannot help believing in Him. Hume speaks in the person of Philo:

Our ideas reach no farther than our experience: we have no experience of divine attributes and operations: I need not conclude my syllogism: you can draw the inference yourself. [Furthermore,] . . . it is a pleasure to me (and I hope to you too) that just reasoning and sound piety here concur in the same conclusion, and both of them establish the adorably mysterious and incomprehensible nature of the Supreme Being.[38]

In the *Dialogues* Hume analyzes the two main types of argument for the existence of God: empirical and rational. The empirical argument is the argument from design presented by Cleanthes:

The curious adapting of means to ends, throughout all nature, resembles exactly, though it much exceeds, the productions of human contrivance. . . . Since therefore the effects resemble each other, we are led to infer, by all the rules of analogy, that the causes also resemble; and that the Author of Nature is somewhat similar to the mind of men; though possessed of much larger faculties, proportioned to the grandeur of the work, which he has executed. By this . . . do we prove at once the existence of a Deity, and his similarity to human mind and intelligence.[39]

Hume criticizes this argument from analogy along the lines indicated in our discussion of Berkeley's argument for the existence of other finite minds, namely that we never have and never can have any experience of other instances of the concluded term in the analogical structure, that we can never experience a God making a world. Philo says:

> When two species of objects have always been observed to be conjoined together, I can infer, by custom the existence of one wherever I see the existence of the other: and this I call an argument from experience. But . . . will any man tell me with a serious countenance, that an orderly universe must arise from some thought and art, like the human; because we have experience of it? To ascertain this reasoning, it were requisite, that we had experience of the origin of worlds. . . .[40]

Philo also sees in Cleanthes' argument from design an instance of the "fallacy of composition":

> . . . can you think, Cleanthes, that your usual phlegm and philosophy have been preserved in so wide a step as you have taken, when you compared to the universe, houses, ships, furniture, machines . . . ? Thought, design, intelligence . . . is no more than one of the springs and principles of the universe. . . . But can a conclusion, with any propriety, be transferred from parts to the whole? . . . From observing the growth of a hair, can we learn anything concerning the generation of a man?[41]

Whether Hume's conception of the argument from design is the best one, however, is another question.*

The rational argument as Demea presents it at the beginning of Part IX begins as a causal argument like those of Aristotle and Aquinas but ends as the ontological argument. Hume's criticism of this ontological argument contains the essential point which has already been noted (Chs. 6-1 and 8-2.2), the point that the existence we conceive God to have may be an

---

* Compare Thomas Aquinas's fifth way in his *Summa Theologica*, Pt. I, Question 2, Article 3.

existence only in our mind, but Hume extends this point in accordance with his theory that all matter-of-fact propositions lack certainty and all certain propositions (relations-of-ideas) lack factuality or existential reference. Cleanthes says for Philo:

> . . . there is an evident absurdity in pretending to demonstrate a matter of fact, or to prove it by any arguments *a priori*. Nothing is demonstrable, unless the contrary implies a contradiction. Nothing, that is distinctly conceivable, implies a contradiction. Whatever we conceive as existent, we can also conceive as non-existent. There is no being, therefore, whose non-existence implies a contradiction. Consequently there is no being, whose existence is demonstrable.[42]

Besides being invalid, these arguments also lead to unwanted conclusions, according to Hume. The argument from design is perfectly compatible with, and even more plausible in, a polytheistic context, for just as human artifacts may be and often are made by many men working together, the world too may have been designed by many Gods. And the argument for God as first cause of all things would seem to make Him also the cause of evil.

Hume's conclusion* from these considerations is that "the dispute concerning theism is . . . merely verbal."[43]

> I ask the theist, if he does not allow, that there is a great and immeasurable, because incomprehensible, difference between the *human* and the *divine* mind. The more pious he is, the more readily will he assent to the affirmative, and the more he will be disposed to magnify the difference: he will even assert that the difference is of a nature which cannot be too much magnified. I next turn to the atheist, who, I assert, is only nominally so, and can never possibly be in earnest; and I ask him, whether, from the coherence and apparent sympathy in all the parts of this world, there be not a certain degree of analogy among all the operations of nature. . . . It is impossible

---

* This conclusion is stated by Philo; and even though the dramatic narrator of the dialogue (Pamphilus) concludes cryptically that Cleanthes comes nearest to the truth, I interpret Philo's position as being nearest to that of Hume. Within the dramatic setting of the dialogues Pamphilus is the pupil of Cleanthes and the son of his intimate friend, so his favoring of Cleanthes is not unprejudiced. Furthermore, Philo, like the Socrates in Plato's dialogues, is the major dramatic character. Finally, only Philo's position follows logically from Hume's basic philosophy.

he can deny it: he will readily acknowledge it. Having obtained this concessi٫n, I push him still farther in his retreat; and I ask him, if it be not probable, that the principle which first arranged, and still maintains order in this universe, bears not also some remote inconceivable analogy to the other operations of nature, among the rest to the economy of human mind and thought. However reluctant, he must give his assent. Where then, cry I to both these antagonists, is the subject of your dispute?⁴⁴

Skeptical empiricism is thus not at all opposed to true religion, Hume argues. Indeed, "a person, seasoned with a just sense of the imperfections of natural reason, will fly to revealed truth with the greatest avidity, . . . [so] To be a philosophical skeptic is, in a man of letters, the first and most essential step towards being a sound, believing Christian."⁴⁵ Though Hume sometimes sounds as if he has his tongue in his cheek, he manages to reconcile apparent opposites with a single argument: he satisfies both the skeptical Empiricist and the man of faith with a liaison of skepticism and fideism. This liaison was noted in the transition from medieval to modern philosophy, and it survives today in a frequent alliance of logical Empiricism and neoorthodox theology.

10-4. *The Story of British Empiricism*

In the final chapter in the story of seventeenth and eighteenth century British Empiricism Hume carries the fundamental theses of Empiricism to their logical conclusion. The two most fundamental characteristics of this Empiricism, nominalism and solipsism (Ch. 10-1.2), arise from its very definition, that all knowledge is confined to sense experience. Nominalism arises from the sensationism of British Empiricism, since sensation presents only unique particulars and never any universal forms. "Abstraction," Hume argues in concert with Berkeley, is an "unintelligible and even absurd" expression.⁴⁶ "An extension, that is neither tangible nor visible, cannot possibly be conceived. . . . Let any man try to conceive a triangle in general which is neither *isosceles* nor *scalenum,* nor has any particular length or proportion of sides; and he will soon perceive the ab-

surdity of all the scholastic notions with regard to abstraction
and general ideas."[47] This is indeed true of sensory images, and
the fact that Hume regards it as true of concepts as well is proof
of his sensationism and nominalism. Since no sensory image has
any necessary connection with any other, since each is complete
in itself and absolutely self-contained, the nominalism of British
Empiricism also produces an atomism similar to that of Descartes and Leibniz—except, of course, that the Empiricists' atoms
are sensory instead of conceptual—in which each sensory atom
is a substance, so far as that term has any meaning. Hume writes:

> Whatever is clearly conceiv'd may exist, and whatever is clearly
> conceiv'd, after any manner, may exist after the same manner. . . .
> Again, every thing, which is different, is distinguishable, and every
> thing which is distinguishable, is separable by the imagination. . . .
> My conclusion . . . is, that since all our perceptions are different
> from each other, and from every thing else in the universe, they are
> also distinct and separable, and may be consider'd as separately
> existent, and may exist separately, and have no need of anything
> else to support their existence. They are, therefore, substances, as
> far as this definition explains a substance.[48]

Thus atomism is one conclusion which British Empiricism
draws in common with Continental Rationalism.

Solipsism is the other fundamental characteristic of British
Empiricism and a second conclusion which it shares with Continental Rationalism. The reason for the solipsism is essentially
the same in the two movements, namely a restriction of one's
knowledge to one's own ideas. As the logical implication of a
tacit theory of cognition as a quasi-physical process, Locke affirms the general principle: "Since the mind, in all its thoughts
and reasonings, hath no other immediate object but its own
ideas, which it alone does or can contemplate, it is evident that
our knowledge is only conversant about them,"[49] although he
deviates from this principle by claiming intuitive knowledge of
the self, demonstrative knowledge of God, and sensitive knowledge of material bodies. Berkeley reaffirms this principle and is
consistent with it in his rejection of matter but inconsistent with
it in his claim of having notions of the self, other finite minds,
and God. Hume, however, not only affirms the principle but

sticks consistently to it, at least in all essentials, rejecting the notions of the self, other finite minds, and God as anything knowable by us, as well as the notion of external bodies. Hume thus shows that the British Empiricist can consistently know nothing but his own atomistically disconnected perceptions. Hume's awareness of this solipsism is presented in his conclusion to his *Treatise* (Section VI) in a picture of the isolation from others in which his philosophy places him:

> I am first affrighted and confounded with that forlorn solitude, in which I am plac'd in my philosophy, and fancy myself some strange uncouth monster, who not being able to mingle and unite in society, has been expell'd all human commerce, and left utterly abandon'd and disconsolate. Fain wou'd I run into the crowd for shelter and warmth; but cannot prevail with myself to mix with such deformity.

Here is a recognition both logical and psychological of the solipsism which has lain at or near the surface of both Continental Rationalism and British Empiricism, a solipsism which was at least predictable if not actually inevitable once Descartes began with his own mind. In this solipsism the self will, of course, be absolute and in that sense God, as Leibniz's own monad seemed to be.

From another more logical and yet paradoxical point of view, however, this solipsism which Hume explicates from both the Rationalist and the Empiricist movements is really not a solipsism at all because, as Hume has shown, the *ipse* or self cannot be known to exist. If *all* that I can know is my own ideas, then I cannot know even the "my" or self which has these ideas. And if that is the case then it is nonsense to say that I can know only myself, or that only I myself exist. Not merely the self but also the *solus* or only in solipsism prevents Hume's statement of the conclusion of the Rationalist and Empiricist philosophies of ideas from being a true solipsism, however, for if I can in fact know *only* ideas I cannot also know that anything exists *other* than ideas which I am incapable of knowing, and if this is so then it makes no sense to say that I know *only* ideas or that my knowledge is *restricted* to them. At this point, therefore, the solipsism logically implied in these two stories turns paradoxically into its opposite. I can no longer say that there is any restriction at all on my knowledge. Though I may call whatever I know an idea or a perception, I must say that everything that I know is fully objective, so far as this term now has any meaning, since there is for me nothing any more objective or any more subjective than these ideas. From this point of view, the world is composed of ideas or perceptions, but these are qualitatively indistinguishable from the rocks, trees, and clouds which constitute the objective world of common sense. This objectivistic, or at least nonsubjectivistic, interpretation of the outcome of the seventeenth and eighteenth century philosophies of ideas as they culminate in Hume has been made by many of Hume's twentieth century followers, especially by the American neorealists and by the logical positivists.[50]

Even if ideas or perceptions are identified with objective things, however, the person who identifies these idea-things still remains, by that very fact, an item which is different from his idea-things and which must therefore be accounted for separately. The work of this unperceivable self is manifest even in Hume in his concept of habit or custom, for without the subjectively or psychologically necessary connections among events introduced by habit or custom, Hume's world would not possess even that reduced degree of unity and interconnectedness which it does. The exploration of this transcendent self and its organizing activities will be the central motif of German Voluntarism in Kant and his followers. Does Empiricism involve an *external* nonempirical *source* of ideas or perceptions as well as an internal organizer of them? Not at all, a consistent appraisal of Hume's philosophy would indicate, and Kant's German Voluntarist followers will agree, but Kant himself, in a reversion to Descartes and Locke, will insist that it does, that there must be an external unperceivable source of the materials of knowledge as well as an internal unperceivable mind.

Thus the British Empiricists end in the Continental Rationalists' circle of ideas, though they follow the way of sense instead of the way of reason; and their way of sense also repeats and even aggravates the atomism involved in the Rationalists' principle of distinctness. Is there any way in which these two conclusions can be avoided? Kant and the German Voluntarists will avoid the conclusion of atomism by stressing that unifying power of the mind which can be glimpsed in the activities of Hume's principle of habit or custom. The conclusion of subjectivism they will not be able to avoid; but they will remove its sting by absolutizing it, thus being true to the developing essence of modernity, by raising the subjective mind to the level of an objective absolute. Let us now see how these two feats are accomplished.

SUGGESTED READINGS

10-1. Locke. *Essay Concerning Human Understanding.* Bk. II, Chs. 1–2, 8, 12, 23; Bk. IV, Chs. 1–2, 3 (Secs. 1–5 and 21), 9–11.

_____. The second of the *Two Treatises of Government.* Chs. 1–3, 5 (Secs. 25–40), 7 (Secs. 87–90), 8 (Secs. 95–99, 119–22), 9.

10-2. Berkeley. *Principles of Human Knowledge.*

10-3. Hume. *Enquiry Concerning Human Understanding.* Secs. 2–5, 7–8, 12.

_____. *Treatise of Human Nature.* Pt. II, Sec. 6; Pt. IV, Secs. 5 and 6; Conclusion; and Appendix.

_____. *Dialogues Concerning Natural Religion.* Pts. II, IX, and XII.

For bibliography, see:

10-1. Aaron, R. I. *John Locke.* 2nd. ed. Oxford: Clarendon Press, 1963. Pp. 309–317.

10-2. Wild, John. *George Berkeley.* Cambridge, Mass.: Harvard University Press, 1936. Pp. 529–46.

10-3. Zabeeh, F. *Hume.* The Hague: Martinus Nijhoff, 1960. Pp. 160–62.

Chapter 11

German
Voluntarism
in
Kant

Immanuel Kant (1724–1804) was influenced by three main strands of thought: Newtonian science, religious pietism, and the history of Western philosophy. The main philosophical influences on Kant are Continental Rationalism (which Kant calls Dogmatism) and British Empiricism (which he calls Skepticism), and Kant sees these two movements as a thesis and antithesis whose synthesis is to be Kant's own philosophy.

The Continental Rationalists regarded the mind as primarily reason, and the British Empiricists regarded it as primarily sensation. Kant concludes that since neither movement could justify possession of universal and necessary truths about the objective world, the knowing mind cannot be reduced to either reason or sensation alone but must involve both in an intimate interplay with each other. Furthermore, the intrusion of the modern knowing subject between itself and the objective world, which was unwanted yet increasingly evident all the way from Bacon's Idols of the Tribe to Hume's custom or habit, Kant concludes was an inevitable and necessary aspect of knowing. Kant thus makes into a virtue the subjectivity which had never wholly ceased being a vice in previous modern philosophy. Let us therefore revolutionize our attitude toward the knowing subject, Kant suggests, and regard it as an active contributor to the objects of knowledge. This starting point was suggested to Kant especially by the active, organizing role of Hume's principle of habit. The knowing mind is no longer a passive spectator mirroring the objective world; it is an active creator of its knowledge, making the objects of its knowledge as the will makes its practical deeds. Because of this productive activity the mind as theoretical reason shall become merged with will as practical reason, a will which is rational in accordance with the Continental Rationalists but which necessarily works on sensory materials in accordance with British Empiricism.

The third and final story within the overall story of modern philosophy, the story of German Voluntarism, begins with Kant basically identifying mind with active will. This period is usually called German Idealism, but its idealism, its identification of reality with mind, is the pervasive characteristic of all modern philosophy—as is becoming increasingly evident—whereas its emphasis upon the productive activity of mind and hence its merging of mind with will is unique to this period and thus demands for it the more distinctive name "German Voluntarism," the growing identification of reality with active will. We shall consider first Kant's theory of knowledge and reality (the *Critique of Pure Reason* and the *Prolegomena to Any Future Metaphysics Which Can Come Forth as a Science*) and then his ethical theory (the *Critique of Practical Reason* and the *Fundamental Principles of the Metaphysics of Morals*).

11-1. *Epistemology and Metaphysics*

11-1.1. *The Problem of Knowledge*

The most fundamental and general problem which Kant attempts to solve is this: How is knowledge possible? That knowledge is indeed possible and even actual—at least mathematical and scientific knowledge—Kant, like Plato, considers a settled fact requiring no proof, for it was clear to Kant that Newtonian science had arrived to stay. What bothered Kant was the problem of the theoretical justification of this knowledge, especially in view of the solipsistic and nominalistic outcome of Continental Rationalism and British Empiricism. This problem of the possibility of knowledge may be stated more specifically and fruitfully in two different ways.

Knowledge requires universality and necessity; Kant inherits this principle from the Continental Rationalists. The propositions of mathematics and science, for example, say what all things of a given class must be. But this universality and necessity which are essential to knowledge are not derivable from experience. This principle Kant inherits from Continental Rationalism, and he finds its confirmation in the story of British Empiricism. Kant accepts without question the Rationalists' and Empiricists' identification of experience with sense experience, and he realizes that the senses present only the particular and contingent aspects of things. From these two principles Kant's problem arises immediately: What is the source of the universality and necessity which are essential to knowledge? It cannot be experience—Kant tacitly regards this as established by both Rationalism and Empiricism—so universality and necessity must arise from some other domain. But what domain? This is the question Kant attempts to answer, a question basically identical with that which gave rise to Plato's epistemological approach to his realm of Forms (Ch. 3-1.1).

Kant's way of stating this problem of knowledge is this: How are a priori synthetic judgments possible? This needs some explaining. An a priori judgment or proposition is one whose truth can be known prior to and independently of experience. For example, one need not go out and try to measure the angles on all the squares that ever have been or will be in order to know that "All squares are rectangles." The opposite of an a priori proposition is an a posteriori one, one whose truth can be known only posterior to experience. For example, one cannot know whether "All farmers vote Republican" without taking a poll. A synthetic proposition is one which synthesizes its predicate with its subject; and its opposite, an analytic proposition, is one which analyzes its predicate out of its subject. For example, "All circles are red" is a synthetic proposition and "All circles are round" is an analytic one because "red" is not present in the meaning of "circle" but is synthesized with it whereas "round" is present in the meaning of "circle" and is analyzed out of it.

Now previous modern philosophers had divided all propositions into just two types: a priori analytic ones (like "All circles are round"), which are Leibniz's "truths of reason" and Hume's "relations of ideas," and a posteriori synthetic ones (like "All circles are red"), which are Leibniz's "truths of fact" and Hume's "matters of fact." The strength of a priori analytic propositions is that they are universally and necessarily true, on pain of contradiction ("All circles are round" cannot be false.), but their weakness is that they are true only of ideas and not of experienced objects, matters of fact, or real existence. The strength of a posteriori synthetic propositions is that they are about experienced objects, matters of fact, or real existence, but their weakness is that they are not necessarily or universally true ("All circles are red" not only may be but actually is false.).

This background helps us to understand what Kant means in his statement of the problem. "How are a priori synthetic judgments possible?"[1] How can propositions possibly be both universally and necessarily true (a priori) and also about experienced objects, matters of fact, or real existence (synthetic)? Note that Kant assumes that they *are* possible; he does so because he assumes that the propositions of mathematics are about real existence in addition to being necessarily true and that the basic propositions of (Newtonian) physics are necessarily true as well as about real existence.

However, Kant does not consider the possibility of the fourth possible combination: a posteriori analytic propositions, propositions which are necessarily and universally true on pain of contradiction because their predicates are analyzed out of their subjects but which are also about experienced objects or real existence because they are derived a posteriori from experience. The reason Kant does not consider this fourth possible combination is simple: this combination presupposes that the universality and necessity required by analytic propositions can be derived from experience, but, as we have just seen, Kant unquestioningly agrees with the rejection of this possibility by Rationalism and Empiricism. This fourth possible combination, this view that universal and necessary forms are imbedded in and derivable from sensory experience of objective nature thus binding the human mind to nature, was held by Aristotle and his medieval followers. Kant's ignoring of the possibility of a posteriori analytic propositions, of sensory experience of nature as containing universal and necessary forms, is another indication of modern philosophy's separation of the subject from the objective world, and it is the most important determinant of Kant's own solution to the problem of knowledge, and thereby, of German Voluntarism as the last chapter in the story of modern philosophy.[2]

11-1.2. The "Copernican" Revolution

How is knowledge possible? How are a priori synthetic propositions possible? What is the source of the universality and necessity essential to knowledge? Kant solves this problem by means of a revolutionary outlook which he compares with Copernicus' revolutionary theory in astronomy. He presents this "Copernican" revolution in the Preface to the second edition of the *Critique of Pure Reason:*

> Hitherto it has been assumed that all our knowledge must conform to objects. But all attempts to extend our knowledge of objects by establishing something in regard to them *a priori,* by means of concepts, have, on this assumption, ended in failure. We must therefore make trial whether we may not have more success . . . if we suppose that objects must conform to our knowledge. This would agree better with what is desired, namely, that it should be possible to have knowledge of objects *a priori,* determining something in regard to them prior to their being given. We should then be proceeding precisely on the lines of Copernicus' primary hypothesis. Failing of satisfactory progress in explaining the movements of the heavenly bodies on the supposition that they all revolve around the spectator, he tried whether he might not have better success if he made the spectator to revolve and the stars to remain at rest. . . .[3]

In this astronomical analogy the object of knowledge is the earth, and the knowing mind is the sun. Where common sense and previous philosophy saw the mind circling around and conforming to its objects, just as common sense and Ptolemaic astronomy saw the sun circling around the earth, Kant postulates that the objects of knowledge conform to the knowing mind, just as Copernicus postulated that the earth circles around the sun. Hume had seen that sense experience presents only discrete, unconnected particulars and that their necessary connection into universal causal laws is the work of the mind by means of its principle of habit or custom (Ch. 10-3.2). Kant extended this organizing power of the mind to all knowledge whatsoever, and his "Copernican" revolution is thus a generalization of Hume's principle of habit. More broadly speaking, Kant's "Copernican" revolution is the logical outcome of the drive toward subjectivism which can be seen all through modern philosophy. If modern philosophers of quite different approaches are all forced to conclude that the mind can know only its own ideas, this must be because the objects of human knowledge conform to the knowing mind.

The objects of knowledge only conform to the knowing mind, however; they are not totally created by it, according to Kant. Only the form or structure of the objects of knowledge comes from the mind, not their matter or content; the content or stuff of our knowledge comes, as with the Empiricists, from our sensory experience of external things. This is Kant's important distinction between the form and the matter of the objects of knowledge, a distinction which is the epistemological corollary of Aristotle's ontological distinction between form and matter. Kant agrees with Aristotle that there can be no form without matter and no matter without form, but for Kant the forms are mental concepts and the matter the "manifold of sensation." Kant's principle of epistemological matter is his legacy from Empiricism, and his principle of epistemological form is his legacy from Rationalism, although it is also from Hume's principle of habit. If the mind's objects lacked form or structure, experience would be only "a blooming, buzzing confusion," as William James called it; and if they lacked matter or content we would know only abstract, static forms. "Concepts without percepts are empty, percepts without concepts are blind."[4]

From Kant's "Copernican" revolution there follows at once

his division of the world into phenomena and noumena. Phenomena (appearances) are things as they appear to us humans, sensory content organized by mental forms; they constitute the world we humans can experience. Noumena (the objects of *nous* or reason) are things as we think they are in themselves independently of the mind's organizing activities. All that we can ever properly know scientifically or theoretically are phenomena, because the "Copernican" revolution makes the objects of knowledge conditioned by the human mind, and this is exactly what phenomena are. Things in themselves *(Dinge an sich)* we can never know since they have not been conditioned by the knowing mind, so they can be objects only of a practical faith. Here Kant killed—or rather saved—two birds with one stone: he saved science by restricting its claims to phenomena organized by the knowing mind, but in so doing he also saved moral and religious faith in things in themselves, in ultimate realities, by placing them beyond scientific encroachment. "I have therefore found it necessary to deny *knowledge* [of things in themselves], in order to make room for *faith,*" Kant writes in the Preface to the second edition of the first *Critique*;[5] thus he vindicates both his scientific and his religious heritage by distinguishing their spheres of jurisdiction. Notice how similar this separation of empirical knowledge from religious faith is to that of the thinkers forming the transition from medieval to modern philosophy (Ch. 7-1).

The logical structure of Kant's general solution to the problem of knowledge is as follows: First, knowledge requires universality and necessity. Scientific truths use the words, "all" and "must"; this Kant learned both from the nature of science and from the Continental Rationalists. Second, sense experience never yields any universality and necessity. "Experience teaches us that a thing is so and so, but not that it cannot be otherwise";[6] Kant learned this especially from the British Empiricists but also from the Continental Rationalists. Third, sense experience is our only cognitive contact with the external world. "The sum of the matter is this: the business of the senses is to intuit, that of the understanding is to think."[7] "The understanding intuits nothing but only reflects."[8] This premise Kant inherited from both Rationalism and Empiricism; and it is this rejection of ancient and medieval philosophy's rational intuition of external universality and necessity, as maintained in both the Platonic-Augustinian and the Aristotlian-Thomistic tradition, which is at the root of Kant's distinctive modernity. This presupposition is the most fundamental and important one in Kant's philosophy. Fourth, from these first three propositions the "Copernican" revolution follows: the universal and necessary features essential to objects of knowledge must be supplied by the mind; they must be a priori, mental or ideal, rather than a posteriori, extramental or real. Fifth, from this "Copernican" revolution it follows that we can never know things as they are in themselves, that we can know things only as they appear to the mind (phenomena) as the result of its imposition of its universal and necessary forms. Sixth and finally, it follows from the "Copernican" revolution and its restriction of knowledge to appearances that we are free to believe or have faith in things as they are in themselves, in ultimate realities, since about them knowledge and science can have nothing to say. Thus has the genius of Kant reinstated genuine scientific knowledge by restricting it to mentally conditioned phenomena while at the same stroke saving religious and moral faith from scientific and logical encroachment.

11-1.3. *Kant's Solution in Detail*

According to the "Copernican" revolution, knowing is constructing phenomenal objects from sensory materials and mental forms. What forms does the mind impose? Exactly which aspects of the objects of knowledge are universally and necessarily present? The mind imposes three types of such mental forms upon sensory material to construct phenomenal objects, three types of features which are universally and necessarily present in human experience; and these three types dictate the overall tripartite structure of Kant's *Critique of Pure Reason* and *Prolegomena to Any Future Metaphysics.* First are the a priori forms of sensation or intuition, space and time; and it is with these that Kant is concerned in the "Transcendental Esthetic" (*Aisthesis* is Greek for sensation.) and in his discussion of the possibility of mathematics. How must we always *sense* or intuit objects? As spatio-temporal. Second come the a priori forms of understanding *(Verstand)*, the twelve categories; and it is with these that Kant is concerned in his "Transcendental Analytic" and in his discussion of the possibility of natural science. How must we always *understand* objects? In terms of the twelve categories. Third are the Ideas of Pure Reason *(Vernunft)*; and it is with these that Kant is concerned in the "Transcendental Dialectic" and in his discussion of the possibility of metaphysics. If we try to extend the categories of understanding beyond sense experience to achieve knowledge of things in themselves, we inevitably fall into contradiction; yet certain Ideas of Pure Reason regulate without constituting our knowledge of phenomena. What must we always *think* in order to give meaning and value to what we experience? The ideas of self, cosmos, and God. Let us now consider these three divisions of Kant's epistemology in somewhat more detail.

The a priori *forms of sensation* or intuition answer the question, How must we always sense objects? Kant ties this epistemological issue to the issue of the nature and justification of mathematics. This fact has unwarrantedly caused most present-day philosophers of mathematics to reject Kant's "Transcendental Esthetic," for they disagree with Kant's claim that *"All mathematical judgments, without exception, are synthetic,"*[9] and maintain instead that they are all analytic, that they depend solely on definitions and the law of noncontradiction. This disagreement is based on a misunderstanding, however, for while Kant's critics are thinking of pure, abstract mathematics Kant is talking about empirical or applied mathematics, mathematics as having objective reality, and especially Euclidean geometry as embodied in Newtonian space.[10] Such mathematical propositions are for Kant empirically true and thus synthetic, since he believes (and here most modern logicians agree) that analytic propositions have no empirical or existential reference. Insofar as they are purely formal and abstract, mathematical propositions may well be analytic, so far as Kant is concerned. But the assumption that Euclid's axioms coincide with empirical space is a synthetic proposition, since there is no contradiction in denying it; and hence every applied mathematical proposition is also synthetic, for it is based on this synthetic assumption. Since practically all present-day philosophers of mathematics and science agree that the coincidence of empirical space with abstract geometry is only a synthetic assumption, that it is not logically necessary, there need be no dispute with Kant concerning the synthetic or analytic character of mathematical propositions. Euclidean space is thus an a priori form of sensation, a way in which we must always sense objects. But time too is an a priori form of sensation for Kant. Space is the a priori form of *external* sensation, of sensation of bodies; and time is the a priori form of *internal* sensation, of sensation of our thoughts and feelings. Moreover, since our sensation of external bodies must also become an internal sensation in our mind, time is the a priori form of all sensation whatever. Sensation is thus incurably temporal and sensation of bodies is incurably spatial as well, so we know a priori that all possible objects of sensation must be temporal and that all possible objects of external sensation must also be spatial. Yet this necessary and universal spatiotemporality applies only to phenomena and not to things in themselves.

The a priori *forms of understanding*, the categories, answer the question, How must we always *understand* objects? This is the topic of the "Transcendental Analytic" in the *Critique of Pure Reason,* and it is Kant's justification of the possibility of scientific knowledge of nature. By "nature" Kant means all possible appearances governed by fixed laws; and appearances become governed by laws to produce natural phenomena, the objective world of nature, by being subsumed under the a priori concepts of understanding, the categories. This objectivity of phenomena and nature is for Kant intersubjectivity, however, not a grasp of extra-mental things in themselves. ". . . objective validity and necessary universality (for everybody) are equivalent terms. . . . What experience teaches me under certain circumstances, it must always teach me and everybody . . . ."[11] The ways in which everybody must always understand objects are the categories, just as space and time are the ways in which we must always sense objects. Kant lists twelve of these categories, the most important of them being substance and cause. Hume had argued that there is no justification for believing that substance and cause are objectively real since they are not to be found in sensory impressions, even though instinct and habit force this belief upon us. But Kant holds that this very fact of being compelled to see substance and causes is a justification of their *empirical* or *phenomenal* objectivity. We must always experience things as substantial and causally connected since we cannot imagine any experience lacking substances and causes, though substances and causes are "transcendentally ideal" or restricted to phenomena and not features of things as they are in themselves. Kant thus avoids the skepticism of Hume by legitimizing the mind's instinctive and habitual way of knowing phenomena and by prohibiting its extension to things as they are to themselves.

Why does Kant have exactly twelve categories? Why not 8 or 10 as Aristotle had, or 122? Kant's answer is that these twelve are dictated by the twelve possible types of logical judgments or propositions which every human mind must use. Yet Kant sometimes seems to say that *all* characteristics of phenomena are a priori, "nay, *all the properties which constitute the intuition of a body belong merely to its appearance.*"[12] On the basis of the "Copernican" revolution it is hard to see how this more sweeping position can be avoided, and this is indeed the position held by the followers of Kant, both the German Voluntarists and present-day pragmatists and analysts.[13]

The "schematism" of the categories is Kant's solution to a problem which is a phenomenalistic analogue of Plato's problem of the relation between Forms and particulars, and Kant's schemata are functionally analogous to Plato's diagrams (p. 49). Phenomena arise by the application of the categories to the spatiotemporal manifold of sensation. But the categories are abstract, unchanging, universal, logical concepts (analogous to Plato's Forms) whereas the spatiotemporal manifold of sensation is concrete, changing, particular, and sensuous. How then can these two opposites meet? How can the categories be applied to concrete experience? Only by means of a bridge grounded in each extreme, a third factor which has something in common with the other two. This bridge Kant finds in time (as Plato found one in soul), for time as the a priori form of all sensation is both a priori like the categories and sensuous like the appearances. By means of time each of the twelve abstract categories is translated into a "transcendental schema" (plural "schemata"), a rule for operating temporally to produce a sensory object in conformity with a category. "The schema of substance is permanence of the real in time, . . . The schema of cause . . . is the real upon which, whenever posited, something else always follows."[14] And so on. Such temporal schematization of abstract concepts is the root of the present-day theory of operationalism which is so much emphasized in the empirical sciences. For something to make sense it must *make sense*; it must be translated into sensorily observable effects.

With the schematization of the categories, the blooming, buzzing confusion of sensation is organized and unified into discrete phenomenal objects with properties and interrelations. Yet these phenomenal objects are further unified into the whole of one's experience. What is the source or principle of this whole of experience, this unity of unities? This final principle of unity must also be an a priori addition of the mind, since sensation never presents such a unity of all experience. What is needed is a final principle of the mind which unifies the unities which the schematized categories produce from the unities in turn produced by space and time. This Kant finds to be the self, "the transcendental unity of apperception," transcendental in the sense of transcending yet ordering experience. As Hume showed (Ch. 10-3.3), the self which Locke and Berkeley thought they knew could not be the ultimate self but only its ideational reflection, which Kant calls the empirical ego, for the self which perceives cannot be the same as the self which is perceived. The eye that sees objects and unifies them into one visual field is not itself a part of that visual field; a searchlight which illuminates a scene does not illuminate itself. In like manner the real self which apprehends all objects and organizes them into a unified cognitive field is not itself found in that cognitive field. While the empirical self is always an object, the transcendental self is always a subject. Hence the transcendental self is an un-knowable thing in itself, like the external things in themselves which are the sources of the material of our knowledge.

The Ideas of Pure Reason[15] form the link between knowledge and faith just as time and the schemata form the link between knowledge and sensation. These Ideas of Pure Reason originate from the "Copernican" revolution itself. We know by the revolution that our knowledge is limited to appearances. From this we are forced to conclude that there is something doing the lim-iting, something beyond appearances; otherwise it makes no sense for us to say that our knowledge is *limited* and extends only to appearances. This conclusion that there is something beyond appearances is *possible* because the categories, the pure a priori forms of understanding, are in themselves abstract and lack sensory content so they can be used to think about some-thing nonempirical. Furthermore, this conclusion that some-thing exists beyond appearances is *necessary* in order to main-tain that we can know *only* appearances, that our knowledge is restricted to them. As we saw in the conclusion of our examina-tion of Hume, if we do not maintain that there is something beyond perceptions, then we cannot meaningfully say that our knowledge is limited to them, but the "Copernican" revolution forces us to say this. Hence we cannot help but think of some-thing transcending the world of phenomena. However, this tran-scendent something which restricts knowledge to phenomena cannot itself be known. As has already been evident several times, this conclusion follows immediately from Kant's general theory, but Kant also attempts to prove this by independent ar-guments. Wherever we claim to have knowledge of things as they are in themselves rather than merely of things as they ap-pear to us, we are immediately bogged down in fallacies. This is the "transcendental dialectic," a "natural and unavoidable dia-lectic of pure reason" which leads to a "transcendental illusion."

This transcendental illusion consists of three more specific il-lusions or dialectics, since there are three things which we must think of as lying beyond all phenomena. The first of these is a transcendent self, subject, or soul; and when we think of this self as a thing in itself which can be known as the object of a purely rational psychology, we are inevitably caught up in the "paralogisms of pure reason" where the soul must be and yet cannot be a simple, self-identical substance. The second of these three is a transcendent world or cosmos; and when we think of the world as the whole of reality which can be known as a thing in itself in a purely rational cosmology, we are inescapably trapped in the "antinomies of pure reason" in which the world must be both limited and unlimited, composed of simple parts and yet infinitely divisible, completely determined and yet also free, and containing and yet not containing a necessary being. The last of these is a transcendent cause, an unconditional condition of all things, a God, and when we think that this bare concept yields objectively true knowledge of such a God as a thing in Himself, then we fall heir to the fallacies of the arguments for the existence of God, the Ideal of Pure Reason.

Kant divides these arguments into three: the teleological or "physicotheological" argument or argument from design, a form of which we glimpsed as Thomas's fifth way, the "cosmological" argument from the existence of changing things which was discussed especially in connection with Aristotle and Aquinas, and the ontological argument which was examined in connection with Anselm, Descartes, and others. Kant's rejection of these three—and all possible—arguments for the existence of God is, like Hume's (Ch. 10-3.4), foreordained by his principle that only phenomena can be known; but he proposes independent reasons for concluding that each argument is fallacious. The main reason he advances is that the teleological and cosmological arguments necessarily involve the ontological argument; and the ontological argument he rejects, as we have already adumbrated, on essentially the same grounds which had earlier been used: that real existence is not a predicate, that the existence which may be built into and logically concluded from the idea of God can only be the *idea* of existence and not real, extra-mental existence.

This dialectic of pure reason is thus a detailed proof of the conclusion laid down by the "Copernican" revolution: transcendent things in themselves cannot be known; they are not possible objects of knowledge. Yet even though they cannot be known they must be *thought,* as we have seen, in order to circumscribe, delimit, and unify the phenomenal world which alone we can know. Therefore, the Ideas of Pure Reason—the ideas of Self, Cosmos, and God—are only *regulative* rather than *constitutive* of our knowledge.

> Pure reason does not in its Ideas point to particular objects which lie beyond the field of experience, but only requires completeness of the use of the understanding in the system of experience. But this completeness can be a completeness of principles only, not of intuitions and of objects. In order, however, to represent the Ideas definitely, reason conceives them after the fashion of the knowledge of an object. This knowledge is . . . completely determined; but the object is only an Idea [invented for the purpose of] bringing the knowledge of the understanding as near as possible to the completeness indicated by that Idea.[16]

Each of the Ideas of Pure Reason thus regulates our knowledge in the sense of giving it an absolute but unattainable goal of complete unity. The Idea of the Self unifies our experience inwardly by supplying the goal of a complete subjective unity, the Idea of the Cosmos unifies our experience outwardly by supplying the goal of a complete objective unity, and the Idea of God unifies these two unities by furnishing the goal of the total unity of all experience under the one first principle or unconditioned condition of God.

These three Ideas of Pure Reason thus have for Kant both an invalid and a valid use. Their invalid use consists in arguing that since we cannot help but *think* that there are ultimate realities which are thus and so, it follows that we *know* that there *are* such ultimate realities. Their valid use in each case consists in realizing that although we cannot know any of these ultimate realities as a thing in itself, we must nonetheless think of them and use these thoughts or Ideas as regulative principles to unify experience inwardly (the self), outwardly (the cosmos), and totally (God). Here Kant synthesizes the antitheses of Rationalism and Empiricism. One of the two pillars of the Rationalists was that what is true of thought is true of reality (Ch. 9-5), so for them from the fact that we must think of self, world, and God it follows that they really exist in just the way we think of them.

To this thesis the antithesis of British Empiricism was drawn by Hume: even though we are led by instinct and habit to believe in extra-mentally real things in themselves, this belief is wholly unwarranted and irrational. Kant's theory that the Ideas of Pure Reason are regulative but not constitutive of knowledge is the synthesis of these antitheses: while it is fallacious to conclude anything about real things in themselves from the nature of thought, it is legitimate and even indispensable to use empty, noncognitive ideas of ultimate realities to delimit and unify the knowable phenomenal world.

To summarize Kant's view of knowledge and reality we may turn to his own statement in the *Prolegomena:*

> The world of sense contains merely appearances, which are not things in themselves; but the understanding, because it recognizes that the objects of experience are mere appearances, must assume that there are things in themselves, namely, *noumena.* . . . That which bounds . . . must lie quite without . . . , and this is the field of the pure beings of the understanding. . . . But as a boundary is itself something positive, which belongs to that which lies within as well as to the space that lies without . . . , it is still an actual positive cognition which reason only acquires by enlarging itself to this boundary, yet without attempting to pass it because it there finds itself in the presence of an empty space in which it can conceive forms of things, but not things themselves. . . .
>
> And thus there remains our original proposition, which is the *résumé* of the whole *Critique:* "Reason by all its *a priori* principles never teaches us anything more than the objects of possible experience, and even of these nothing more than can be known in experience." But this limitation does not prevent reason from leading us to the objective boundary of experience, namely, to the relation to something which is not itself an object of experience but is the ground of all experience. Reason does not, however, teach us anything concerning the thing in itself; it only instructs us as regards its own complete and highest use in the field of possible experience.[17]

11-1.4. *The Problem of Unknowables*

The very nature of Kant's "Copernican" revolution requires that we know that there are unknowable things in themselves lying beyond the mentally constructed phenomena which alone we can know. This situation immediately creates the most fundamental problem in the philosophy of Kant: the problem of how we can possibly even state that philosophy or know that it is true. If Kant's philosophy is true, then Kant's knowledge must be restricted to phenomena, and if Kant's knowledge is restricted to phenomena, he cannot know that there are any things in themselves. And if he cannot know that there are any things in themselves, he cannot know that they supply the materials for the constructive forms of the mind; and if he cannot know that, then he cannot know the "Copernican" revolution, the very heart of his philosophy. Hence if Kant's philosophy is true he cannot know that it is true. This contradiction of knowing that there are unknowable things in themselves, and of knowing something about them, occurs in three main areas—as it also did in Continental Rationalism and British Empiricism—material things in themselves, other minds, and one's own mind.

The knowledge of unknowable material things in themselves comes out sharply in the *Prolegomena:*

> . . . things as objects of our senses existing outside us are given, but we know nothing of what they may be in themselves, knowing only their appearances, that is, the representations which they *cause* in us by *affecting* our senses. Consequently I grant by all means that there are bodies without us, that is, things which, though quite unknown to us as to what they are in themselves, we yet know by the representations which their *influence* on our sensibility procures us. These representations we call "bodies," a term signifying merely the appearance of the thing which is unknown to us, but not therefore less *actual.* Can this be termed idealism? It is the very contrary.[18]

Kant might have followed Hume in holding that we can have no knowledge of any kind beyond phenomena or perceptions, that the very expression "things in themselves" is utterly without meaning. But this would conflict with the "Copernican" revolution which holds that the objects of knowledge only conform to the mind, that their matter comes from things in themselves. To say with the "Copernican" revolution that the objects of knowledge are *joint* products of the mind and of real things in themselves is both to say that real things in themselves are not possible objects of knowledge and yet also to know something positive about them: that they *actually exist* and *cause* the content of our phenomenal objects which are the appearances of them, as the immediately preceding quotation says. However, this is a contradiction. If the mind can know *only* its own phenomena, ideas, or perceptions, it cannot also know that there is anything else beyond them which produces their content; this was the main lesson both of British Empiricism and of Continental Rationalism. On the other hand, if Kant does indeed know by virtue of the "Copernican" revolution that there exist independently real things in themselves which produce the content of our experience, then of course he really knows something about them, and he can no longer consistently maintain that we can know only phenomena.

The knowledge of unknowable other minds comes out in Kant's identification of objectivity with intersubjectivity. The objective validity of my knowledge of phenomenal nature means, according to Kant, that it is also valid for all other minds like mine. If the "Copernican" revolution is true, however, whatever I can know is transformed by my own mind. And if I can know only what my own mind has transformed, how can I possibly know that any other minds exist to experience things in the way that I do? Of course I can know other minds as phenomena, as transformed by my own mind; but these phenomenal minds are not the other minds as they are in themselves. If I cannot know other minds as they are in themselves, how can I know that my judgments have intersubjective or objective validity, that they are also true for other minds which I cannot know? This problem of reconciling the objectivity of knowledge with the theory that one can know only one's own ideas Berkeley had solved by means of his concept of God; the objective truth of some of our beliefs and ideas consists in the fact that they are also God's. In a logically similar fashion Kant solves the problem by asserting that the mind to which the "Copernican" revolution makes all objects of knowledge conform is reason in general *(Vernunft überhaupt)*, not your particular mind, or mine, and the a priori forms of sensibility and understanding are the cognitive forms of this general mind. Yet this solution only transfers the problem to a different locus, as it also did for Berkeley. Even though its *esse* is *percipi,* Berkeley's tree continues to be since it is observed by God; but how was it possible for Berkeley to know God as a real, independent being if the objects of Berkeley's knowledge were always his own ideas? Hume concluded that it was not possible, that all that one can know is one's own perceptions. In like manner Kant holds that the phenomena which he experiences constitute the objectively true world of nature because the mind to which they conform is mind in general, but how can Kant know this general mind as a determining thing in itself if he can know only the phenomena which he experiences?

The knowledge of the transcendent self is the third case of knowing an unknowable, and we have already seen it emerge in Kant's account of the transcendental unity of apperception. The situation with respect to the transcendent self is exactly the same as with transcendent matter and other minds. Since the "Copernican" revolution says that I can know only phenomena, then I cannot know my transcendent self as a thing in itself any more than I can know other minds or the transcendent source of the content of my knowledge. Yet Kant apparently knows this transcendent self anyway, and knows that it is the ultimate principle of the unity of his experience.

Kant is quite similar to Locke in thus restricting knowledge to phenomena while knowing three things which are not phenomena: the transcendent material source of phenomena, the transcendent overall mind which supplies the a priori forms for phenomena, and the transcendent self which unifies phenomena into one total experience, though the last two are perhaps the same. Correspondingly, Kant's followers will be quite similar to Locke's followers in rejecting these unknowable things in themselves, in concluding that phenomena must be things in themselves, and in insisting that the mind which knows them must be the only mind and hence absolute. Yet there are differences between the Empiricist sequence and the Voluntarist one. First, in Empiricism the phenomena are atomistically disconnected sensations and the mind which knows them is an utterly passive sensory receptacle, while in Voluntarism the phenomena are necessarily connected unities organized by an active mind or will. Second, while Locke's position is verbally self-contradictory in applying the term "knowledge" to the unknowable things in themselves as well as to the knowable ideas, Kant's position avoids this verbal contradiction explicitly (though not implicitly) by affirming that our relation to unknowable things in themselves is not the theoretical and scientific one of knowledge but the practical and moral one of faith. "I have therefore found it necessary to deny *knowledge* [of what lies beyond experience], in order to make room for *faith*,"[19] Kant tells us, and let us see just what this practical, moral faith is like.

11-2. *Ethics*

Kant's ethical theory is a consistent application of the creativity of the mind established by the "Copernican" revolution. This moral philosophy he presents in his second *Critique* (the *Critique of Practical Reason*) and also in his *Fundamental Principles of the Metaphysics of Ethics* which is to the second *Critique* what the *Prolegomena to Any Future Metaphysics* is to the first *Critique*. In examining Kant's ethics we shall consider first the moral law and then the moral postulates.

11-2.1. *The Moral Law*

Like the laws of knowledge the law of morality is a priori, according to Kant. Why? Because the moral law like scientific law is universal and necessary, and because, as we have seen, universality and necessity are not a posteriori, not derivable from experience, when experience is identified with sense experience. Kant's ethical theory therefore rejects from the beginning the natural law ethics of Plato and Aristotle because Kant rejects their view that there is a rational or intellectual intuition whose universal and necessary objects are real independently of the mind. Like the objects of scientific judgments, the objects of moral judgments must, in obedience to the "Copernican" revolution, conform to the mind for their universality and necessity. Just as sense experience teaches us what sometimes is the case but never what always must be the case scientifically, so also it teaches us only what happens to be the case but not what always must or ought to be the case morally. Thus

Kant makes morality formal, rational, or a priori, an ethics of rational laws or principles. ". . . an action . . . derives its moral worth, *not from the purpose* which is to be attained by it, but from the maxim by which it is determined," Kant writes. "Therefore the action does not depend on the realization of its objective, but merely on the *principle* of volition by which the action has taken place, without any regard to any object of desire. . . ."[20]

From this location of morality in the principle of an action rather than in its purpose or consequences, Kant draws the conclusion that it is not enough for an action to be merely *in accordance with* duty or the moral principle; to be truly moral an action must be done *for the sake of* duty or the moral principle. The business man who always acts honestly but only because honesty is the best policy for making money is not, for Kant, a moral man. Neither is his action strictly *im*moral, however; it is rather *a*moral or *non*moral—which Kant seems to place even lower than immoral—because it arises from our animal nature or inclinations rather than from our rational nature or reason. Even motives which many of us would deem noble, such as love of family or country, cannot produce truly moral actions, though they may be *in accordance with* duty, because such motives are mere passions or inclinations which we share with the animals and which are therefore not distinctively human and rational. Indeed, only when an action is contrary to the agent's every inclination or passion, going completely against the grain, can we be quite sure that the action is performed for the sake of duty, since in this case there is obviously no other possible motive. If a person enjoys performing a certain action, the possibility always exists that he may be doing it for the sake of the enjoyment rather than for the sake of duty, and therefore at least a slight suspicion always exists that the action may not be truly moral. Here is a feature which we can recognize also in American Puritanism and which doubtless springs in part from Kant's own pietistic or Puritan background. Kant never goes so far as to say that everything that is fun is thereby bad, however. In fact, as we shall see, Kant holds (Ch. 11-2.2) that moral actions must *eventually* be rewarded with happiness, even though they must never be done for the sake of this happiness.

This same point is made by declaring that every moral imperative is categorical rather than hypothetical. "If the action is good only as a means *to something else,* then its imperative is *hypothetical,*" Kant writes. "[On the other hand,] if it is conceived as good *in itself* and consequently as necessarily being the principle of a will which of itself conforms to reason, then it is *categorical.*"[21] No matter how good an action may be hypothetically, as a means to an end, if the end is bad the action is bad. Hence to be moral an action must have intrinsic or categorical worth. Morality is thus not concerned with what is right *if* you happen to want something else; morality is concerned rather with what is categorically right with no ifs, ands, or buts. Thus the moral law is the "categorical imperative."

What is the categorical imperative specifically? We have seen that the morality of an action depends "on the *principle* of volition by which the action has taken place, without any regard to any object of desire. . . ."[22] Kant then adds that "the simple conformity to law in general, without assuming any particular law applicable to certain actions, . . . serves the will as its principle. . . ."[23] Hence the very essence of the moral law or categorical imperative is pure lawfulness, and as was evident in the presentation of Kant's theory of knowledge, the very essence of lawfulness is universality and necessity. This point immediately leads to the first form of the categorical imperative: *"Act only on that maxim by which you can will that it, at the same time, should become a universal law,* [or] . . . *Act as if the maxim of your action were to become by your will a universal law of nature."*[24]

Kant regards the violation of the categorical imperative as a matter of self-contradiction of either of two types considered in connection with Descartes's reason for believing in his own existence (Ch. 8-2.1.): a strict, conceptual, logical contradiction in which the universalized maxim of the immoral action is internally self-contradictory or contradicts the maxim *it*self, or a less strict, volitional, practical contradiction in which the universalized maxim of the immoral action contradicts the willing or the willer *him*self. Making a lying promise to return borrowed money, for example, is immoral in the first, strict sense, in the sense that its maxim when universalized would logically contradict itself, since if everyone made lying promises no one would make lying *promises,* a promise having meaning only against a general background of truthfulness. Resolving not to help other people who are in distress in order to have more for oneself, however, is immoral in the second, less strict sense, in the sense that its maxim when universalized would contradict, not the maxim itself, but the willing and willer of the maxim, since a person cannot will that others refuse to help him when he is in distress. Abstinence from actions of the first type whose universalized maxims are logically self-contradictory Kant calls a perfect or strict duty, while abstinence from actions of the second type whose universalized maxims are volitionally self-contradictory is an imperfect or less strict duty.

The main point behind the perennial criticisms of the first form of Kant's categorical imperative is that no concrete action contains only a single maxim or principle. Consider for example Jean Val-Jean in Victor Hugo's *Les Miserables*. He breaks into a store and steals a loaf of bread to feed his starving family. Is this action right or wrong? To answer this question we must consider whether the maxim of that action can be consistently universalized. But what is the maxim of that action? Is it stealing, or is it feeding one's family? Feeding one's family is consistently universalizable, but—at least for Kant—stealing is not. And supposing that the maxim of Jean Val-Jean's action is stealing, is it stealing *period,* or is it stealing at a particular moment by a particular individual at a particular place? If the former, the maxim presumably cannot be universalized, but if the latter it seems perfectly universalizable, since in this case the universe contains only one item and that item has willed the maxim. The point is that morality is a matter of concrete actions (whether volitional or bodily), and every concrete action can be classified under many different principles—as every judge realizes when he is confronted with the problem of fitting a unique case under some law or precedent. Hence an abstract moral principle, like the first form of Kant's categorical imperative, can never be a sufficient criterion for judging actions. While consistent universalizability may be, and probably is, a *necessary* condition or *sine qua non* of morality, its abstractness prevents it from being a *sufficient* condition. This defect Kant attempts to remove, however, in the second form of the categorical imperative. *"Act so as to treat man, in your own person as well as in that of anyone else, always as an end, never merely as a means."*[25] This second form of the categorical imperative gives the content needed to supplement the abstract formalism of the first form. This second form would condemn slavery, racial discrimination, and all forms of exploitation, for example, since these consist in using other people merely as means toward one's own ends. Notice, however, that this second form of the categorical imperative does *not* prohibit using other people as means; it only prohibits using them *merely* as means and not also treating them as ends in themselves. Indeed, the necessary dependency of human beings upon each other requires that they use each other as means. We must use the butcher, the baker, and the candlestick maker as means; but it would be immoral to treat them *only* as means and not *also* as ends in themselves. The reason that every person is an end in himself is, for Kant, that he is the habitat of that rationality which defines morality and of that will which alone is unqualifiedly good. We should treat other persons as ends in themselves because they, too, are moral beings possessing the rational wills without which there would be no morality. "Nothing can possibly be conceived in the world, or even out of it, which can be called good without qualification, except a *good will.*"[26] And this takes us to the last form of the categorical imperative.

The third and final form of the categorical imperative Kant frames as follows: *"Always act so that the will could at the same time regard itself as giving in its maxims universal laws."*[27] Here the important word is "giving." While the first form of the categorical imperative states that we should always regard ourselves as *subjects under* universal law, this third form states that we are to regard ourselves, as rational beings, as the *legislators of* universal law. Just as the understanding or reason in its theoretical capacity actively creates the laws governing experience and our knowledge of it, so also the will or reason in its practical aspect creates the laws governing action and our willing of it. In both cases what is of fundamental importance is self-legislation. This self-legislation Kant calls autonomy, being subject to one's own law; and its opposite he calls heteronomy, being subject to a law other than one's own. In rejecting heteronomy Kant rejects what we today call conformism—doing something merely to conform to some outside pressure without freely choosing it for ourselves. Now this autonomy or self-legislation is self-determination or freedom; "What else then can freedom of the will be but autonomy; that is, the property of a will to be a law unto itself?"²⁸ Therefore, freedom is the very essence of morality; ". . . a free will and a will subject to moral law are one and the same."²⁹ We shall shortly see that for Kant freedom is also a precondition of morality, as well as its very essence; but at this point to be moral is to be rational, and to be rational is to be autonomous or free.

Kant regards these three forms as expressing just one categorical imperative, although from three different points of view. The first form gives the form or unity of the categorical imperative as universality, the second form gives the matter or plurality of the categorical imperative as rational beings as ends in themselves, and the third form gives the synthesis or totality of the categorical imperative as autonomy of the will. Read in reverse, morality is rational autonomy (third form) which means that intrinsic value is rationality (second form) and that consistent universality is the general form of all moral action (first form). Thus, again, nothing is unqualifiedly good save a good will; and a good will is simply an autonomous practical reason, a reason which creates the law out of itself and then obeys it.

11-2.2. The Moral Postulates

What does morality, living for the sake of one's own rational laws, presuppose or postulate? This is Kant's next and final question; and his answer is freedom, immortality, and God.

According to the third form of the categorical imperative freedom is the essence of morality as autonomy. However, freedom is also a precondition of morality, and one which is postulated or presupposed by the meaning of morality. Kant holds that we cannot possibly give a logical or scientific demonstration of free will, since the will is a noumenon or thing in itself which is therefore unknowable. Yet freedom is a necessary postulate of practical reason, of being subject to moral law. Kant's argument is basically that "I ought" implies "I can." We cannot acknowledge moral obligation without at the same time believing ourselves to be free. If we were told that we ought to do something and yet were convinced that we were not free to do it, we would conclude that we really had no obligation to do it at all. According to Kant man must act *as if* he were free, for man is the being who cannot help but feel moral obligation; man is the being with a conscience. Since man must act as if he were free, then it follows tautologically that man really *is* free for all *practical* purposes. Thus freedom is established as a necessary practical faith even though, according to Kant's epistemology, one cannot possibly demonstrate freedom as a scientific or a metaphysical fact. This practical or moral freedom requires and arises from Kant's distinction between phenomena and noumena. As phenomena, as empirically observable natural events, man's actions are completely determined because they are all necessarily subsumed under the category of causation. But the category of causation cannot be applied to man as a noumenon, as a thing in himself, so the possibility of man's noumenal freedom is dictated by Kant's epistemology. Man is thus a citizen of two worlds: the world of phenomena and the world of noumena. As a citizen of the world of phenomena man is just as determined as everything else, but as a citizen of the world of noumena he cannot help but believe that he is free.

According to the third form of the categorical imperative the freedom of autonomy, the essence of morality, is not a freedom of alternatives or choice, for in this freedom there is only one thing to "choose": the moral law. If a man possessing the freedom of autonomy were to choose something other than the moral law, he would be heteronomous, not autonomous, and would by that fact no longer be free, according to this identification of freedom with autonomy. As a matter of fact, if a person were purely rational, and therefore purely moral, he would necessarily always do only one thing, what is right. He is not free until after he is moral, and he is free only so long as he continues being moral. But then how can he be free to *become* moral? By means of the freedom which is a moral postulate, apparently, a second kind of freedom which is a choice from alternatives rather than necessary determination to the good; however, Kant does not explicitly discuss this second, lower freedom of choice apart from the first, higher freedom to do only the right.

Kant's other two moral postulates, immortality and God, are derived from the concept of the *summum bonum,* the greatest good. The *summum bonum,* Kant says, is the union of virtue with happiness. By happiness Kant means the greatest possible satisfaction of sensory desires or inclinations. Kant has completely separated inclination, pleasure, and happiness from virtue, as we have seen, on the ground that action motivated by happiness is heteronomous or externally determined rather than autonomous or internally determined. How then can happiness possibly enter the greatest good as one of its necessary constituents? By virtue of the fact that man is a citizen of two realms, not just one. As a rational, noumenal, thing in himself, man is concerned solely with virtue as rational autonomy, and happiness is absolutely excluded. As an animal, sensual, phenomenal being, however, man is concerned with happiness or pleasure; in fact, pleasure is here his sole concern, so Kant is a psychological hedonist even though not an ethical hedonist. Yet these two natures with their diverse goals are united in one and the same being. Hence, it follows that the greatest or most complete good for man, the *summum bonum,* must unite virtue (man's rational nature) and happiness (man's animal nature).

From this concept of the *summum bonum* Kant derives the moral postulates of immortality and God. The *summum bonum* requires perfect virtue, but man as a finite rational being is incapable of achieving perfect virtue in any finite length of time. So man's obligation to become perfectly virtuous requires that he live on forever to make an infinite progression toward the asymptotic goal of perfect virtue. Hence the virtue part of the *summum bonum* requires the moral postulate or practical faith that man is immortal. Since "I ought" implies "I can," the infinite "I ought" of perfect virtue requires an infinite "I can" of immortality. Moreover, the happiness part of the *summum bonum* also postulates or practically requires immortality, for every person deserves the reward of happiness in accordance with the degree of his virtue, so the achievement of perfect happiness as the reward for perfect virtue must require the same infinite amount of time as the achievement of perfect virtue. Note that this latter argument implies that the after-life includes our animal nature, since happiness is for Kant the satisfaction of our animal inclinations or sensory appetites. This makes the after-life rather like a fundamentalist heaven, or rather more like a Dantian purgatory because of the infinite striving toward perfect virtue and perfect happiness. Though immortality is not a proven fact, all proven facts being phenomena, it is, Kant holds, a necessary belief or practical faith for man, since his rational nature drives him toward perfect virtue and his animal nature drives him toward the reward of perfect happiness.

The third moral postulate is God, the unitor of virtue and happiness. The fact that man is both rational and animal requires a necessary connection between virtue and happiness, but this world contains no such connection. Virtue has no internal or analytic connection with happiness, nor happiness with virtue, as we have seen; and, as a matter of fact, experience with this world shows that all too often the wicked prosper and the virtuous suffer. Hence this connection between virtue and happiness which constitutes the *summum bonum* must be a synthetic one effected by a being in another world; and this being must be both perfectly good, in order to want to unite virtue and happiness, and sufficiently powerful to be able to do so. Such a being is God. Thus God, freedom, and immortality are established but only as practical postulates or articles of moral faith about unknowable things in themselves.

11-3. *Summary Analysis*

The most fundamental point in the philosophy of Kant is the "Copernican" revolution which makes objects of knowledge conform to the knowing mind. This revolution has two immediate logical consequences.

The first is the central importance of the mind as the autonomous, productive source of both knowledge and action. In its theoretical or cognitive capacity, this productive reason or mind imbues sensory content with its own universal and necessary forms to produce knowable phenomena. In its practical or moral capacity, this active reason or will imbues sensory desires or inclinations with its own universal and necessary rational laws to produce moral actions.

The second consequence of the "Copernican" revolution is that the mind is incapable of knowing real things in themselves, since Kant's productive mind can know only what it has made. Productive mind or will must know both that real things in themselves exist and yet also that they cannot be known, for the phenomenal objects which alone can be known are defined as the joint products of external and internal things in themselves. The mind cannot know the material source of its constructed objects, it cannot know other minds or the mind in general whose a priori forms it imposes in its constructive activity, and it cannot know even itself as the productive mind-will which constructs its objects and actions and experiences them. Kant attempts to remove this paradox of knowing unknowables by means of the Ideas of Pure Reason and the moral postulates: those things in themselves which the "Copernican" revolution prevents us from knowing in a theoretical and factual way must be thought about and believed in to make sense of the activity of the productive mind-will, not only in the moral sphere, but even in the theoretical sphere.

The first of these two consequences of the "Copernican" revolution—that the mind is just as active and productive in its knowing as in its willing—will be accepted by Kant's followers as the guiding spirit of his philosophy and as the developing essence of German Voluntarism. The second of these two consequences—that constructive mind-will is incapable of knowing real things in themselves—will be rejected by Kant's followers, however. It will be rejected, in the first place, on the ground that the paradox of knowing unknowables is a genuine contradiction, in spite of Kant's attempt to hide it by means of his Ideas of Pure Reason and moral postulates, but it will also be rejected, second, on the more fundamental ground that this inability to know real things in themselves is a restriction of that creative power of the mind which is the true spirit of Kant's philosophy and the developing essence of German Voluntarism. Hence in the sequel to Kant's chapter in the story of German Voluntarism will be the mind as fully creative and therefore as absolute will.

SUGGESTED READINGS

11-1. *Critique of Pure Reason*, Preface to the Second Edition, Introduction, B 176–87, and B 131–9.
Prolegomena to Any Future Metaphysics.
11-2.1. *Fundamental Principles of the Metaphysics of Morals.*
11-2.2. *Critique of Practical Reason*, Bk. II, Chs. 1–2.

For bibliographies, see:

Körner, S. *Kant.* Baltimore: Penguin, 1955. Appendices B and C.
Beardsley, M. C., ed. *The European Philosophers from Descartes to Nietzsche.* New York: Modern Library, 1960. Pp. 366–69.

Chapter 12

German
Voluntarism
Through
Hegel

Where reason was supreme in Continental Rationalism and sensation was supreme in British Empiricism, will becomes supreme in German Voluntarism—though all three are instances of the supremacy of the subject and therefore characteristically modern. The main theme of the story of German Voluntarism is the increasing creativity of mind. While Kant's predecessors tried to make the mind conform to its objects, he made it creative of the form of its objects and his followers made it a totally creative subject.

The story of German Voluntarism starts with Kant's "Copernican" revolution which views the objects of knowledge as conforming to the mind. Therefore the mind as cognitive is creative of the universal and necessary forms, and perhaps of all the forms, of its objects, and in this the mind is like the will. Kant's moral philosophy is a consistent application of his "Copernican" revolution, especially in his theory of the autonomy of the will, for in it the mind is creative of the universal and necessary form of its moral actions and hence explicitly will. But this creative will is limited to the forms of its objects and actions; beyond its own created forms it is confronted, rather like Plato's divine

Craftsman (Ch. 3-2.2), by the surd of unknowable things in themselves. Thus ends the first chapter in the story of German Voluntarism. In the second chapter, written by Fichte, Kant's independent surd of unknowable things in themselves is seen as an obstacle of the mind's own making, and mind-will is therefore creative of the content or material of its objects and actions as well as of their forms. Hence, in this second chapter the mind becomes all-creative and thus pure, unlimited will. The third chapter in the story will be written by Schelling; objective things in themselves are reinstated in opposition to the subject, but they are ultimately united with the subject in an Absolute which is neither subject nor object but neutral. The fourth and last chapter of the story will be written by Hegel; Schelling's fundamental opposition of the object to the subject is retained and justified, but with Fichte it is an opposition of the subject's own creation. The story of German Voluntarism through Hegel is thus the story of the increasing creativity of the mind or subject which dialectically requires its own opposite precisely to obtain and express its full creativity.

12-1. *Fichte*

Johann Gottlieb Fichte (1762–1814) takes his starting point from the autonomous, creative will of Kant's moral philosophy, which, as we have seen, reflects Kant's "Copernican" revolution. As Schelling, Fichte's immediate successor, writes: "Fichte's peculiar merit . . . [is] that he extends the principle which Kant places at the head of practical philosophy, the principle of the *autonomy of the will,* so as to make it the principle of all philosophy, and thus becomes the founder of a . . . higher philosophy, since in its spirit it is neither theoretical nor practical alone, but both at once."[1] Fichte rejects the things in themselves which were for Kant the source of the content of the objects of our knowledge, and in so doing he makes the mind creative of that content as well as of the form. The mind therefore becomes all-creative and hence absolute, which is another statement of the metaphysical idealism or mentalism espoused by Leibniz (Ch. 9-4.1) and Berkeley (Ch. 10-2.2).

This rejection of external things in themselves and this absolutizing of mind Fichte believed to be required by the spirit of
Kant's philosophy in order to render Kant's system consistent.
As might be expected, however, Kant himself protested against
any attempt to discover the doctrines of Fichte in his own writings; and he insisted that they were to be judged literally rather
than in accordance with some supposed spirit of his philosophy
which was in contradiction to what he actually said. Furthermore, Kant declared that Fichte's creation of the world out of
the mind alone, without any sensory content supplied by independently real things in themselves, radically opposed his own
doctrine of the interaction of mind and reality. Yet Fichte maintained that Kant's distinction between things as they appear to
us and things as they are in themselves was "certainly intended
to be accepted only provisionally and conditionally,"[2] and he
held fast to his conviction that no things in themselves exist
independently of the conscious subject, no non-ego apart from a
correlative ego. Furthermore, Fichte contended that this theory
alone corresponded to the spirit of the Kantian philosophy and
that the "holy spirit in Kant" was closer to the truth than Kant
was himself. While Fichte is thus not true to Kant, in absolutizing the creative mind he is true to the spirit of Kant's philosophy, true to its logical implications, especially of the "Copernican" revolution.

According to Fichte, this creative ego or infinite will strives
endlessly toward the unattainable ideal of pure, self-conscious
activity. Here it is clear how much Fichte is influenced by Kant's
theory of the everlasting asymptotic approach of the moral will
toward perfect virtue. This striving toward completely free
activity requires that the absolute will create or posit obstacles
to overcome. Thus arise both the evils of this world and the supposedly independent external things in themselves or non-ego
of Kant; both are necessary for the struggle of the absolute ego
toward its ultimate goal. While this creative subject is the emphasis of Fichte's earlier philosophy, in his later writings he
begins to place more stress on the idea of an Absolute which synthesizes this conflict between the creative subject and the object

which it posits. In this tendency toward an Absolute which comprehends both subject and object, Fichte is influenced by Schelling.

12-2. *Schelling*

Friedrich Wilhelm Joseph von Schelling (1775–1854) writes the third chapter in the story of German Voluntarism. Beginning with Fichte's doctrine of the absolute ego or subject, Schelling uses Spinoza's philosophy, especially the equal status of the attributes of thought and extension in the one Substance, to reinstate the objective pole which he was convinced Fichte had neglected. The result is a "System of Identity" in which the absolute reality is the identity and indifference of subject and object, ego and non-ego, mind and nature.

This theory of the Absolute as the identity of subject and object Schelling finds to be the true interpretation of Kant. Like Fichte he rejects Kant's external things in themselves; however, while Fichte concluded that this external, objective pole must be created by the subject and thus be secondary to it, Schelling maintains that the objective pole is coeval with the subjective. He also holds that each pole is in tension or conflict with the other so that the ultimate reality must be, not the subject or ego, but an Absolute which resolves in itself this tension between subject and object. Schelling also finds confirmation for his theory of the Absolute as the identity of object and subject in Kant's moral postulate of God as the being who overcomes the conflict between virtue (subject, mind) and happiness (object, nature) by uniting them in the one *summum bonum*. Schelling concludes that Kant's *Critiques*, when rightly understood, show that reality must consist of two conflicting systems, subject and object, morality and happiness, mind and nature, which repel and yet require each other in a tension which is the Absolute. Kant's two realms of which man is a citizen, phenomena and noumena, Schelling views as mutually opposed and yet mutually entailing; like man and woman, they cannot get along with each other but they cannot get along without each other either.

Reality is thus a process of centrifugal repulsion and centripetal attraction of polar opposites, an identity of opposites which is both a return to the theory of Heraclitus and an anticipation of the dialectic of Hegel (Ch. 12-3.2).

This Absolute is the identity of mutually entailing opposites and has in itself no character whatever, according to Schelling in his earlier and principal philosophy; it is simply the total identity and indifference of subject and object. The Absolute knows no object and therefore has no consciousness at all, since consciousness requires a distinction between subject and object which is overcome in the Absolute. Here Schelling's Absolute is quite like Plotinus' One; however, Plotinus' One is prior to the opposition between subject and object which arises only in the first emanation, Reason, whereas Schelling's Absolute is posterior to and defined as the identity of subject and object. Schelling's Absolute so lacks positive content that Hegel rejected it as a merely verbal solution to the problem of the dialectical tension between mind and nature. In Schelling's later "positive" philosophy in contrast to his earlier "negative" philosophy, he tried to answer Hegel's charge by giving more content to the Absolute; but this later philosophy was mystical, theosophical, lacked the rigor of the earlier philosophy, and exercised less influence on Schelling's immediate successors.

While Schelling thus counters the one-sidedness of Fichte's emphasis upon the subject by making the object equally necessary in the indifferent Absolute, this Absolute is so indifferent that it tends to abandon that primacy of the subject which is the very essence of Kant's "Copernican" revolution and of the resulting movement of German Voluntarism. Hence Schelling's Absolute must be given a content and that content must be essentially of the nature of mind, spirit, or subject. Furthermore, though Schelling claims that subject and object necessarily involve each other in a union of opposites, he does not show why this must be so nor how it actually is so in the detailed activities of mind and nature. These two lacunae will be filled by Hegel, the first lacuna by emphasizing that the Absolute is mind, spirit, or will, and the second by showing why and how the nature of reality or absolute mind requires a dialectical opposition and union of subject and object in every sphere of its activity. These two points, subjectivity and dialectic, will form the two principles of Hegel's conclusion to our story.

12-3. *Hegel*

12-3.1. *The Synthesis of Modern Philosophy*

Georg Wilhelm Friedrich Hegel (1770–1831) essentially concludes two stories: the story of German Voluntarism and the story of modern philosophy. Hegel himself regarded his philosophy as the synthesis of all preceding philosophy whatsoever, of ancient and medieval philosophy as well as of modern—and indeed, of all human knowledge. He had a high regard for the ancients, and he believed he had incorporated the objectivism of ancient and medieval philosophy as well as the subjectivism of modern philosophy within his own system. Yet this self-judgment is exaggerated. In fact, as we can perhaps see already and as we shall shortly see more fully, Hegel's philosophy is a synthesis only of modern philosophy, for in Hegel the subject is absolute, and the objectivism of the tradition of ancient and medieval philosophy is preserved only by being inverted in Hegel's subjectivized version of it.

As the synthesis of modern philosophy Hegel's system is.analogous to the systems of Aristotle and Aquinas, the former a synthesis of ancient philosophy and the latter of medieval philosophy—though also of ancient philosophy because of Thomas's Aristotelianism. Where the Continental Rationalists took reason and the British Empiricists took sensation, the German Voluntarists take will as the key to reality; but in all three movements the subject or self predominates. Descartes started with the self, and each movement and the whole modern period ends with the self. While this self or subject officially remained a passive mirror for Rationalism and Empiricism, however, with German Voluntarism it becomes the active creator of its objects as the will creates its actions. This creative subject or will begins with Kant's "Copernican" revolution as creative of only the universal and necessary forms of things, but it ends in Hegel's philosophy as Absolute Spirit which creates everything whatever out of and for itself. Kant's Voluntarism is dualistic with a radical distinction between phenomena and noumena; Fichte's Voluntarism is subjectivistic with the objective world merely a non-ego posited by the ego; Schelling's Voluntarism is a contentless identity of subject and object which seems to abandon the primacy of the subject, and Hegel's synthesis, as we shall now see, makes the object absolutely necessary in the dialectical process which is the life of the Absolute Subject or creative will. This sequence within German Voluntarism is thus somewhat analogous to those in Continental Rationalism and British Empiricism: each movement begins with a dualism (Descartes, Locke, and Kant) and ends with a reconciliation of the dualism through a synthesis of subject and object, though a synthesis in which the subject still predominates (Leibniz, Hume, and Hegel).

The fundamental principle of Hegel's philosophy, and of all modern philosophy, is thus the creativity of the subject. But this creativity of the subject logically implies another fundamental principle which is Hegel's main contribution and which makes possible the previously mentioned necessity of the object to the subject in Hegel's synthesis of German Voluntarism. This second fundamental principle which is logically implied by the principle of the creativity of the subject (though not logically implying it, Marx claimed) is Hegel's famed dialectic, a dialectic which is not at all to be confused with Plato's dialectic. Hegel's dialectic is implied by his principle of the creativity of the subject because a subject which is *creative* must of course create an object, and this union of opposed subject and object is the heart of Hegel's dialectic.

12-3.2. *The Dialectical Union of Opposites*

Hegel's dialectic is the culmination of two themes we have seen in modern philosophy: the Rationalists' paradoxical union of atomism and monism (the modern version of the ancient problem of the one and the many) and the opposition between subject and object, mind and external thing, which permeates the whole of modern philosophy.

The Rationalists' paradoxical union of atomism and monism

was implied in their principle of distinctness (Ch. 9-5). According to this principle, everything must be absolutely distinct and isolated and yet necessarily involved in everything else to constitute one interconnected whole. For the Rationalists this situation was a predicament to be avoided rather than a truth to be affirmed, so Descartes favored the atomistic pole, Spinoza the monistic pole, and Leibniz held them side by side in an unreconciled opposition. Kant also noted this paradox of atomism and monism in his transcendental dialectic and especially in his antinomies of pure reason. For him too, this situation revealed illusion rather than truth—though it is an inevitable and unavoidable illusion—so he concluded therefrom that reason is incapable of comprehending ultimate reality. Surveying this story Hegel reasons as follows: Since the mind cannot help but *think* that reality involves this dialectical union of opposites, as the Continental Rationalists and Kant have shown, and since it is nonsense to state that there is an unknowable realm of things in themselves different from this thinkable reality, as Fichte showed in criticizing Kant, then we can only conclude that reality itself must consist of this dialectical identity of opposites.

The other main theme which gives rise to Hegel's dialectic is the opposition between subject and object, the mind and the external world, which pervades all modern philosophy. All modern philosophy prior to Hegel indicates that the mind must know extra-mental things and yet that it cannot, that the subject can know only its own ideas and yet that it must thereby also know an objective realm outside it. Like the tension between atomism and monism, this tension between subjectivity and objectivity had been interpreted by the other modern philosophers as an embarrassing predicament rather than as a revelation of truth. Surveying this egocentric predicament of modern philosophy Hegel reasons much as he did in surveying the story of the paradoxical union of atomism and monism: Since modern philosophy has shown that the subject can know only itself, since it has also shown that this restriction of the subject to its own states requires the subject to think of an objective realm outside itself, as Kant held with his Ideas of Reason, and since, finally, it is nonsense to say that this objective realm is unknowable (Fichte's criticism of Kant), then we must conclude that the objective realm of things in themselves is necessarily created by the subject as its own opposite with which it becomes reidentified when it sees that this objective realm exists for the subject itself. Fichte had recognized part of this truth when he saw that the objective realm of the non-ego is posited by the ego to be overcome by it, and Schelling had glimpsed the rest when he saw that reality is an identity of the opposites of subject and object. But neither had clearly comprehended the logical, dialectical necessity of the object to the subject.

When Hegel's conclusion of the story of the union of atomism and monism is combined with his conclusion of the story of the union of subject and object, the result is his famed dialectic. Thought, and therefore reality itself, is a process of the creation and synthesis of opposition in which the many opposites form a pluralism which is also an atomism when their interrelations are not seen and in which the synthesis of this opposition is a monistic creative subject or mind. An idea or being is first taken in isolation as a thesis (e.g., one's own egoistic self-interest). This idea or being is then viewed as necessarily involving its polar opposite—this thesis becomes its very antithesis—as the pursued policy of egoism gives rise to its antithesis in altruism when one concludes that having one's own desires satisfied requires that one satisfy the desires of others. When thesis and antithesis are viewed as involving each other necessarily, finally, the synthesis or union of the two opposites arises, as when the opposition between egoism and altruism is overcome in the policy of working for mankind. In thus being synthesized, each opposite is taken up to a higher level *(aufgehoben)* at which its truth, value, and reality are preserved while its error, evil, and unreality are transcended. In this way "Spirit is essentially the result of its own activity, [and] its activity is the transcending of immediate, simple, unreflected existence, the negation of that existence, and the returning into itself."[3]

The paradigm of this dialectical process from thesis through antithesis to synthesis goes from being through nonbeing to becoming in a way reminiscent of the ancient problem of change in

Heraclitus. When we posit being as the ultimate thesis in an ontology, we are abstracting from all differences and therefore leaving out all beings, for it is not physical being or mental being or human being or any other kind of being that we are considering in this thesis. In thus abstracting all beings in our concentration upon pure being, however, we find that we have taken away everything whatsoever and are, therefore, left with a notion so utterly empty that it is indistinguishable from pure nothing. Thus does the thesis of being give rise to the antithesis of nonbeing. Yet the converse is also true, for the concept of nonbeing is something, after all, and thus necessarily involves being. In this contradictory union of being and nonbeing we find, however, the first concrete, contentful notion, for that which both is and is not is precisely process or becoming. The contradiction between being and nonbeing is thus preserved and yet transcended *(aufgehoben)* in the synthesis of becoming: *Sein, Nichts, Werden.* And this most basic instance of the dialectic is repeated in every part of every level of thought and reality.

This universality of the dialectic, this fact that everything involves everything else, leads to a theory of truth as coherence and of relations as internal which is essentially the same as that of Spinoza (Ch. 9-3.2) except that for Hegel the items which are internally related in the coherent whole are in dialectical contradiction to each other. The truth is the whole and error is partiality, the absolutizing of any particular persuasion which tragicomically turns into its opposite when it is pursued and enacted.[4] To be an egoist is to become an altruist, since the achievement of selfish desires requires satisfying the other who is needed for that egoistic end. To be a pleasure-seeker is to be a pain-seeker, as was evident in the story of the Cyrenaic philosophers (Ch. 2-5), since the experience of pleasure entails antecedent and subsequent pains and wants, and so on. Everything necessarily involves its opposite; determination is negation and negation is determination. What a thing positively and determinately *is* is precisely all that it is *not*, and what a thing is not is just what it is. Man's humanity, for example, is his *distinctiveness* from all other things; "humanity" is essentially defined by all the things which it excludes. Since each thing is thus constituted by all the other things which it repels, to achieve truth one must grasp the dialectical unity of all oppositions in the one supreme whole which is the Absolute.

Thus does Hegel's dialectic make the object necessary to the subject, the many necessary to the one, and everything whatever necessary to everything else, for reality or truth lies in the *relation* between these opposites. For Descartes there were many isolated things but no unified world, and so also for Hume. For Spinoza one Substance tended to absorb and fictionalize all the many things, and so also for Schelling. Furthermore, all the modern philosophers tended to have a subject without any object. From Hegel's point of view the common mistake of all these theories was their location of reality in some *thing*, some term of a supposed relation, for when they did this they could never find the relation of that term to all others. If we place reality in things, their interrelations must lie outside reality and can, therefore, never be found. But if we revolutionize our point of view and locate reality in relation, then, by the very meaning of "relation," we will also have the terms of that relation, the object connected with the subject, the many things united in one universe. From this point of view modern philosophy is the search for relations, and when no one could find relations among things Hegel made reality itself relation. To be is to be related.

12-3.3. *Absolute Subjectivism*

Hegel's most fundamental principle, the creativity of the subject, solves that most fundamental and definitive problem of modern philosophy: the problem of subjectivism or solipsism. Ever since Descartes began modern philosophy within his own mind, modern philosophy has been plagued with the problem of how to get outside the mind to external, objective reality. Every modern philosopher found himself in the same impasse of being confined by his principles to his own mental states and being logically unable to get outside himself to objective reality. Most modern philosophers tried to escape this impasse through an illogical tour de force: Descartes through interactionism, Geulincx and Malebranche through occasionalism, Spinoza through Substance with the attribute of extension, Leibniz through preestablished harmony, Locke through sensitive knowledge, Berkeley through notions of God and other spirits, and Kant through noumenal awareness of things in themselves. Even Hume was forced to invoke the unperceivable principles of memory and habit, and Schelling had his neutral Absolute. Perhaps Fichte came closest to consistency, but in doing so he remained in the impasse of subjectivism, giving inadequate status to the posited non-ego. If all modern philosophy, whether Rationalist, Empiricist, or Voluntarist, is forced to conclude that only the subject and its mental states can be *known,* then this must be because only the subject and its mental states truly *exist.* This is Hegel's conclusion of the main theme of the story of modern philosophy.

All modern philosophy has thus been driven toward solipsism. Rationalism teaches us that all that reason can know is the self, Empiricism teaches us that all that sensation can know is the self, and Voluntarism teaches us that all that will can know is the self. All right, concludes Hegel, then all that there *is* is the Self. But if the Self is *all,* if there is nothing beyond the Self, then the Self is no longer confined, there is no longer any *solus* (only) in the solipsism, and therefore, properly speaking, solipsism no longer exists at all.* Thus modern solipsism turns dialectically into its very opposite; thus Hegel draws the sting from modernity's solipsism, by absolutizing it to make reality the Absolute Self or God from Whom all things flow and unto Whom all things return. This point is made in an amusing and instructive story titled, "Solipsist":

> Walter B. Jehovah, for whose name I make no apology since it really *was* his name, had been a solipsist all his life. A solipsist, in case you don't happen to know the word, is one who believes that he himself is the only thing that really exists, that other people and the universe in general exist only in his imagination, and that if he quit imagining them they would cease to exist.
>
> One day Walter B. Jehovah became a practicing solipsist. Within a week his wife had run away with another man, he'd lost his job

---

* Compare this with the way in which solipsism becomes nonsolipsism at the hands of Hume (Ch. 10-4).

as a shipping clerk and he had broken his leg chasing a black cat to keep it from crossing his path.

He decided, in his bed at the hospital, to end it all.

Looking out the window, staring up at the stars, he wished them out of existence, and they weren't there any more. Then he wished all other people out of existence and the hospital became strangely quiet even for a hospital. Next, the world, and he found himself suspended in a void. He got rid of his body quite as easily and then he took the final step of willing *himself* out of existence.

Nothing happened.

Strange, he thought, can there be a limit to solipsism?

"Yes," a voice said.

"Who are you?" Walter B. Jehovah asked.

"I am the one who created the universe you have now just willed out of existence. And now that you have taken my place—" There was a deep sigh. "—I can finally cease my own existence, find oblivion, and let you take over."

"But—how can *I* cease to exist? That's what I'm trying to do, you know."

"Yes, I know," said the voice. "You must do it the same way *I* did. Create a universe. Wait till someone in it really believes what you believed and wills it out of existence. Then you can retire and let him take over. Goodby now."

And the voice was gone.

Walter B. Jehovah was alone in the void and there was only one thing he could do. He created the heaven and the earth.

It took him seven days.[5]

Rationalism, Empiricism, and Voluntarism, restricted by and in conflict with an alien objective reality, have thus given way in Hegel to an unrestricted Absolute Voluntarism in which the creative Subject is reality itself.

This dialectical process which is the life of the Absolute Will or Spirit moves through many theses and antitheses up to the final synthesis in the Absolute's own self-consciousness. In Aristotle's philosophy all nature also moved toward the Absolute, God, since for Aristotle as for Hegel God is the complete actualization of all natural things. For Aristotle, however, natural things never reach God, but they always aspire toward Him. According to Plotinus and Spinoza, on the other hand, all things aspire toward God and yet are eternally identical with Him, and life is a process of realizing the already existent identity of all things with God. Here Hegel follows Plotinus and Spinoza rather than Aristotle, *except* that for Hegel the aspiration of things toward God, and thus of God toward Himself, is a clash of contradictories, a strife of opposites. As Heraclitus had said, "War is lord of all."[6] The temporal manifestation of this dialectical development of Absolute Spirit through strife is history, the march of God through the world, and the state is the idealization of history and therefore the temporal idealization of God.

This dynamic, dialectical striving toward Absolute Self–consciousness has in Hegel's philosophy three grand stages or "moments": the life of common sense which is spirit as initially subjective, the life of science which is spirit objectivized out of itself, and the life of philosophy which is spirit returned to itself in a synthesis of the objective with the subjective. The life of common sense, which uses the categories of being (quality, quantity, and measure), sees each thing subjectively as isolated and complete unto itself. The life of science, which uses the categories of relation (essence-existence, force-expression, and cause-effect), sees each thing objectively as internally related to and constituted by every other thing. And the life of philosophy, which uses the categories of ideal unity (final cause and organic unity), sees all these objectively interrelated and mutually determining things as internally related to, as determining and being determined by, the subject which knows them. Here objects are dialectically interconnected not only with each other but also with the creative subject in one Absolute whole. These three grand moments in the overall dialectical process of Spirit are analogous to the ladders of wisdom presented by earlier philosophers:

Plato	*Aristotle*	*Plotinus*	*Spinoza*	*Hegel*
(the Good)		(the One)		
reason	metaphysics	Reason	intuitive reason	philosophy
thinking	mathematics	Soul	discursive reason	science
belief	physics	Body	opinion	common sense
(imaging)		(Matter)		

12-3.4. History and the State

The meaning of Hegel's synthesis of modern philosophy in his Dialectical Voluntarism may be seen more concretely by considering its application to two main areas of human concern: history and the state.

History, according to Hegel, is the objective manifestation of the dialectical process of the Absolute Subject; it is the march of God through the world. Hegel writes:

> The principle of Development involves . . . the existence of a latent germ of being—a capacity or potentiality striving to realize itself. This formal conception finds actual existence in Spirit, which has the history of the world for its theatre, its possession, and the sphere of its realization. It is not of such a nature as to be tossed to and fro amid the superficial play of accidents, but is rather the absolute arbiter of things, entirely unmoved by contingencies, which, indeed, it applies and manages for its own purposes.[7]

The goal of this dialectical process of history is thus the same as the goal of the Will itself; it is freedom as complete self-determination, completely autonomous self-conscious creativity. This conception of freedom is similar to that of Spinoza, and therefore it also involves the same essential difficulties. Indeterminist freedom of choice from alternatives does not exist, for everything is entirely determined by the nature of the Absolute Will; true freedom is self-determination, freedom from outside forces. Complete freedom lies only in the Absolute; the individual is free only insofar as he identifies with the Absolute, only insofar, that is, as he is no longer merely an individual. How the individual can be ethically free to realize or not to realize this fact remains, as with Spinoza, a problem. While the goal of history is freedom, the method of realizing this goal is the dialectic, the creation and overcoming of opposition and contradiction. "Thus Spirit is at war with itself; it has to overcome itself as its most formidable obstacle. That development, which in the sphere of Nature is a peaceful growth, is in that of Spirit a severe and mighty conflict with itself."[8] This dialectical thrust toward freedom culminates, Hegel believed, in the state, and especially in the German state of his day.

For Hegel the state is the idealization of the historical process and therefore also of the temporal manifestation of the Absolute. "... the Universal is to be found in the State, in its laws, its universal and rational arrangements. The State is the Divine Idea as it exists on Earth."⁹ Since the Absolute is a dialectically interconnected, organic whole, so is the state; in this respect it is like the Leviathan of Hobbes except that for Hegel the state is not a human fabrication but the outward life of God himself. And since the state is the highest temporal manifestation of God, the appropriate attitude to take toward the state is one of worship, awe, and reverence. Furthermore, as the highest outward expression of the Absolute, the state also requires conflict and war for its life and development. As Hegel puts it, "War has the deep meaning that by it the ethical health of the nations is preserved . . ."¹⁰ Just as all growth requires the creation and overcoming of opposition, according to Hegel, so also does the state; and its creation and overcoming of opposition is war. From the fact that the state is dialectically opposed to other, alien states Hegel draws the conclusion, finally, that there can be no universal or world state, for a universal state would, by definition, have no alien state outside itself to stand over against it as its opposite, and it, therefore, would have nothing to determine it as a state at all. However, Hegel fails to apply the dialectic of the Absolute completely to the state, for the dialectic of the Absolute produces finally a synthesis of all syntheses which is the Absolute itself. Since the dialectic involves a synthesis as well as an antithesis, one would expect Hegel to maintain that the conflicts among states would finally be resolved in a single world society; this is the conclusion which Marx later drew in his materialistic application of Hegel's dialectic. But Hegel himself stops short with the antithesis, maintaining that the only final synthesis is the nontemporal one achieved in the Absolute itself.

12-4. *The Story of German Voluntarism*

The story of German Voluntarism begins with Kant's "Copernican" revolution which was itself the end of the stories of Continental Rationalism and British Empiricism. Since those stories ended in the predicament of the mind's knowing only its own particular, contingent, discrete ideas with the only universal and necessary organizing power coming from the mind itself, Kant concluded that knowable objects and moral actions must conform to the mind for their universal and necessary or scientifically knowable and rationally moral characteristics. But this solution left Kant still in the Rationalists' and Empiricists' subjectivistic predicament, for according to the "Copernican" revolution, unknowable things in themselves must exist to supply the materials for the mind's organizing activities. Thus mind became productive like will, though limited by a material surd. Fichte insisted that Kant's knowledge of these "unknowable" things in themselves is self-contradictory, and he concluded that the mind must create the content as well as the form of knowable objects and moral actions. Fichte thus wrote the second chapter in the story of German Voluntarism by making the mind into all-creative will. But Fichte's solution failed to account adequately for the reality of the objective world, according to Schelling, so Schelling reinstated the objective realm as equally necessary with Fichte's subjective realm and identified both in a neutral Absolute, thus writing the third chapter in the story of German Voluntarism.

According to Hegel, however, Schelling did not show why or how subject and object are necessarily identical in the Absolute; and in making the Absolute utterly neutral and contentless he gave a merely verbal solution which even rejected the primacy of the subject which was the essence of Kant's "Copernican" revolution. Hegel attempted to correct both of these defects. The first he corrected through his theory of dialectic by showing, both in general principle and in concrete detail, why and how subject and object must necessarily involve each other. The second he corrected through his theory that the Absolute reality is subject, spirit, or will, thus absolutizing the subjectivism of modern philosophy and the Voluntarism of his immediate predecessors. Thus Hegel concludes both the shorter story of German Voluntarism and the longer story of modern philosophy. Reality is an absolute creative subject or will which necessarily creates the objective world out of itself in order to overcome it to achieve full self-determination and self-consciousness. Reality is will, but will requires opposition and opposition must be overcome in the successful reaffirmation of Absolute Will. To Hegel as to Heraclitus apply the last lines of Coffin's "Crystal Moment":

> Life and death upon one tether
> And running beautiful together.

SUGGESTED READINGS

12-1. Fichte. *The Vocation of Man.* Bks. II and III.
12-2. Schelling. *System of Transcendental Idealism.*
12-3. Hegel. *Lectures on the Philosophy of History.* Introduction.

For bibliographies, see:
Calkins, M. W. *The Persistent Problems of Philosophy.* New York: Macmillan, 1926. Pp. 564–66, 568–69, 571–75.
Beardsley, M. C. *The European Philosophers from Descartes to Nietzsche.* New York: Modern Library, 1960. Pp. 488–89, 534–36.
Friedrich, C. J. *The Philosophy of Hegel.* New York: Modern Library. 1954. Pp. 551–52.

Epilogue: The Story of Western Philosophy[1]

The main theme of the story of Western philosophy, as outlined in the Prologue and presented in the various chapters of this book, is a movement of human awareness from the whole of reality to that part which is the human self and then to the reunion of this self with the whole. This three-stage movement is the philosophical expression of the history of Western culture generally and of the natural development of the human individual.

Erich Fromm, in his book, *Escape from Freedom,*[2] sees the social and political phylogeny of Western man as recapitulating his psychophysiological ontogeny. Man begins life in his mother's womb, functionally and, to a large extent, physically one with her. At birth his physical tie with his mother is cut with the cutting of his umbilical cord, but his functional ties continue for many years. When he leaves home to go out into the world this primal tie is severed, and the individual experiences himself as a subject, a self, an ego free from everything else. This subjective freedom from external determination is bought at a price, however, the price of isolation and loneliness, a loneliness which Fromm claims the individual finds intolerable.

To overcome this dreadful freedom the individual has two alternatives. One is to attempt to restore his primal tie, to return to the womb, to obliterate his newly acquired sense of individuality and selfhood by identifying with something larger than himself, say with church or with state. This first alternative is an undesirable "escape from freedom," however; and it is even impossible because man can no more annihilate his newly acquired subjective selfhood than he can literally restore his umbilical cord and reenter his mother's womb. The other alternative is for man to accept his freedom from external determination, his new subjective individuality, and to try to create a new kind of relation to that whole of which he was once an unconscious part but from which he has now been cast out. This alternative would be a creative synthesis of his original objective state in the whole and his new-found subjective freedom from it, a synthesis which would retain both antitheses but fuse them together into an harmonious unity.

Ancient and medieval man had no life apart from the whole community, and modern man has been cast out into an unbearable individual isolation and freedom. Modern man is thus faced with the dilemma of an impossible return to his primal, natural ties versus an intolerable acceptance of his modern isolation. The positive solution of this dilemma in a new relation of the free individual subject to the rest of reality is the fundamental challenge now confronting modern man, according to Fromm, and if and when this synthesis is achieved a new, postmodern man will have been born.

This social and political recapitulation of ontogeny has a still higher recapitulation in the story of Western philosophy. The story begins with the Cosmological philosophers' exclusive attention to the objective whole of which man is an unnoticed part; the individual subject or human self is still in the womb of the world, at one with reality, hardly conscious of any distinct existence. With the Anthropological philosophers man is born from the world, but the conscious subject or self remains in the womb. The man (who in this period was the measure of all things) is thus still objective man, man as an object, rather than the subjective individual who is acutely self-conscious. Evidence for this may be seen in the fact that the Sophists (and later the Skeptics) are skeptical only of any stable, universal truth; they are never skeptical of the very existence of the external world or of their interaction with it. For this reason the concentration upon man in the Anthropological Period of ancient philosophy remains an anthropomorphism and never comes close to the solipsism which stamps modern philosophy. In the Systematic Period of Plato and Aristotle a synthesis is achieved between man and his world, but again it is man as object that is synthesized with the world, not man as introverted, self-conscious subject. This same sequence is repeated in the Hellenistic and Roman Period from post-Aristotelian Skepticism, Epicureanism, and Stoicism to Neoplatonism: man is separated out of the world and then rejoined with it, but it is man as object and not man as subject.

Medieval philosophy repeats again the same sequence, but at a deeper level. Though man begins to be freed from the world and begins to establish himself as a subject by way of his contrast with objective nature whose existence he puts into question, the rift is quickly closed through God's reassurance that man and nature are still affiliated by their common Father. Though man as subject, acutely aware of his alienated state, begins to be born, not man as subject but man as object tied to nature is reestablished by the reassurance granted by God.

The story of ancient and medieval philosophy is the story of the birth of man from his natural matrix and his reunion with that home, but it is the story of man and his world as objects and not of man as a free and isolated, self-conscious subject. Thus it is the story of objectivism in which the object is the measure of all things. In ancient and medieval philosophy man still retains his primal tie with the world. His cord has not yet been cut; he still feels at home in the world because he has not yet been made aware of himself as an existing, self-conscious subject free and separate from his world.

The story of modern philosophy is the antithesis of objectivism: subjectivism. Labor begins with the loss of the medieval unified God of reason and faith Who could reassure man of his home in nature, and the umbilical cord is cut by Descartes's *"Cogito, ergo sum."* Not "Man is the rational animal" as with

Aristotle, but "I think, and therefore I am." I am or exist as a separate, free being unto myself just because I have turned inward to myself and can see no other. Although the self was intended to be in Descartes's philosophy a new, modern reassurance of the reality of man's external world, its clear distinctness from all else succeeded only in cutting it off from that external world. Now the primal tie has been severed, the cup has been broken. Man stands alone and apart from a distant and alien world; the individual self-conscious subject has been born. Adam now knows himself in his nakedness because he has eaten of the fruit of the tree of knowledge. Man has now gained his freedom as an autonomous self but at the cost of his security in and solidarity with the world. What does it profit a man if he shall gain his free soul but lose the whole world? The individual is now free *from* his world, but what is he free *to* do? He is free to try to establish a relation with the world with which he was once one, in unrelated unity, and to try to establish this relation out of himself since this is all he now has.

Reason is the modern philosopher's first attempted relation with his lost world. But the new, modern reason of the Continental Rationalists is not at all the same as the old reason of the ancient and medieval philosophers. The old reason was a part of man's primal tie with nature which has now been severed; it was the *nous* or reason seeds of Anaxagoras, a reason sprinkled through man and his world to make them connatural. In the medieval philosophers it was the divine *logos* or word implanted equally in nature and man and binding them together. But the new, modern reason of the Continental Rationalists is the reason of clear and distinct subjective ideas, a reason which belongs properly only to the reflecting subject and which can, therefore, never be successfully used as a new tie or relation of the subject to his lost objective world. When the Continental Rationalists insist, to the contrary, that their modern reason of subjective ideas is indeed a tie with the objective world because of their principle that what is true of thought is also true of reality, their supposedly objective world necessarily becomes only an objectified reflection of their own inner subjective reason.

Sensation is the modern philosopher's second attempted relation with his lost world, perhaps because sensation seems necessarily to be physical as well as psychical. Once more, however, the new, modern sensation of the British Empiricists is inevitably, because of modern philosophy's subjectivity, a screen of impressions and ideas which hides the objective realities which are supposed to be their causes. Even though Hume realizes that this world of impressions and ideas has to be the objective world so far as it now makes sense to talk about one, he views this residual "objective" world as only the projection of the inner world of the sensing subject cut off from "nature's secret powers" which long ago she disclosed to man. Now, however, "these ultimate springs and principles," Hume sighs, "are totally shut up from human curiosity and inquiry."[3]

Will is the modern philosopher's third and final attempted relation with his lost objective world, since Kant sees in his "Copernican" revolution that for modern philosophy the objective world can only be a world formed by the creative knowing and willing subject. However, this new, modern will, just like modern reason and modern sensation, is necessarily different from its ancient and medieval counterpart, for the latter will presupposed—and for some philosophers was directed and determined by—an antecedent, independent reality, while the modern will of Kant and his Voluntarist followers is the maker of modern man's very world. For Kant this means that man's original home in the objective world is still unattainable, but it remains as a noumenal wraith dreamed by a nostalgic subject.

With the help of Fichte and Schelling and under the prophecy of Hume, Hegel finally draws from these repeated attempts to forge from the subject a relation to his lost world the only conclusion which can consistently be drawn by the isolated subject of modernity—the conclusion that the objective reality nostalgically dreamed as the self's original home can only be the self's projection of its own inward nature, that no objective reality exists, other than that which the absolute subject creates for itself. With Hegel the isolated subject, whose self-consciousness is the essence of the story of modern philosophy, is so isolated that he is no longer isolated; he is so cut off from his original home that independent, objective, extra-mental reality can no longer even exist for him. Thus the story of modern philosophy as it culminates in Hegel is the story of the growth of self-conscious subjectivity from its birth out of an objective world to its encompassment of that world as the outward reflection of its own inward nature. Brought to fruition by Hegel, it is thus the story of subjectivism in which the subject or self is the measure of all things.

Thus the self which was to be modern man's reassurance of his bond with an antecedently real world of nature becomes instead the creator of the very existence of that world. Within the context of modern philosophy, German Voluntarism, especially as fully developed in Hegel's philosophy, may be regarded as a statement of the third stage, reunion of subject and object; Rationalism and Empiricism together form the modern statement of the second stage, self-alienation, and medieval philosophy gives the first stage, original union, in a three-stage sequence constituting modern philosophy. Yet modern philosophy as a whole and as brought to fruition by Hegel is most basically the deepest level of the second stage, the stage of the freedom of the self from the world, with ancient and medieval philosophy together forming the first stage, the stage of primordial union, in the context of the whole of Western philosophy. Ancient and medieval objectivism and modern subjectivism thus represent the first two stages in the total three-stage sequence, and they form the most basic structure of the whole of Western philosophy through Hegel.

Thus this story of Western philosophy ends with Hegel. This is not to say, of course, that philosophy itself ends with Hegel, even though Hegel himself sometimes seemed to have thought that it should. On the contrary, a great deal of important philosophizing has occurred in the hundred-odd years since Hegel's death, in the East as well as in the West. Not only does the period since Hegel have its lively Platonists, Aristotelians, Augustinians, Thomists, Rationalists, Empiricists, and Voluntarists; it also contains new movements which have sprung from Hegel and his modern predecessors. The Dialectical Idealism of

Hegel has been stood on its feet (after Hegel himself "stood it on its head")—or vice versa—by Marx and his followers in their Dialectical Materialism. Hegel's own Absolute Idealism has been continued by such philosophers as Green, Bosanquet, Bradley, Royce, and Blanshard; and a pluralistic, personal idealism has been developed, especially from Leibniz and Berkeley, by Lotze, Bowne, Brightman, Flewelling, and Bertocci. The voluntarism of the German Voluntarists has been continued by Schopenhauer, Nietzsche, Bergson, Royce, and Whitehead; and the movement known as pragmatism, developed by Peirce, James, Schiller, Dewey, Mead, and Lewis, is, at least in large part, a naturalizing and pluralizing of Kant's voluntarism and especially his schematism. Positivism also derives in large part from the destruction of the possibility of metaphysics at the hands of Hume and Kant; and twentieth century neorealism and critical realism, in such philosophers as Moore, Russell, Perry, Montague, Santayana, Lovejoy, Pratt, and Sellars, derives primarily from the sources studied, especially from Platonism, Aristotelianism, and British Empiricism.

While philosophy, therefore, has not ended with Hegel—and will doubtless continue as long as human life continues—the *story* of *modern* philosophy does logically or essentially end with Hegel since he has expressed in absolute form the subjectivism which is that story's defining essence. Philosophy since Hegel has so far been either a perpetuation of the modern emphasis upon the primacy of the subject or a return to the objectivism of ancient and medieval philosophy. Even those two movements which are paramount in contemporary Western philosophy— phenomenology and existentialism on the one hand and analytic philosophy or linguistic analysis on the other—seem to approach the world from the point of view of the knowing and acting subject, the self, and thus to fall within the framework of modern philosophy, as we have seen its essence unfold, although we are perhaps still too close to them to tell for sure. By the same token, any further philosophizing which approaches the world from the point of view of the self-conscious subject will by that fact fall within modern philosophy, and any future philosophizing which approaches the world from the standpoint of objective things will, of course by that fact, fall within the tradition of ancient and medieval philosophy.

While the story of ancient and medieval philosophy, on the one hand, and that of modern philosophy, on the other, have thus essentially ended, the story of *Western* philosophy has not. At least the story of Western philosophy has not yet been finished *logically*—even though it is an unhappy fact that it may at any time be finished temporally. For every story, if not every history, must logically have a beginning, a middle, and an end; and the story of Western philosophy has so far presented only a beginning and a middle, a thesis and an antithesis. The beginning or thesis of the story of Western philosophy is the objectivism of ancient and medieval philosophy; and its middle or antithesis is the subjectivism of modern philosophy. The end of the story of Western philosophy should be a reconciliation of its traditional and modern parts, a synthesis of objectivism and subjectivism, analogous to but grander than the ancient synthesis of Plato and Aristotle of the super-objectivism of their Cosmological predecessors and the quasi-subjectivism of their Anthropological predecessors. Such a synthesis has, however, not yet emerged; although its nature can be envisaged logically and abstractly, its concrete character and full development remain works of the future. With the emergence of such a synthesis a new age would evolve and its story would complete the story of Western philosophy.

Ancient and medieval objectivism, with the subject at one with objective reality, and modern subjectivism, with the individual subject born free from objective reality and isolated by inward self-consciousness—these are Parts One and Two of the grand story of Western philosophy which we have followed. However, this story is certainly not the only one to be found in the history of Western philosophy, and it may perhaps not be the most important story. It is also an unfinished story, for its conclusion, the synthesis of traditional and modern philosophy which sacrifices the integrity of neither, still remains hidden in the future. May one of the readers of this book be its creator.

SUGGESTED READINGS

Interpretations of Modern Philosophy

Gilson, E. *The Unity of Philosophical Experience.* New York: Scribner, 1937. Modern philosophy (and also in Part I medieval philosophy) interpreted by a contemporary but premodern philosopher, a brilliant and lively criticism of modern philosophy by a great disciple of Thomas Aquinas.

Royce, J. *The Spirit of Modern Philosophy.* New York: G. Braziller, 1955 (1892). Modern philosophy interpreted by a modern idealist philosopher, spirited lectures by a great American idealist and voluntarist.

Dewey, J. *Reconstruction in Philosophy.* New York: Beacon, 1948 (1920). Modern philosophy interpreted by a great modern pragmatist philosopher, the outline of Dewey's own philosophy as arising out of his critical survey of modern philosophy.

Whitehead, A. N. *Science and the Modern World.* New York: New American Library of World Literature, 1948 (1925). Modern philosophy interpreted by a great modern and would-be postmodern philosopher, the outline of Whitehead's own system as it arises out of his critical survey of modern philosophy.

General Histories of Western Philosophy

Ueberweg, F. *History of Philosophy,* trans. G. S. Morris. 2 vols. New York: Scribner's, 1871, 1889, 1903. The history of philosophy arranged by authors, a mine of material.

Windelband, W. *History of Philosophy,* trans. J. H. Tufts. New York: Macmillan, 1901. The history of philosophy arranged by ideas, has slight Kantian leanings.

Copleston, F. C. *A History of Philosophy.* 7 vols. Westminster: Newman, 1946-63. Extremely thorough and detailed.

Russell, Bertrand. *A History of Western Philosophy.* New York: Simon & Schuster, 1945. Often brilliant, sometimes profound, but also sometimes distorted; the inimitable Bertrand Russell, one of the great twentieth-century philosophers.

Notes

Chapter 1. The Cosmological Philosophers

1. See F. M. Cornford, *Principium Sapientiae* (Cambridge University Press, 1952), or H. A. Frankfort, et al., *Before Philosophy: The Intellectual Adventure of Ancient Man* (University of Chicago Press, 1946), especially the Conclusion.
2. Note the beginning of the Gospel according to St. John.
3. The last lines of Robert Peter Tristram Coffin's "Crystal Moment."

Chapter 2. The Anthropological Philosophers

1. This interpretation I learned substantially from Gregory Vlastos of Princeton University.

Chapter 3. Plato

1. For this point of view, see Paul Desjardin's essay in a volume of Yale studies of Plato edited by Robert S. Brumbaugh and John Brentlinger to be published by the University of Southern Illinois Press.
2. Cf. Robert S. Brumbaugh, *Plato for the Modern Age* (New York: Crowell Collier, 1962), pp. 63–66.
3. I cannot here go into the matter of the significance, if any, of the fact that the middle two segments must have the same length. See Robert S. Brumbaugh, "Plato's Divided Line," *Review of Metaphysics*, V (1962), 329–34.

4. Plato, *Republic* 435E.
5. Ibid., Bk. VIII.
6. Ibid., 352E–354A.
7. Ibid., 435E.
8. Ibid., 369B–C.

Chapter 4. *Aristotle*

1. See especially Aristotle, *Metaphysics*, Bk. I, Chs. 3–10.
2. *Physics*, Bk. II, Ch. 3.
3. Ibid., Bk. III, Ch. 1, 201A 10–11.
4. Ibid., Bk. IV, Ch. 11, 219B 1.
5. *Metaphysics*, Bk. XII, Ch. 7, 1072B 28–29.
6. *De Anima*, Bk. II, Ch. 1, 412A 29–30.
7. *Nicomachean Ethics*, Bk. I, Ch. 7, 1098A 17–19.
8. Ibid.
9. Ibid., Bk. II, Ch. 6, 1107A 6–9.
10. Ibid., Bk. I, Ch. 7, 1098A 17–18.
11. Ibid., Bk. X., Ch. 7, 1177B 26–28.
12. Ibid., 1178A 4–9.
13. *Metaphysics*, Bk. IV, Ch. 3, 1005B 19–20.
14. *Nicomachean Ethics*, Bk. X, Ch. 7, 1178A 4–9.

Chapter 5. *Hellenistic and Roman Philosophy*

1. For a modern case of the same apparent blindness, see the last chapter of Ruth Benedict's *Patterns of Culture* (New York: Houghton Mifflin, 1934).
2. Epicurus, *Letter to Menoeceus*.
3. Ibid.
4. Epictetus, *Manual*, Sec. 43.
5. Ibid., Sec. 16.
6. Ibid., Sec. 3.
7. Epictetus, *Discourses*, Bk. II, Ch. 8.

Chapter 6. *Medieval Philosophy*

1. Etienne Gilson, *The Spirit of Medieval Philosophy* (New York: Scribner's, 1940), p. 69.
2. E.g., J. N. Findlay, "Can God's Existence Be Disproved?" in A. Flew and A. MacIntyre, *New Essays in Philosophical Theology.* (New York: Macmillan, 1955), pp. 47–56.
3. See, for example, Norman Malcolm, "Anselm's Ontological Arguments," *Philosophical Review*, LXIX (January 1960), 41–62, and the various replies to this article in the same volume. See also

Charles Hartshorne, *The Logic of Perfection* (LaSalle, Ill.: Open Court Pub. Co., 1962).

4. For a very instructive ontological argument for the nonexistence of God see again J. N. Findlay's essay in Flew and MacIntyre, pp. 47–56.

5. Aquinas, *Summa Theologica*, Part I, Question 2, Article 3, from Thomas Gilby, trans. and ed., *St. Thomas Aquinas Philosophical Texts* (Oxford University Press, 1951), p. 56, italics added.

6. Ibid., p. 57.

7. Gilson, p. 5.

8. For a recent expression of this reduction of reason to faith, see Henry Margenau, *The New Faith of Science* (Northfield, Minn.: Carleton College, 1953), 20 pp.

9. See, for example, Flew and MacIntyre, Ch. 6.

10. Tertullian, *On Prescription Against Heretics,* Ch. 7.

11. This position was also held in modern times, by Pascal in the seventeenth century (Ch. 9–1), and by Kierkegaard in the nineteenth century, for example. See also Flew and MacIntyre, Ch. 10.

12. Aquinas, *Summa Theologica,* Pt. I, Question 32, Article 1.

13. See, for example, Arthur O. Lovejoy, *The Great Chain of Being* (Cambridge, Mass.: Harvard University Press, 1936) and the subsequent debate of Lovejoy with Henry B. Veatch and Anton C. Pegis in *Philosophy and Phenomenological Research,* Vol. VII and IX.

14. See James F. Anderson, *The Bond of Being* (St. Louis: Herder, 1949).

15. Noted by Gilson, p. 59.

Chapter 7. The Beginnings of Modern Philosophy

1. William of Ockham, *Commentary on the Sentences,* Bk. I, Distinction 27, Question 2.

2. Bacon, *Novum Organum,* Bk. I, aphorism xlix.

3. Ibid., Bk. II, aphorism xvii.

4. Ibid., Bk. II, aphorism xv.

5. Ibid., Bk. II, aphorism xiii.

6. Ibid., Bk. II, aphorism xx.

7. Ibid., Bk. II, aphorism xxi ff.

8. Ibid., Bk. I, aphorism xcv.

9. Hobbes, *Leviathan,* Ch. 1.

10. Ibid., Ch. 13.

11. Ibid., Ch. 14, originally italicized.

12. Ibid., Ch. 17, originally italicized.

Chapter 8. Continental Rationalism in Descartes

1. Italics added.
2. Descartes, *Meditation* II, italics added.
3. Ibid., italics added.
4. Ibid., III.
5. Ibid., II.
6. Ibid.
7. Ibid., III.
8. Ibid.
9. Ibid.
10. Ibid.
11. Ibid.
12. Ibid.
13. Ibid., italics added.
14. Descartes, *Discourse on Method*, Pt. IV.
15. Descartes, *Meditation* V.
16. Ibid.
17. Ibid., "Reply to Arnauld."
18. Ibid., III.
19. Ibid., VI.
20. Ibid.
21. Ibid.
22. Descartes, *Discourse on Method*, Pt. II.
23. Descartes, *Meditation* III.

Chapter 9. Continental Rationalism After Descartes

1. Pascal, *Thoughts*, No. 277.
2. Spinoza, *Ethics*, Pt. I, Prop. 17, note.
3. Ibid., Prop. 11, italics added.
4. Ibid., Def. IV.
5. Ibid., Pt. II. Prop. 21, note.
6. Ibid., Prop. 7, note.
7. Ibid., Pt. I, Def. V.
8. Ibid., Pt. II, Prop. 40, note 2.
9. See, for example, ibid., Def. IV.
10. Ibid., Prop. 36.
11. Ibid., Prop. 8.
12. Ibid., Prop. 41.
13. Alfred Lord Tennyson, "Flower in the Crannied Wall."
14. E.g., in Spinoza, Pt. II, Prop. 43, end of note.
15. Ibid., Prop. 35, note.

16. Ibid., Pt. I, Prop. 35.
17. Ibid., Prop. 33.
18. Ibid., Pt. II, Prop. 49, note, item 2.

Chapter 10. *British Empiricism*

1. Locke, *Essay Concerning Human Understanding,* Bk. II, Ch. 23, Sec. 11.
2. Ibid., Sec. 4.
3. Ibid., Sec. 2.
4. Ibid., Sec. 29.
5. Ibid., Bk. IV, Ch. 1, Sec. 2.
6. Ibid., Bk. IV, Ch. 2, Sec. 14.
7. Ibid.
8. Ibid.
9. Ibid.
10. Ibid., Ch. 9, Sec. 9.
11. Ibid., Ch. 10, Sec. 6.
12. Berkeley, *Principles of Human Knowledge,* Intro., Sec. 6.
13. Ibid., Sec. 10.
14. Ibid., Sec. 12, italics added.
15. Ibid., body of book, Sec. 2.
16. Ibid., Sec. 17.
17. Ibid., Sec. 8.
18. Ibid., Sec. 5.
19. Ibid., Sec. 20.
20. Ronald Knox, quoted in Bertrand Russell, *A History of Western Philosophy* (New York: Simon & Schuster, 1945), p. 648.
21. Ibid.
22. Berkeley, *Principles,* Sec. 148.
23. Ibid., Sec. 147.
24. Ibid., Sec. 142.
25. Ibid., Sec. 89.
26. Ibid., Sec. 86.
27. Ibid., Sec. 88.
28. Hume, *An Enquiry Concerning Human Understanding,* Sec. II.
29. This example is drawn from Charles Morris, *Signs, Language, and Behavior* (New York: Prentice-Hall, 1946), p. 163.
30. Hume, *Enquiry,* Sec. II.
31. Ibid., Sec. IV, Pt. I.
32. Ibid., Sec. VII, Pt. I.
33. Ibid., Sec. VII, Pt. II.
34. Ibid.

35. Ibid., Sec. V, Pt. I.
36. Ibid., Sec. XII, Pt. I; cf. Hume, *A Treatise of Human Nature,* Pt. II.
37. Hume, *Treatise,* Pt. IV, Sec. V.
38. Hume, *Dialogues Concerning Natural Religion,* Pt. II.
39. Ibid.
40. Ibid.
41. Ibid.
42. Ibid., **Pt. IX.**
43. Ibid., Pt. XII.
44. Ibid.
45. Ibid.
46. Hume, *Enquiry,* Sec. XII, Pt. I.
47. Ibid.
48. Hume, *Treatise,* Pt. IV, Sec. V.
49. Locke, *Essay Concerning Human Understanding,* Bk. IV, Ch. 1, Sec. 1.
50. See, for example, E. B. Holt, *The Concept of Consciousness* (London: G. Allen, 1914), and A. J. Ayer, *Language, Truth, and Logic* (New York: Dover, 1952), Ch. 7.

Chapter 11. German Voluntarism in Kant

1. Kant, B 19. *B* refers to the second edition of this work.
2. On this topic see my "Traditional Reason and Modern Reason," in *Faith and Philosophy,* ed. Alvin Plantinga (Grand Rapids: Erdmans, 1964), pp. 37–50; reprinted in *Philosophy Today,* VII, 44 (Winter 1963–64), 235–44.
3. Kant, *Critique of Pure Reason,* B xvi.
4. Ibid., B 75.
5. Ibid., B xxx.
6. Ibid., B 3.
7. Kant, *Prolegomena to Any Future Metaphysics Which Can Come Forth as a Science,* Sec. 22, p. 305. Page numbers are those in the edition of this work edited by Benno Erdmann, IV (Preussische Akademie der Wissenschaften, 1911).
8. Ibid., Sec. 13, Remark II, 289.
9. Kant, *Critique,* B 14.
10. See Kant, *Prolegomena,* Sec. 13, Remark 1, pp. 287–88.
11. Ibid., Sec. 19, p. 299.
12. Ibid., Sec. 13, Remark II, p. 289.
13. See, for example, Hans Vaihinger, *The Philosophy of As If* (New York: Harcourt Brace, 1924); C. I. Lewis, *Mind and the World*

Order (New York: Scribner's, 1929); and Alfred J. Ayer, *Language, Truth, and Logic* (New York: Dover, 1952).

14. Kant, *Critique*, B 183.
15. Which Kant discusses in the "Transcendental Dialectic" in the *Critique* and in Pt. III of the *Prolegomena*.
16. Kant, *Prolegomena*, Sec. 44, p. 331.
17. Ibid., Sec. 59, pp. 360–61.
18. Ibid., Sec. 13, Remark II, p. 289, italics added.
19. Kant, Critique, B xxx.
20. Kant, *Fundamental Principles of the Metaphysics of Ethics*, Sec. I, p. 19.
21. Ibid., Sec. II, p. 39.
22. Ibid., Sec. I, p. 19.
23. Ibid., p. 22.
24. Ibid., Sec. II, p. 47.
25. Ibid., p. 57.
26. Ibid., Sec. I, p. 11.
27. Ibid., Sec. II, p. 63.
28. Ibid., Sec. III, p. 79.
29. Ibid.

Chapter 12. German Voluntarism Through Hegel

1. Quoted in Friedrich Ueberweg, *History of Philosophy*, II (New York: Scribner's, 1889), p. 216.
2. Ibid., p. 208.
3. Hegel, *Lectures on the Philosophy of History*, Intro., Pt. IV, Sec. 3.
4. See Jacob Loewenberg, ed., *Hegal Selections* (New York: Scribner's, 1929), pp. ix–xliii (Loewenberg's Introduction).
5. From the anthology by Frederic Brown, *Star Shine* (New York: Bantam Books, 1956); originally published as *Angels and Spaceships* (New York: E. P. Dutton & Co., 1954) and brought to my attention by Christopher Glass.
6. Heraclitus, Fragment 215.
7. Hegel, *Lectures on the Philosophy of History*, Intro., Pt. IV.
8. Ibid.
9. Ibid., Intro., Pt. III, Sec. 3.
10. Loewenberg, p. 464. Quoted from Hegel's *Philosophy of Law*.

Epilogue: The Story of Western Philosophy

1. This Epilogue follows in part my essay on "The Temporal Being of Western Man," *Review of Metaphysics*, XVIII, 4 (June 1965), 629–46.

2. (New York: Holt, Rinehart, & Winston, 1960). Fromm's main idea may be obtained best from p. viii, Ch. 2, and pp. 256–65. For support for his idea and for some of his materials he draws on Jacob Burckhardt, *The Civilization of the Renaissance in Italy*, trans. S. G. C. Middlemore (London: G. G. Harrop & Co., 1929).

3. Hume, *An Enquiry Concerning Human Understanding*, Sec. IV, Pt. I, pgf. 12.

Index